Translating the English Bible

For my beloved wife Estelle

Translating the English Bible
From Relevance to Deconstruction

Philip W. Goodwin

James Clarke & Co

James Clarke & Co
P.O. Box 60
Cambridge
CB1 2NT

www.jamesclarke.co
publishing@jamesclarke.co

ISBN: 978 0 227 17391 6

British Library Cataloguing in Publication Data
A record is available from the British Library

First Published, 2013

Contents

Figures and Tables

Preface

This work forms the substance of my thesis for a PhD, awarded in 2010 by the University of Manchester. Perhaps more importantly, it represents a thorough (if, perhaps, not final) scratching of an itch I have felt practically as long as I can remember an intellectual life. The problem of translation has always fascinated me, and translation issues seem to me to form the knotty, many-stranded interpretive puzzle at the centre of the puzzle of puzzles that is the Bible. As an earnest and bookish young Christian in the 1970s, I learned to love the Bible – especially the one I was given by my parents on my sixteenth birthday. I have it in front of me now, inscribed 1977. It is a black-bound RSV, with Metzger's Oxford Concordance in the back. To me, the heft of the thing, its smell and feel, and above all the words inside, with their quiet, firm insistence, are *the* Bible. The calm assurance conveyed by these dignified words, though, gave way to confusion, doubt and anxiety as I matured intellectually; this doubt was compounded during my time studying philosophy, politics and economics at Oxford. It continued during adulthood, though covered over by many things, as I found a path through life. I always had a thought that 'one day' I would get to the bottom of some of these doubts. Certain developments in my career led at one stage to a lot of long distance commuting and being away from home, and (after exhausting the less edifying ways to spend the time) I decided to learn ancient Greek, and later Hebrew. The studies that this opened up led towards the present work, and in 2006 I finally had the opportunity to take an extended break from a career in business finance to do something full time.

I would like to take the opportunity to thank my erstwhile colleagues at Montagu Private Equity for facilitating that break. I would also like to thank Tom Deidun at Birkbeck College (University of London) for opening up the Greek language. Todd Klutz at the University of Manchester supervised my PhD, and was a constant source of criticism, observation, encouragement and, above all, sheer enjoyment – his good humour and positive frame of mind, as much as his intelligence and knowledge, were a vital source of energy during the marathon that is a doctorate. I also benefitted from input from Peter Oakes, Alan Williams and Mona Baker at the University of Manchester, Ward Blanton of the University of Glasgow, and my long-standing friend Richard Young. I have gained enormously from talking about communication and translation issues with many business people over the years, working in various parts of the UK but also Europe, Scandinavia, the USA, Japan and Africa. I owe especial thanks to my colleagues at Fusion Capital in Nairobi and elsewhere in East Africa, who have helped me (just occasionally) to glimpse how the world looks from another's eyes and in another's language.

Finally, and above all, I would like to thank my wife, Estelle, for her love, encouragement and forbearance over many years.

Phil Goodwin,
31 May 2012

Note to the reader

This is a book about translation. As such, it frequently cites source texts in their original languages. In order to assist readers who are unfamiliar with those languages, I provide 'translations' alongside. It is to be understood that these 'translations' (which are my own, unless stated otherwise) are there simply to establish the point of reference for such readers, and not to anticipate the discussion of what is, or is not, the appropriate translation, which forms the main body of the work.

Abbreviations

Cited biblical versions

Barclay	*The New Testament*, 1968, Collins, UK (William Barclay)
BigS	*Die Bibel in gerechter Sprache Gütersloher Verlagshaus*, 2006, Germany (Bail, Crüsemann, Crüsemann, Domay, Ebach, Janssen, Köhler, Kuhlman, Leutzsch, Schottroff)
CEV	*Contemporary English Version*, 2000 (1995), British and Foreign Bible Societies, UK
CJB	*Complete Jewish Bible*, 1998, Messianic Jewish Publishers, USA (David H. Stern)
CV	*The Concordant Version of the Sacred Scriptures* 1930 Concordant Publishing Concern, Los Angeles, USA (A. E. Knoch)
Cotton Patch	*Clarence Jordan's Cotton Patch Gospel*, 1969, Smyth & Helwys, USA (Clarence Jordan)
DVB2	*Die Volxbibel 2.0*, 2005, Volxbibel-Verlag, German (Martin Dreyer) Elberfelder, Die Bibel, Elberfelder Übersetzung, 2005 revidierte Fassung, Voltmedia, (Revision of Elberfelder Bibel)
EHNT	*New Testament*, 1768, London, UK (Edward Harwood)
ESV	*Holy Bible, English Standard Version*, 2001, Good News Publishers, USA ('adapted' from RSV)
GAN	*Good as New: A Radical Retelling of the Scriptures*, 2004, English, Winchester UK and Washington USA (John Henson)
GNB/TEV	*Good News for Modern Man: The New Testament in Today's English Version*, 1966,1976,1992, American Bible Society, USA (Eugene Nida)
Gothic	*The Gospels*, 360? Joseph Bosworth (4th edition, 1907) Visigothic (Ulfilas?)
JB	*The Jerusalem Bible*, 1966, Publisher: various, UK (English version of La Bible de Jérusalem)
Jérusalem	*La sainte Bible traduite en francais sous la direction de l'École biblique de Jérusalem*, 1955, Publisher: various, Paris, France

King	*The New Testament, Freshly translated*, 2004, Kevin Mayhew Ltd, UK (Nicholas King, SJ)
KJV	*The Holy Bible*, 1611, (New Cambridge Paragraph ed. 2005) 'The King James Version' or 'Authorised Version', rights vested in the Crown, UK
La Colombe	*La Sainte Bible, Nouvelle Version Segond Révisée*, 1978, Société biblique française, France (Revision of Louis Segond's revised translation of 1910)
Luther	*Die Bibel, Luther Übersetzung*, 1984, Deutsche Bibelgesellschaft, Germany (revision of Luther)
LXX	*Septuaginta Id est Vetus Testamentum graece iusta LXX*, 260 BCE? interpretes ed. Alfred Rahlfs, Editio altera (2006) Greek (Ptolemy II Philadelphus)
Message	*The Message: The Bible in Contemporary Language*, Eugene H. Peterson, 1993, Nav Press, USA
Moffatt	*The New Testament: A new translation*, James Moffatt, 1926, Hodder and Stoughton, UK
NA27	*Nestle-Aland Novum Testamentum Graece*, 1993, 27th edition, 9th correction, 2006, Greek New Testament, Deutsche Bibelgeselschaft
NASB	*New American Standard Bible*, 1963, Lockman Foundation, USA (Revision of American Standard Version, 1901)
NEB	*The New English Bible*, 1961, Oxford University Press, UK
NIV	*New International Version*, 1978, Zondervan, New York Bible Society International, USA
NKJV	*The New Testament, New King James Version*, 1979, Thomas Nelson, USA (Arthur Farstad)
NLT	*Holy Bible, New Living Translation*, 1996, 2004, Tyndale House Publishers, Inc, USA
NRSV	*Holy Bible, New Revised Standard Version*, 1989, Anglicized Version 1995, National Council of the Churches of Christ in the United States of America publishers various
Phillips	*New Testament in Modern English*, 1958, Harper Collins, UK (J.B Phillips)
R-D	*The New Testament of Jesus Christ translated faithfully into English*, 1582, English, Douai, The English Roman Catholic church, (Gregory Martin)
REB	*The Revised English Bible* (the New Testament), 1989, Oxford University Press, UK (revision of NEB)
RNT	*Restored New Testament: A New Translation with Commentary, Including the Gnostic Gospels*, Thomas, Mary and Judas, 2009, W.W. Norton & Co, New York and London (Willis Barnstone)
RSV	*Holy Bible, Revised Standard Version*, 1952, Publishers: various, UK (Revision of RV 1901, see below)

RV	*Holy Bible, Revised Version*, 1901, Publishers: various, UK (Revision of KJV 1611 and RV 1885)
Stier	*Das Neue Testament*, 1989, übersetzt von Fridolin Stier Kösel-Verlag, Patmos-Verlag, Germany (Fridolin Stier)
T5G	*The Five Gospels: What did Jesus Really Say?* 1993, Polebridge Press, USA (Robert Funk/Roy Hoover, The Jesus Seminar)
THG	*Tha Halgan Godspel on Englisc*, 990? (4th edition, 1907), George Putnam, New York, USA (ed. Benjamin Thorpe)
TODB	*Traduction Œcuménique de la Bible*, 1988, Société biblique francaise, France
TSB	*The Street Bible*, 2003, Zondervan, USA (Rob Lacey)
TUNT	*The Unvarnished New Testament*, 1991, Phanes Press (Andy Gaus)
Tyndale	*The newe Testament as it was written and caused to be written, by them which herde yt.*, 1526, (Cooper ed. 2000) The British Library (William Tyndale)
Vulgate	*Biblia Sacra Vulgata*, 390-405? (5th ed,2007), Latin (Pope Damasus/St Jerome)
Wycliffe	*The Later Version*, 1388, (Cooper ed. 2002), The British Library (John Wycliffe? The Lollards)
Zürcher	*Zürcher Bibel*, 2007,Genossenschaft Verlag, Germany

Abbreviations: Other

BAGD	Danker etc., *A Greek-English Lexicon of the New Testament and other early Christian Literature*, 2000, 3rd Edition
GEC	*The Exhaustive Concordance to the Greek New Testament*, 1995, Goodrick and Kohlenberger, Zondervan, (based on the text of the 26th edition of the Nestle-Aland Novum Testamentum Graece)
LS	Liddell and Scott, 1996, 6th Edition
NIBC	*New International Bible Commentary*, Paternoster Press
RTT	Relevance Theory of Translation
TDNT	*Theological Dictionary of the New Testament*, 2006 (1964) Eerdmans (English version of TWNT, tr. Bromily)
TWNT	*Theologisches Wörterbuch zum Neuen Testament*, 1933 ed. Kittel und Friedrich

Chapter One

The Holy Marriage

David Daniell and the lost art of translation

'The main thrust of what I want to say is that translating the Bible is an art that we seem to have lost, for mysterious reasons.' So said David Daniell, the distinguished Tyndale scholar, at a conference in London in February 1995. There has been, to my knowledge, no decisive answer offered to the question implied by his statement. Daniell himself points out some of the central paradoxes of this situation. The 'we' of his statement refers, of course, to the community of English-speakers, a language which 'has never been in better shape . . . It is healthier than ever before, alive and kicking in mainstream, dialects, pidgins and creoles, across the world.' Surely, he suggests, a language whose expressive power is in such robust health, should be able to accommodate a new scriptural translation of comparable excellence to Tyndale's? Moreover, as he goes on to say, our knowledge of the relevant source languages and contexts, of the transmission of the texts, has never been better. These two facts alone, he argues, suggest that we should be able to do so much better than Tyndale, who, almost five centuries earlier, was translating into a target language which had limited vocabulary and conceptual apparatus, and with only a comparatively sketchy knowledge of the source language and culture.

We might add to the sense of paradox by observing the enormous flowering of thinking about translation, beginning after Tyndale in the early modern period but taking off in the 19th Century and blooming especially vigorously since the 1960s: if there is still no generally accepted theory of translation, it is not for want of trying. Nor has this theoretical enterprise been conducted only in an academic corner: translation studies has become mainstream, and the problems it considers are widely recognised as important and perhaps urgent in a world where the global flow of goods, people and ideas require constant translation, and where peoples' inability to understand each other threatens the peace and stability of that world.

We could consider also the amount of scholarly effort and money which has been expended on new Bible versions in English. The NIV, for example, was ten years in planning and a further ten years in execution. It involved more than 100 scholars working intensively in a hierarchy of committees, from the best available source texts, to produce a brand new translation of the whole Bible. Even Ptolemy and his LXX translators could not match this scale of commitment and resource. The NIV, published first in 1978, is only one of several mainstream versions and revisions which appeared in the second half of the twentieth century. Not all of them were quite so well-funded, but each involved a similar army of scholars working with the best resources available.

There is more: besides these major efforts – versions which we will describe as 'institutional' for reasons which will become clear – there have also been a series of attempts by scholars, mostly working on their own, sometimes in very small groups, to produce innovative new translations. This tradition, which reaches back well into the 18th Century in English (as well as in German) has only accelerated with the passage of time. Daniell's provocative statement appears half way through a decade in which no fewer than twenty such versions appeared in English, including some like *The Message* which have had a major, if controversial, impact. The trend for new versions continued into the 21st Century and shows no sign of abating. Highlights of the continuing process include not only complete Bibles and Testaments, but also many versions of individual books or portions. Everett Fox's *The Five Books of Moses* (from 1983), which is self-consciously an 'Englishing' of the text along the lines of the *Verdeutschung* of Buber and Rosenzweig; Ariel and Chana Bloch's beautiful *Song of Songs* (1995); Robert Alter's metrically sensitive renderings of the Psalms (2007), which follow on his acclaimed Pentateuch (2004); Stephen Mitchell's *Job*, and so on.

In what sense, then, does Daniell's comment deserve consideration? Perhaps he is, quite simply, wrong? At the least, we might suggest a degree of arrogance in the statement. It is as if a distinguished keynote speaker at the International Automobile Manufacturers' Conference said: 'The art of making cars is one which we have lost, for mysterious reasons.' Such a speaker risks being booed from the stage, his assertion being so manifestly contradicted by the gleaming, high technology product on display all around. Yet the record does not show that Daniell was pelted with vegetables, and in fact his dissatisfaction with contemporary Bible translation is widespread. It is a dissatisfaction which he expresses by way of contrast with Tyndale, but for many more the comparator is the King James Version.

The present work is partly directed at responding to Daniell's implied questions. Is translating the Bible an art we have lost? Are there identifiable reasons for this? And is it an art which we can recover? My answer to all three questions is 'yes'.

The rules of the art

Let us look at the evidence Daniell adduces for his statement. The procedure is by way of example, and the first concerns the interaction of Laban and Jacob in Genesis 31. Daniell is able to show that whereas Tyndale successfully and economically conveys 'some sense of the voice of Laban as something to be afraid of', the REB makes Laban sound 'like an inadequate – and patronising – personal counsellor.' The problems identified with the REB include lack of gravitas, incorrect register and woolly vocabulary. The next example, from John 14, cites the TEV '"Do not be worried or upset", Jesus told them.' Tyndale's rendition was 'Let not your hearts be troubled . . .' Again, register is a key issue: Bible translation should be recognisable spoken English, but in a 'heightened' register. 'The TEV 'is wrong on every single count: for the Greek, for the occasion, for the register; and John's spiritual perception is simply wiped out – the words belong to cheering the disciples up when they had missed a bus. . . . To lose 'a troubled heart' as a concept is a terrible loss indeed.'

My own intention in citing Daniell's paper is not either to agree or disagree with his assessment of the REB or the TEV: as a matter of fact, I find his points well-made and his criticisms of the newer translations very effective, but this is irrelevant to the argument I want to make. What I want to notice here is more procedural.

The first thing to notice is that the argument proceeds almost entirely on an intuitive level. The examples are used to illustrate six general criteria which, Daniell argues, a biblical translation should meet. These can be summarised as follows:

- To be accurate;
- To make sense (no 'holy rubbish' such as may occasionally be found in KJV prophets – Daniell cites Habakkuk 1.9);
- To deal boldly with difficulties (for example the many *hapax legomena* which must be decided in translation from the Hebrew scriptures);
- To accommodate the stylistic differences of the different biblical writers;
- To achieve 'heightened every-day register' such as may be found in present-day use of proverbs;
- To be memorable, such that it can be heard once and remembered.

The first three criteria here are such that it is very unlikely we will find anyone to disagree: are there *any* translators who aim to be inaccurate, to not make sense, to shy away from difficulties? 'To be accurate'-- of course. But what does accuracy mean? What is it that should be accurate to what, and how should it be done? At what level should accuracy be assessed – word, sentence, verse, book or some other level? Is accuracy a question of semantics only, or are there other dimensions – and if so, how should those dimensions be weighed against each other and against semantics? How can accuracy be measured, and who is the judge? The puzzles multiply. Similarly: 'To deal boldly with difficulties.' There is widespread agreement amongst translators that courage is required for what they do: we will explore some of the dimensions of this required fortitude in Chapters Three to Six. For now, though we should observe that, however they are defined, there are 'difficulties' in every single line of biblical translation. It is worth emphasising this point because quite a different impression would be gained from reading much of the literature on biblical translation. Daniell himself focuses on examples involving *hapax legomena*: the word which appears only once in the literature, and where we must resort to guesswork and comparative etymology to arrive at a translation. He cites the treasure arriving on ships in 1 Kings 10, which Tyndale charmingly (and, yes, we must concede, boldly) translates as 'gold, silver, ivory, apes and peacocks.' Similarly, we find highly theoretically-oriented writers on translation citing difficulties in translating technical terms for harvest processes and so on. The problem with such examples is not that they are not real translation issues – of course they are, and when there is 'thin' evidence for how a particular word is used, or when very 'alien' objects or processes are assumed, it does indeed require some ingenuity in the translator. The problem is the implication that all the *other* words used in a given passage are quite straightforward. In fact, as Steiner reminds us, 'Though they deny it, [even] phrase-books and primers are full of immediate deeps.' When the difference between source and target language spans millennia, the deeps are deeper still, and may be especially impenetrable in the case of very common, everyday words. Only our habit of placing absolute trust in a lexicon, which lists the canonically approved 'equivalents' for an ancient word, leads us to think otherwise. It is the very wealth of evidence which creates the difficulty: like an archaeologist trying to understand an ancient midden heap, we find ourselves much better able to interpret the occasional gem, the oddly-shaped artefact, and quite at a loss to interpret the ubiquitous shards and fragments. When we find in a passage a common word such as καρδία ('heart') or ἱερεῦς ('priest'), γίνομαι ('become') or ἄγγελος ('angel') we may reach confidently for our canonically approved 'equivalent', but if we stop to consider what makes us so sure that this is an appropriate translation, doubt sets in. It is another major objective of the present work to instil and foster such doubt, and in the course of the discussion I will attempt to destabilize the sense of certainty in the case of a number of very common words found in Luke's writings.

In all this there is a weird sensation that the last fifty or so years of effort in the area of translation theory have simply not happened, or are irrelevant. Daniell's comments would have been quite appropriate in the period of innocence before any of this work took place. The early 20th Century German-Jewish thinker, Rosenzweig, for example, had this to say about Kautsch's German *Textbibel* as long ago as 1926: 'Perhaps there are, in a book as stylistically diverse as the Bible, passages for which this provincial bureaucratic diction is precisely right. But diffused equally over the whole story, it falsifies the tone and thus the"music"'. Rosenzweig's objection is against what he calls *wissenschaftlich* translation, which at best is 'superficial' and at worst allows a passage to be 'transposed from its austere, concrete, sublimity to a relentlessly chatty idiom that scribbles all over the original clarity . . .' Rosenzweig was of course at this point defending the Luther translation against a newer kind of 'scientific' practice, and he was engaged at the time (with Buber) on his own monumental biblical translation project. I cite Rosenzweig (to whom we will return) not negatively against Daniell, but to point to another of the major themes of the present work; and this is the problematic relationship between translation theory and biblical translation practice. For whilst it is obvious that, in making his criticisms, Daniell has ignored the progress of translation theory, it must also be clear that the actual translations coming under his scrutiny are subject to the same criticisms as a translation (in German) appearing three quarters of a century earlier. Perhaps, then, all this putative 'progress' is not really making much progress at all. At the very least, as we will see, the relationship between theory and practice in biblical translation is not a straightforward one, and the complications of this relationship operate at both the institutional and at the individual psychological level.

Daniell's second triad of criteria are in a way more interesting, but also intriguingly in sympathy with Rosenzweig's agenda of 70 years earlier. The question of the different biblical writers' styles is one which could be added to the list of paradoxes: how is it that, in a period when understanding of genre and stylistics has made such huge strides, this does not seem to be reflected in biblical translation? Daniell's points are made against the TEV and the REB, but he might equally have observed the same uniformity of style in the NRSV or the NIV – in the former a certain limpid, elegant blandness; in the latter a relentless, robust literalness. The problem with such observations is that they seem to boil down to just a question of style. So we might say Daniell admires Tyndale's style, and he doesn't like the TEV style; so be it, let them agree to differ and all is well. Stylistics are notoriously subjective; or to make the point in the language of translation theory, stylistics are part of the audience-orientation of a text, of its *skopos*. Daniell's assertion that the register for biblical translation 'should' be a heightened everyday language such as that used in proverbs is just that – an assertion. Even if we could agree in some measure to this assertion (perhaps on the grounds of memorability, Daniell's final criterion?) , we would still have to determine what would count as 'heightened', and to whose 'everyday' speech this heightening should relate. What I find 'heightened' may not at all coincide with what he does, and so on.

This brings us to the main procedural point about Daniell's paper. This is that at no point is any comparison made to the source text. Although we are once or twice told that something is, or is not 'true to the Greek', there is no reference to what that Greek (or Hebrew, as the case may be) is. As it is not clear what being 'true' might mean for Daniell, we would perhaps not be much wiser if there was. But, how can two translations, qua translations, be compared at all, other than by reference to the source text? If there is no attempt to do so, then we do end up with what we have observed: with the statement of personal preferences. Although I have chosen to make this point with reference to Daniell, whose preferences are stated in terms of stylistic issues, the same observations could be offered in countless other cases, including cases where the commentators' preferences are theological rather than stylistic. I would include in this those conservative scholars who from time to time object to a certain, perhaps idiomatic, translation on the grounds that it is 'wrong' theologically.

What this omission points to is quite serious. There are, I think, two reasons why Daniell is reluctant to assess the translations as translations – that is, in relation to the source texts they purport to translate. These reasons are related, to each other, and, crucially, to the 'mysterious reasons' to which Daniell alludes in his opening remark.

The problem of fidelity

Perhaps the fundamental issue is this: in order to engage with the issue of how the translation relates to the source text, one must have some working notion of fidelity to that text, of how such fidelity is to be described and discussed, how it might be measured – in short, one needs a definition of faithfulness. Here, Daniell senses a problem: isn't the whole idea of fidelity a suspect one? On introspection, instead of a clear, theoretically grounded definition of fidelity, he finds a theoretical lacuna. Lacking this grounding, he resorts to his intuitions. When he says that he wants a translation 'to be accurate' he is articulating those intuitions, or, if we prefer, making common sense.

In so doing, he is, I believe, making a perfectly reasonable – perhaps the only intelligent - response to the central problem in contemporary translation theory, at least as it pertains to biblical translation. From the late 1960s onwards, the notion of 'fidelity' in biblical translation was increasingly expressed in terms of 'dynamic equivalence' or, as the theory later developed 'functional equivalence'. Nida and Taber's 1969 book perhaps marks the decisive arrival of this theoretical approach, but it has been elaborated by an entire generation of theoreticians and been the major influence on nearly all the biblical translation projects of the last fifty years. Although the most noticeable surface feature of the theory is its mandating of 'idiomatic' or 'non-literal' translations, its theoretical mainspring is or certainly was an appropriation from Chomskian linguistics; 'fidelity' is defined in terms of 'back-translatability', via the deep structures which are purported to be common to all human languages.

Nida seemed to promise that any utterance in any language can be 'back-translated', via these deep structures, to an 'equivalent' utterance in any other language. For the first time, then, faithfulness in translation could be defined and (in principle, at least) demonstrated. What one had to do was to look behind the utterances to the 'kernels' of meaning, authorising a very 'free' translation style: providing the 'kernels' were the same, fidelity was guaranteed. This idea had understandably caused great excitement in biblical translation circles: here, at last, was a standard of fidelity which not only mandated the kind of idiomatic, democratic translations which the major mission-oriented institutions were itching to commission (and which some individual efforts had already, as we will see, embarked upon), but also was thoroughly *scientific*. A translation such as the TEV could, it seems, at least in principle be *scientifically proved* to be a faithful translation of the source text. Nida and his followers would certainly (and increasingly, as time went by) admit that in practice the proof was hard to come by. The 'kernels' of meaning were difficult to establish with certainty; the 'deep structures' of language were perhaps deeper and less easily recoverable than originally thought. There was an increasing uncomfortable awareness that the theory did not really deal with contextual difficulties. However, with more work, better understanding and more sophisticated techniques, fidelity could in principle be shown to operate (or not operate) in a given translation. Not since the infallible 'translation committee' of the LXX had such a guarantee been offered, and the great missionary translation bodies seized it eagerly. Fuelled by their enthusiasm, Nida's project achieved a life and momentum of its own.

As Nida's project began, in fact, the currents of linguistic philosophy were already moving strongly against him. From within the Anglo-Saxon philosophical tradition, Quine had, for example, already in 1960 put the very idea of synonymy in translation in doubt. Soon, and coming from an entirely different angle, Derrida was undermining the notion of textual determinacy upon which the idea of back-translation also depends. Then Steiner's critique of Chomskian linguistics in *After Babel* in 1975 called the whole project into question. What part could 'deep structures' really play in translation theory if they were so deep that they could never be brought to light? Shouldn't we be suspicious of a model which claims to be scientific but can neither demonstrate its operation, nor make verifiable predictions? How could a purely linguistic model possibly deal with the infinite variety, complexity and nuance of human expressive powers? Above all, as languages represent different ways of introspecting and of interacting socially with others – different ways of being human – is a scientific/mathematical model the right paradigm at all? Isn't there something ineluctably social and contextual about language? These criticisms, and many others, put the attempt to found translation theory upon Chomskian linguistics into a pattern of long-term retreat, and led, via a more socio-culturally informed *socio-linguistics*, to the modified form of 'functional equivalence'. Chomsky himself had already disowned the attempt to use his theory to underpin an approach to translation: 'The existence of deep-seated formal universals . . . implies that all languages are cut to the same pattern, but does not imply that there is any point by point correspondence between particular languages. It does not, for example, imply that there must be some reasonable procedure for translating between languages.'

The theory of 'dynamic equivalence' was, then, subject to early and highly effective criticism. In response, 'dynamic equivalence' morphed into 'functional equivalence', with a much more nuanced notion of how language functions in a context which has extra-linguistic as well as linguistic dimensions. The idea of the *function* of a text replaced that of its dynamic effect, and began to deal much more effectively with the question of how reception context might affect that function. For example Vermeer talks of two texts from different cultures which could 'differ to a greater or lesser extent, but . . . would be culturally equivalent, both being considered natural behavioural acts with the same 'function' in their respective culture specific settings.' What is interesting about this for our purposes is that the idea of fidelity (the 'equivalence' part of dynamic equivalence) has been absorbed into that of function (the 'dynamic' part). It has, in other words, been quietly dropped. Equivalence is now defined in terms only of the functions which texts play – functions which may be determined by any number of actors in the process, and which can certainly not be straightforwardly 'read off' from the text.

The term 'equivalence', therefore, represents a ghost concept – it is the ghost of the concept of fidelity, which has quietly died and been buried without a funeral. A number of contemporary translation theorists have noticed the hollowing-out of the term 'equivalence', and try not to use it. Tellingly, though, even though Chomskian 'scientific' equivalence has been shown not to exist, this ghost concept continues to lurk in the literature: – Derrida would describe it as a 'trace' – particularly in the biblical translation community. This is because fidelity is not, in the field of biblical translation, an optional concept in the way it seems to be in much 'secular' translation. This leaves translation theory in a peculiar position. Nida's 'dynamic equivalence' was always a two-stroke engine: the 'dynamic' describes the effect (or function, as it became) of the text; the 'equivalent' describes the relation of fidelity. If the latter fails, the engine won't work. This, I would like to suggest, is the reason why new Bible versions tend to be very reticent about their approach to translation: the preface or 'To the reader' section is usually quite clear, for example, about the approach which has been taken on source-critical issues, but remarkably *unclear* as to translation theory. Metzger's preface to the 1989 NRSV may serve as an example: in amongst several pages of explanation, he has only one sentence on translation theory. 'The Committee has followed the maxim: As literal as possible, as free as necessary.' Similarly, the Good News Bible says only that it is 'faithful . . . to the meaning'.

This brings us back to Daniell's problem in assessing these translations. He is aware that some standard of fidelity should be in operation, but is also aware that the mainstream notion of 'equivalence' as it has been used in biblical translation is at best highly problematic. More importantly, he also knows that it is this notion of 'equivalence' which has given him the TEV and all the other 'have-a-nice-day Bibles', as he calls them. 'By their fruits shall ye know them', as his beloved Tyndale would say, and the fruits in this case are not good. So all he can do is resort to his intuitions and give us the commonsense statement that a translation should be 'accurate.'

The curse of the Holy Marriage

There is a second reason why Daniell doesn't make the comparison with the source text. This is that he already has his fixed reference point – and it is the Tyndale Bible. For him, the only relevant comparison to make is with Tyndale's translation, not with any Greek or Hebrew source text. Although he would doubtless disagree with the proposition thus baldly expressed, it is nonetheless the hidden assumption behind every line of his paper. Tyndale has become, for him, what Rosenzweig named *Schriftum*, 'scripture': the product of a holy marriage between a language and a text. The idea of the holy marriage is that at a certain point in the development of a natural language, a text is encountered which is of such cultural importance that it becomes 'the book everyone must have read.' The fact that it is so means that it is not only an instance of that language, but becomes a determinant of it. This text may be either a home-grown text (such as Dante, for Italian), or a translation – such as the Luther Bible, for *Hochdeutsch*. Translations are, for him, subject to a 'certain law of uniqueness . . . (E)very great work of language can in a certain sense be translated into another language only once.' Although Rosenzweig did not express himself in these terms, we might say that the 'holy marriage' text establishes a certain set of agreed and 'authorised' 'equivalents'. Once Luther has decided that πίστις (pistis) 'means' Glaube ('faith'), then it does so mean, and becomes embodied in the language.

'What God has joined, let no man put asunder.' The ἱερὸς γάμος, the holy marriage, is the perfect union, achieved at just the right time, unrepeatable, and authoritative for all time. At least 'It remains immortal as long as the connection between this moment and the past is not catastrophically ruptured.' Rosenzweig articulates a schema of translation history in which, when a language and text first 'encounter' each other, sketchy, tentative attempts at translation begin to appear. These 'trots' are followed by a good 'working draft', and then, finally, the holy marriage occurs: text and language find each other. For Rosenzweig, this unrepeatable moment tends to arrive just as a *Schriftsprache*, a literary language, is being formed. At this point, a community of language speakers is longing for the text: 'it is the time when the receiving people comes forth of its own desire and in its own utterance to meet the wingbeat of the foreign work- the time when the act of reception is motivated not by curiosity, by interest, by edification, not even by aesthetic pleasure, but by the whole range of a historical movement.'

Now, Rosenzweig was thinking about Luther and the German Bible in naming the holy marriage. However it will be very obvious that, if he is right, we could make the same observations about the English tradition, in which Tyndale and the KJV play such a significant part. The KJV meets the requirements of a 'holy marriage' translation: it comes along shortly after a period of vigorous development of the language; it is of overwhelming cultural importance; and it has stood the hackneyed 'test of time.' One of the evidences evinced by Rosenzweig for the existence of an ἱερὸς γάμος translation, is that despite the passage of time it is still readily understandable by a modern language user. The Luther Bible, the KJV and Tyndale all pass this test; their predecessors, even by only a few years, don't. The holy marriage is facilitated by a willingness of the host language to accept innovation: Tyndale was, we might say, 'right' to translate Job 19.20 'by the skin of my teeth'. He was 'right' because his rendering of the difficult Hebrew source was not only accepted but savoured and enjoyed and remembered, and became part of English, so that modern, more semantically 'correct' renderings are simply '*not* right'. No subsequent translator can ever be accorded this privilege. teiner shares this view of great translation, which 'can only occur once' for a given work. For him, though, that moment might occur only once the reception *Schriftsprache* has some history: the KJV was accepted so quickly and so completely because it was written not in a contemporary Jacobean idiom, but in an earlier, Elizabethan form. It arrived in the world fully formed, pre-packaged with a certain nostalgia, and with the 'weight' which can only come from familiarity and repetition. It also had a magnificent forerunner, in the form of Tyndale.

In English Bible translation, we might regard the Anglo-Saxon Gospels, the fragmentary efforts of the Middle Ages, Aelfric's glosses and the various Psalters as the 'trots'; the 14th Century Wycliffite Bible as the 'good working draft'; and Tyndale and the other 16th century translations (which all, to a greater or lesser extent, had some dependence on Tyndale) as the 'final drafts'. The KJV then represents the holy marriage itself, a marriage which was institutionalised and given the full authority and majesty of the state. Although there are of course different ways of schematising translation history, the view which Rosenzweig expresses is comfortably in accord with many scholarly accounts of the translation of the Bible into English. For example, Lynne Long evaluates the Wycliffite Bible translators thus: 'Their achievement lay not so much in the quality of the work, but in the addressing, however crudely, of the specific problems of translating the Scriptures into English . . . Theirs was the first complete rough draft in a lengthy process that was not to be completed satisfactorily until centuries later.' We should carefully note here the tell-tale word 'completed'. The process of translation is presented here in an almost teleological mindset, with one generation of translators providing a 'rough draft' for another which follows. Once Tyndale and the KJV had 'completed' the work, the Holy Marriage was in place.

After the promulgation of the Holy Marriage in 1611, there was a long, contented honeymoon. English and the Bible had found each other, and following the moment of ecstatic union, all was well for two and a half centuries. Renewed translation work did begin in the form of more or less idiosyncratic individual efforts in the 18th Century, but the possibility of institutionally sanctioned revision did not appear until the late 19th Century. Only in the 20th Century did the floodgates really open, with the results which we observe.

Figure 1, below, provides a greatly simplified schematic representation of this interpretation of the translation history:

Such a schematic is, of course, highly simplified. Amongst the features which it ignores are: the complex web of influences between the various versions; the influences from outside – particularly Luther but also the Roman Catholic Douay version; and the differences which arise from the various source texts used (including the major factor of the Latin Vulgate, which was the source for all of the translations until Tyndale). It also ignores the fact that not everyone was completely satisfied with the holy marriage, when it came: the Geneva Bible of 1560, for example, lingered for a long time after 1611 in certain circles.[1]

The purpose of this schema is not to attempt an accurate and complete portrayal of translation history, but to gesture towards the indisputably important position which the KJV has, and towards certain problems associated with that position. All lines of influence pass through it: it is the fulcrum of English Bible translation. Rosenzweig's main concern was to draw attention to the dangers involved in the phenomenon of the holy marriage. It may, of course, prove to be both a blessing and a curse. The key danger is that the translated text may *itself* come to be regarded as 'Scripture' or *Schriftum*. An authoritative interpretation

---

1   Famously, it was the Bible taken by the Pilgrim Fathers to Massachusetts in 1620, and seems to have been the only version used by the Plymouth and Virginia settlements. See Berry, 2007, p.22.

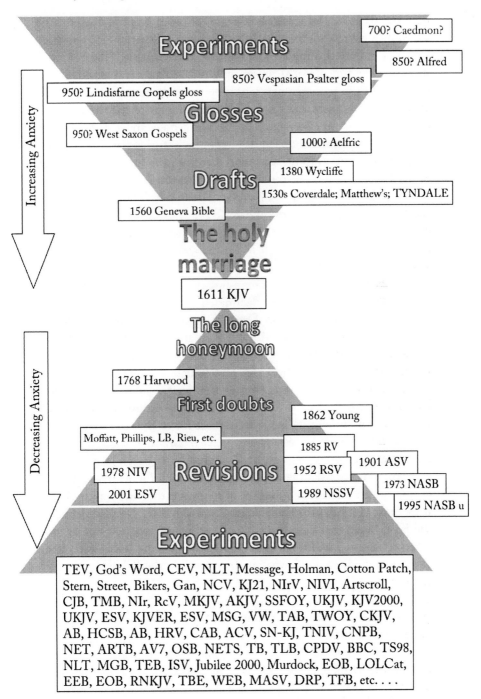

The Story of a Marriage

then stands as an obstacle to *further* acts of interpretation. Rosenzweig
was fully alive to the dangers of idolatry in this situation: in protestant
German culture, Luther's Bible became and remained 'the bearer of
its [the church's] physical presence,'[1] and idolatry was avoided only
by virtue of the presence of a vigorous oral culture surrounding it. In
sermon and exegesis, the implacable permanence of the monumental
translation was ameliorated. The holy marriage must not, in other
words, be taken too seriously: if it becomes 'set in stone', it effectively
prevents any further translation, and therefore any further true reading
of the Bible. For this reason, Rosenzweig was in favour of continually
updating and revising the *Lutherbibel*. 'Every translation is a messianic
act, which brings redemption nearer.'[2] He was also keen to produce a
completely different version of the Hebrew scriptures, one which bore
as little relationship as possible to Luther's work. This impulse resulted
in the collaboration with Martin Buber and the marvellous *Die Schrift*
whose publication only began many years after his death, and once its
potential readership had been decimated by the holocaust.[3]

We may postulate that in Daniell's mind, the Tyndale Bible has
become *Schriftum*, the authoritative standard by which other versions
(including the original) are measured. Daniell's 'angle' on all of this
is that he has gone behind the text which we most naturally see
as the holy marriage translation, to the draft, which in his opinion
contributes what is best to it; however, this is an unimportant detail for
the present argument. What is important for us to see is that a ἱερὸς
γάμος translation can effectively *prevent* any new translation. Nor
can this be remedied simply, as Rosenzweig suggests, by permitting
revision and retranslation. In the chapters which follow below, we will
encounter an enormous quantity of evidence that translation of the
Bible into English effectively ceased in 1611 with the completion of
the KJV. Since that date there have been many revisions but no new
interpretations. I will work hard to substantiate this audacious claim:
amongst the phenomena we will encounter are the following:

The tramlines of interpretation

In version after version, what we find are endless revisions of the
same basic translation. Although it is evident throughout the text,
it may be illustrated by examples from poetic passages such as the
Magnificat (Luke 1: 46-55) and the other Lukan hymns. It is
especially noticeable here because it is the characteristic of poetry to

1   Rosenzweig, 1925 (in Rosenwald, tr.1994), p.54.
2   Preface, I *Die Schrift*, 1954.
3   Publication of *Die Schrift* began in 1954 and was completed in 1962.

admit of a wide range of interpretation; and yet we find that, however many times the re-translation is attempted, the interpretation which emerges is always mysteriously the same. However many times we revisit Mary's opening statement, we cannot escape from the beautiful 'My soule magnifieth the lorde. And my sprete reioyseth in god my savioure . . .' There are, of course, many different interpretations of Mary's song amongst commentators and exegetes. Even a mainstream commentator like Fitzmeyer observes that the piece can be interpreted as a reiteration of Hannah's song in 1 Samuel 2, as a canonical psalm, as a Maccabean victory hymn, or even along the lines of the Qumran War Scroll.[1] Feminist interpreters have, naturally, taken great interest in the Magnificat, and have noticed that there is something very odd about it as a song on the lips of a young woman who has just heard that she is to bear a child: the political and economic themes, the focus on power and overturning of the social order. Schaberg interprets Mary's exaltation as the reaction to being rescued from the shame of rape or seduction, the ταπείνωσις from which she is saved then referring to the law on this matter in Deuteronomy 22.24.[2] It is also possible to see a certain self-preoccupation in the song – Mary's focus is not on the baby to be born, but on herself, as is clear from the five-fold repetition of the first person pronoun in vv 46 to 49. In mentioning these possible interpretations, my purpose is not to choose between them, but to observe that – not surprisingly for a poetic passage – there are *many* possible ways of reading it. What *is* then surprising, is that there are (to my knowledge) no translations in English which substantially stray from Tyndale's:[3] none which pick up on Mary's astonishment at the way the shape of her life has been changed, or the questions she has about it, or her preoccupation with the apparently chaotic nature of divine power, for example. None, even, which draws out Mary's disgraced condition at the time or the pathos of her naive motherly optimism, an optimism very soon to be shattered by Simeon (Luke 2.34-35). The tramlines of interpretation are encountered even (or perhaps especially) in those versions which attempt a 'radical re-telling.'[4] What *The Message* yields, for example, is, as so often, a 'jazzed

---

1   Fitzmeyer, 1970, I, p.358.
2   Schaberg, J., 1990, p.100.
3   I am not suggesting here or elsewhere that Tyndale's interpretation was novel at the time; in fact, his rendition was quite well in accord with Wycliffe's, Luther's and even the Vulgate. The 'holy marriage' does not necessarily represent, and probably will not be, a work of remarkable innovation: rather, it is the point at which a tradition, which may be long established, crystallises.
4   This is the self-appointed task of 'Good as New' (see Appendix) but it

up' version of the same familiar interpretation: 'I'm bursting with God-news; I'm dancing the song of my Savior God.' Long before *The Message* appeared, Steiner summarised a certain kind of translation practice thus: 'Too often, the translator feeds on the original for his own increase. Endowed with linguistic and prosodic talents, but unable to produce an independent, free life-form, the translator . . . will heighten, overcrowd, or excessively dramatize the text which he is translating to make it almost his trophy.'[1] *The Message* here, rather than attempting a genuine, present day interpretation of Mary's song, merely produces an inflated version of the traditional interpretation. This accounts for what we can only describe as the somewhat grotesque, almost comic nature of much of the work: it is as if we were to take a 17th Century Englishman and ask him to deliver the Bible in rap. *The Message* (and other versions with same agenda) represent a 17th Century interpretation of the Bible, wrapped in 20th Century speech-forms.

Recurrent fascination with 'literal' translation

The argument that scriptural translation should be 'literal' or 'essentially literal' has a very long and respectable history, and it will not go away.[2] As we will see in Chapter Six, there are some important respects in which literal translation is to be preferred to 'functional equivalence'. Here, though, I would like to point to a feature of the arguments used, which illustrates the continuing stultifying effect of the Holy Marriage on translation practice. When advocates of literal translation make their case, they often do so by invoking a list of canonical words which 'should' be present. For example Grudem, approaching the Magnificat says: 'The verse contains both the Greek word for "soul" (psyche) and the Greek word for "spirit" (pneuma). Essentially literal translations all translate them as "soul" and "spirit" (KJV, NKJV, RSV, NRSV, NASB, NET, ESV and HCSB. . . .). But dynamic equivalence translations leave out Mary's spirit and mostly leave out her soul as well . . .'[3] This statement of the case is so thoroughly steeped in the 'holy marriage' that it is almost indistinguishable from it: the 'essentially literal' translations, we note, are all those stemming from the authoritative KJV which is set at the head of the list. Its authority, moreover, is so total that the ancient Greeks even anticipated it; so they even had a 'Greek word for "soul"' and a 'Greek

---

could equally be applied to many other recent versions.
1   Steiner, 1975, p.423.
2   Competent recent statements of the case include Ryken, 2002, and Grudem, in Ryken, Collins, Poythress, Winter, 2005.
3   Grudem et al, 2005, p.39.

word for "spirit"' and so on! The literalist case is often stated thus, and is
entirely based on the unstated assumption that it is the KJV (representing
the holy marriage between English and New Testament Greek) which
gives us the authoritative list of which English words are 'for' which
Greek words (or even, as Grudem seems to be saying, vice versa). I have
not been able to find a living advocate of 'literal' translation who does
not share this assumption,[1] which is, of course, not logically integral to
'literalism': it would be perfectly logical to argue in favour of 'essentially
literal' translation, whilst proposing that ψυχή be translated 'breath'
and πνεῦμα be translated 'wind'. In Chapter Six we look at 'essentially
literal' translation again, naming Grudem's variety of literalism 'Gametic
literalism', but noting at the same time that it is not necessarily so.

The missionary project

We will encounter in Chapter Three a case where the translator (Nida, in
this instance) seems to be attempting to translate not the Greek original
of Acts, but an English version, into the target African language. I will
argue that this practice is, in fact, the norm in missionary translation.
What the translator or translator's aid is attempting to do is to facilitate
the target language's encounter with *our interpretation of the Bible*, not
with the original text. This may be observed both in how the text is
translated, in the provision of textual notes, commentaries, and study
aids. The reference point is always the translator's favoured version of
the ἱερὸς γάμος, the Holy Marriage. So, for example, we are told by
Ernst Wendland that in translating Ruth 1.22 for a certain audience,
we have to note that 'The time reference is important, since in a Tonga
sociocultural setting it would immediately arouse the suspicions of the
people whose village Naomi was entering. A person does not usually
move during the period extending from after the fields have been
planted until after the harvest has been completed. One's crops mean
life, and therefore it must have been some serious offence which drove
Naomi away from her former home at such a time. Perhaps it had been
that she was guilty of practising witchcraft – after all, were not all her
men now dead?[2] Wendland's point is that the translator has to find some
way of preventing the Tongans from forming a 'highly plausible, though
mistaken, interpretation for the receptor language audience.'[3] What
seems to be important to Wendland is that the target audience for his

---

1   Examples of non-living proponents of non-gametic literalism include the
early 20th Century dispensationalist, A.E. Knoch, whose *Concordant Version*
represents an independent-minded literalism. See *Abbreviations*.
2   Wendland, 1987, p.171, cited in Gutt, 2000, p.94.
3   Gutt, 2000, p.95.

translation forms an interpretation of it in line with his own – in this case, including the idea that the chronological information conveyed carries no significance as to Naomi's motivation for the journey or her state of mind,[1] The projected Tongan translation must, in other words, conform to the ἱερὸς γάμος: no other interpretation could be valid. If this is not sufficiently clear in the translation itself, it must be rammed home by footnotes. This is presumably because, in the words of another missionary translator, 'People from cultures that are just now coming in contact with the Bible do not have the benefits of a Christian heritage and so have more to learn . . .'[2] The arrogance of this standpoint is breathtaking: there is not a hint of recognition that the Tongan obsession with witchcraft, which Wendland finds so unacceptable, might be just the right interpretive 'key' for this aspect of Ruth. What, exactly, is it which makes him so certain that his 'early-modern scientific' interpretation is better? There is a double tragedy here: the Tongans are prevented from having their own genuine 'first encounter' with this piece of scripture; and we are prevented from learning from that encounter. The tragedy is all the more poignant because it is irremediable: the Tongans (or the Adioukrou, or the Silt'i, or whichever minority language group we are discussing) can never re-live this moment.

The history of translation and re-translation

One thing which Daniell does not do, we should note, is condemn translation *per se*. This positive approach to translation is on the whole the dominant one in the Western Judeo-Christian tradition, though always with strong dissenting voices. There are three decisive moments in this tradition: the LXX was the first, and perhaps the most important. Because it became the authoritative scripture of the Christian church, it is easy to forget that it was conceived within a Jewish context as a 'holy marriage' between Greek and Hebrew. Initially certainly tolerated and perhaps welcomed within Judaism,[3] it only became unacceptable once it had become the authoritative translation for the early Christian church,

1 As a matter of fact, some commentators suggest that Naomi may indeed be feeling guilty about something at this point in the story – see Robertson Farmer, in NIBC 1998.
2 Hill, 2006. To be fair to Hill, she goes on to say that 'we are all learners', and her study of the Adioukrou of West Africa does acknowledge that that people may have something to teach us about the first century Jewish conception of the supernatural.
3 Philo, certainly, was enthusiastic in his endorsement of the marriage. See *On the Life of Moses*, 2.6.36, 37. Some scholars also see the Letter of Aristeas as also representing a Jewish view of the translation. See Seidman, 2006, p.47.

and implicated in disputed readings – this is, perhaps, an example of the 'fundamental rupture' which Rosenzweig talks about, as the only way a holy marriage can be broken.[1] The next decisive moment is the acceptance of the Greek gospels (which represent a double-translation, from oral Aramaic to written Greek); and the translation of the Greek scriptures into Latin, most particularly into Jerome's 'Vulgate'. There have always been dissenting voices, but this positive tradition remains dominant. The key documents of Christianity, unlike those of Islam, were not dictated by God to a scribe who simply wrote them down; there has usually been an acceptance of the secondary nature of scripture, as penned by individuals who were indeed inspired by God, but whose autographs we have lost. The key texts of the Reading of the Law (Nehemiah 8), the Great Commission (Matthew 28) and Pentecost (Acts 2) seem to mandate such translation as may be necessary to take God's word to all his people in a form which they can in some sense understand.[2]

Daniell, of course, speaks from within the broad Protestant English tradition, and for him it is perhaps self-evident that translation is possible, necessary and desirable; yet there is also within his statement the trace of an anxiety that none of these things are so. The Holy Marriage is the balm for this anxiety. Seidman's recent study of the history of Jewish-Christian translation provides a fascinating survey of the successive building and resolution of this anxiety, which will not go away, because it arises from something quite fundamental; namely the Christian's anxiety that his or her faith relies on the translation of another religion's foundation documents.[3] One way of viewing the history of translation of the English Bible is in terms of the progressive build of anxiety during the period of 'trots' and 'working drafts' (i.e. up to and including Wycliffe and Tyndale), to the point of ecstasy, at which the holy marriage is achieved (Tyndale/the KJV). Thereafter, anxiety progressively declines: the *Schriftum* is in place and inviolable, therefore everybody can relax. During the period of building anxiety, the arguments against translation form themselves on the lips of those in authority, those who have

---

1   That this particular 'holy marriage' begins as a romance and ends in bitter divorce can be deduced even from the language of scholarship on the subject. Seidman observes that Aristeas 'lovingly details the social intricacies, the hesitations and flirtations of the Septuagint romance . . . '(p.50). The divorce can be represented by the new Jewish Greek translations by Aquila, Symmachus and Theodotian – usually thought of as unsuccessful 'affairs', they nevertheless spelled the end of the marriage.

2   Further texts may be cited in this vein: Zephaniah 3.9, and Acts 8.26-39 perhaps have important translational elements.

3   Seidman, 2006, especially pp.1-36.

'political' responsibility.[1] The anxiety is not that people will be able to access the Scriptures, but that a new translation will represent a new interpretation, and that this novelty will cause dissension and division in the Body of Christ.[2] This anxiety is, as we well know from the bloody history of the Reformation, both well-founded and rational; in this context, the putting to death of recalcitrant translators and would-be translators is completely understandable.

Once the ἱερὸς γάμος is achieved, though, the 'political' argument begins to wane. The authorities begin to appreciate that though new translations may continue to appear, they will not contradict the supreme interpretive act embodied in the holy marriage. Subsequent attempts at re-translation are thus viewed with progressively more tolerance, and finally are even welcomed; the role of recalcitrant is thrust on the poor lay-Christian, who is asked to struggle with yet another 'up to date' version of the same interpretive act. Church bodies are happy to commission and finance what are either explicitly or implicitly revisions. By the beginning of the 21st Century, incumbent church leaders show themselves eager to endorse a variety of new translations of very different complexions.[3]

---

1   St Augustine; Archbishop Arundel; the earlier Henry VIII, Thomas More, etc.

2   St Augustine's famous correspondence with St Jerome on the latter's Latin translation work, which became known as the Vulgate, provides the paradigm for what will follow. Augustine's arguments are essentially political: '. . . it will cause extreme difficulty if your translation is widely adopted: the Latin churches will then differ violently from the Greek churches.' Letter 71.6, tr. Kelly. Although different arguments are used to address the expediencies of different times, the common theme is not the evil of translation itself but (in the words of More) the fear 'lest if it were had in every man's hand there would great peril arise and that seditious people would do more harm therewith than good and honest folk should take fruit thereby.'(More, Complete Works, v.6, p.332).

3   In 2004, Rowan Williams, Archbishop of Canterbury, endorsed Nicholas King's new rather literal translation of the New Testament as 'a fine and quite distinctive addition to the ranks of Scripture translations. As a guide to the kind of study that will nourish a robust and grown-up faith, it will be hard to beat.' In the same year 'Good as New' appeared, a translation exercise of a very different kind, involving substantial re-writes, ditching parts of the traditional canon and adding new parts. It, too, received a ringing endorsement from Williams. The role of political/pastoral leadership is interpreted here as embracing and welcoming variety, and to this extent is in part merely 'political correctness'; what is surprising, nonetheless, is the great latitude in interpretation of what is, after all, the foundation document for the institution of which he is head. Such latitude is born only from a complete confidence that, whatever interpretation it is which emerges, it will only be a new manifestation of the ἱερὸς γάμος.

We may, then, venture some tentative answers to David Daniell's implied questions. Yes, the art of biblical translation is something we have lost. The reasons for this are not, in fact, mysterious: the key problems are the overwhelming presence of the ἱερὸς γάμος, which inhibits any subsequent act of interpretation, permitting only revisions; and the absence of clear theoretical criteria of fidelity, which criteria would give a foothold from which the Holy Marriage could be challenged. The problem paradoxically turns out to be the very 'model of excellence' which Daniell holds up for our consideration.

Is there a remedy? To my mind, the only possible solution is to approach the problem from a theoretical angle. Only from the firm ground of a robust theory of translational faithfulness can the beast of 'the holy marriage' be tackled. Without such a foundation, the translator is always going to be overwhelmed; and in this respect his or her position is very different from that of Tyndale (or Jerome, or Luther, for that matter.) Tyndale proceeded without what we would recognise as a clear theory of translation, we may conjecture. As πρόδρομος to the ἱερὸς γάμος he did not need one. The purity and innocence of his approach is not available to latter-day translators: just to manoeuvre our frail craft around the huge monument which our predecessor created, we need far better navigation equipment than he ever had.

The need for theory

Our critical examination of David Daniell's paper serves as an example of what happens when the examination of translation issues takes place in a theoretical vacuum. In the absence of a firm platform from which to survey the issues, the only approach is to rely on common sense and intuition. Part of my argument is that this is a permissible strategy up to and including the consummation of the ἱερὸς γάμος , but not thereafter. The principal reason for this is that one of the effects of a ἱερὸς γάμος translation is to govern the intuitions of the relevant language community: it just seems so obvious and natural that the text should be translated a certain way, that intuition alone is never going to suggest an alternative.

A pioneer, arriving in a new and lushly fertile country, but one that is empty of human habitation, may proceed by responding to his new environment in simplicity, and with a certain spontaneity: there will be problems, but they will be overcome each in their turn. There is also a certain sense of provisionality, of improvisation: the settler knows that the rude huts he is building today will, if colonisation proves successful, be rebuilt and improved by his successors. Thus, for example, the two versions of the Wycliffite Bible in the 1380s have this air. As soon as the first version was complete, in 1384, a quite substantial revision began. In the Prologue to the latter, the author (possibly John Purvey) declares that, 'a symple creature haÞ translatid Þe Bible out of Latyn into English,' and appears to encourage future translators to continue the work.[1]

Should the traveller arrive in the new country and find, on the other hand, that it is already populated, that there are thriving settlements with already established customs and practices, he must adopt a different strategy. He or she has to deal in some way with what is already there. She or he would be wise to remain on ship for a while, and work out a strategy, whether it is one of positive engagement, hostility, or 'neutral' disengagement. There is no viable strategy in which the efforts of predecessors can be simply ignored.

The KJV, even as it arrives, is already showing some consciousness of its status as the holy marriage between English and Bible. 'The Translators to the Reader' with which it is prefaced acknowledges the efforts of predecessors, saying,

> Truly, good Christian reader, we never thought from the beginning that we should need to make a new translation, nor yet to make of a bad one a good one (for then the imputation of Sixtus had been true in some sort, that our people had been fed with gall of dragons instead of wine, with whey instead of milk); but to make a good one better, or out of many good ones one principal good one, not justly to be excepted against, that hath been our endeavour, that our mark.[2]

The KJV acknowledges predecessors but is careful not to encourage successors; it is self-consciously seeking to establish an authoritative 'principal' translation, 'not justly to be excepted against.'

Despite this discouragement, the Bible, or substantial parts of it, has been translated into English several hundred times and all but a few handfuls of these efforts have been undertaken after 1611; that is, after the consummation of the 'holy marriage'.[3] This is the Bible which we call the Authorised Version, and every translation produced after it has had to deal with its existence, and therefore in some sense to bear its imprint. Anyone with the temerity to attempt yet another English translation is

1   KJV, Hudson ed., 1978 (1388), The Prologue, pp.67-72.
2   Norton, ed 2005, (1611)'The Translators to the Reader', xxxi.
3   There is no way of being certain about the numbers: both because many translations achieve only a small circulation and are hard to track down, and because there is so much current translation activity. See the Appendix for a taste of translation activity since 1990.

highly likely simply to produce another child of this fruitful marriage. Some do so deliberately, their retranslation being more or less explicitly positioned as a revision or 'update' of the ἱερὸς γάμος, a renewal of vows, as it were . So, for example, the ESV, which declares itself to be 'in the classic mainstream of English Bible translations over the past half-millennium.'[1] The starting point for the exercise was the 1971 RSV, but 'our goal has been to retain the depth of meaning and enduring language that have made their indelible mark on the English-speaking world and have defined the life and doctrine of the church over the last four centuries.' In the statement of its translation principles, nothing more is said than that it is 'essentially literal'; and this is understandable – to perform such an update, no particular theory is required, because the ἱερὸς γάμος is not being challenged, only brushed up for the present day.

Others seek to position their translation work more radically. So, for example, Andy Gaus'"The Unvarnished New Testament"[2] declares, in its blurb, 'The fresh approach taken by this gifted translator strips away the thick layers of convention and 'Biblical' language which often clouds the meaning of the original words.' Unfortunately, Gaus does not explain to us on what theoretical basis he has approached the work. The author of the introduction (not Gaus, but George Witterschein) states, absurdly, that 'what Gaus has done is to translate the Greek as if the nearly two thousand years of Christian history had not occurred. He has translated the Greek into modern American English, period.' A glance at any page of the translation is enough to show that this, of course, is not true;[3] nor could it be true. The words, the very categories of thought available to Gaus are, in part, the product of this Holy Marriage. What if Gaus had been locked in a sound-proof box for his entire life, and forbidden to read or hear any word from outside? He would thereby escape the influence of the ἱερὸς γάμος , but, if this had been his fate, he would not, of course, have been able to do the translation – for he would not know English, or have any idea of how to communicate with modern American English speakers about how they viewed the world.

Gaus cannot, of course, escape the influence of the holy marriage. Any translator must deal with it. And as is often the case, those who naively

1   ESV, Preface, vii.

2   Gaus, Andy, 1991.

3   For example, and to continue the 'case study' opened in the Introduction to the present work, the Magnificat begins: 'My soul magnifies the Lord,/ And the breath within me has been delighted by God my savior.' The 'breath' is a welcome innovation – but everything else remains 'holy marriage', and, most importantly, the interpretation of Mary's song which is offered does not stray one iota from the specification entrenched in the KJV.

assume that they can ignore it are the ones most likely to be steeped in it.[1] Willing or not, all bear the genetic likeness of their parents.

It is important to appreciate the attitude toward theory which I seek to advocate here. I am *not* suggesting that there is any final theoretical solution to the problem of translation (George Steiner famously refused to call his 'poetics' of translation a theory at all.)[2] The open-ended human problem of understanding and misunderstanding each other is not susceptible to a magic bullet. What I *am* saying, though, is that if, in the case of biblical translation, we approach the work thinking that we are guided by 'common sense' or 'intuition', we are sure to simply reproduce the ἱερὸς γάμος. The purpose of theory is to give us a platform outside the field of forces created by the series of 'equivalents' in the holy marriage, from which we can look at the problem again.

What kind of theory?

In 1975 George Steiner bewailed what he termed 'the sterile triad' which had characterised English discourse about translation 'at least since Dryden.'[3] The idea that a translation can be too literal, too free, or just right is as long-lived a notion as the story of *Goldilocks and the Three Bears;*[4] to confirm that it is alive and well, we need to look no further than Metzger's 'To the Reader' for the NRSV of 1989, which we have already mentioned.[5] Steiner pointed out that the approach we have chosen Metzger to exemplify (there are many, many other examples in biblical translation) seems to suggest that translation is a one-dimensional problem, whose issues relate only to the mechanical question 'How literal should we be?' He wanted to return translation to the hermeneutic fold: to try to position translation as the interpretive question at its most acute -- 'How should we understand this other?'[6] This agenda is picked up by Paul Ricoeur, who speaks of translation as 'linguistic hospitality . . . the act of inhabiting the word of the Other paralleled by the act of receiving the word of the Other into one's own home, one's own dwelling.'[7] Steiner and Ricoeur and all sympathisers in between,

---

1   One is reminded of John Maynard Keynes' famous dictum that 'everyone who claims to be practical is a slave of some usually defunct theory.'
2   Steiner, 1992, (Preface to the Second Edition of Steiner 1975), xv.
3   Steiner, 1975, p.249ff.
4   See Porter, p.144 in Porter and Boda, 2009.
5   Another example is Barnstone's explanation about his own *Restored New Testament* (see *Abbreviations*). Using Dryden's schema, he finds himself in 'the difficult middle way'. Barnstone wants to 'make the literal literary', a nice slogan but not developed in theoretical terms.
6   Steiner, 1975, p.18.
7   Ricouer, 2006 (2004), pp.19-20.

insofar as they can be said to have a 'programme' to change approaches to translation, have failed – certainly as regards biblical translation. Steiner's famous 'Hermeneutic Motion'[1] offers a four-fold approach to translation which, I argue elsewhere,[2] provides an 'ethics of translation' of enormous explanatory power and subtlety, yet it has not been successful as a guide to the actual nitty-gritty of translation. It is too philosophical, too elevated in tone, and insufficiently reproducible. In the intellectual atmosphere of the 1970s, when so many of the large-scale efforts at Bible re-translation were launched, the available options did, to those holding the purse-strings, seem to be ranged along that same one dimension: either one went for 'literal' (ESV, NKJV, NASB, etc.) or one went for 'free' (TEV, CEV, and later The Message), or something in-between (NIV, NRSV etc.). If one opted for the 'free' end of the scale, it was usually felt that some theoretical justification was required, and this was without exception sought and found in Eugene Nida's exposition of the doctrine of 'dynamic equivalence', or, as it later became, 'functional equivalence.'

What is of interest for our argument here is that Nida's approach, even while apparently mandating great latitude in translation practice, did nothing to loosen the grip of the Holy Marriage on biblical translation. His concept of 'equivalence', when combined with his own profoundly conservative theology, simply reproduced the ἱερὸς γάμος in another form. It encouraged the 'one dimensional' view of translation, and dragged the argument back onto this ground, away from the hermeneutic approach which Steiner and others were advocating, so that the opponents of 'dynamic equivalence' (and 'functional equivalence', as it became) found themselves able to argue *against* it only by arguing *for* literalism.

We might, then add to the list of baleful consequences of the Holy Marriage, the enslavement of theory to its purposes. To reiterate the argument: (1) The ἱερὸς γάμος appears at a certain point in history. It is the unique moment when a language community 'accepts' a foreign text. (2) From this point onwards, the Holy Marriage is part of that language community's common life – it establishes a set of agreed correspondences between source and target languages, which find themselves enshrined in lexica, dictionary and commentary – in an entire interpretive community. (3) Theoretical explanation for these correspondences is sought, and found in concepts such as 'functional equivalence'. (4) Once this theoretical framework is established, it becomes possible to produce new versions of the ἱερὸς γάμος, which can be shown to be (more or less – there is scope for argument within the community) 'functionally

---

1   Steiner, 1975, p.312ff.
2   Goodwin, 2010, p.5ff.

equivalent' to it. In this way the Holy Marriage behaves like a particularly successful meme – it spreads through the entire language community like a virus, seizing control of important neural pathways in the process.[1] Most effectively, even when a 'carrier' thinks he or she is producing a new version of the text, it turns out to be just another successful mutation of that interpretation. It becomes impossible for a language user to challenge this dominant interpretation. It is important to note in passing here, that I am not advocating any foolish conspiracy theory: there is no villain to accuse of 'suppression' of rival interpretations. As we saw in the Introduction, official, institutional anxiety about translation reached its peak in the period up to production of the Holy Marriage, and subsided rapidly thereafter. It is in the nature of viral infection to spread all on its own; there is no need for a guiding hand.

Nor, in using the language of 'infection', do I intend to suggest that there was something wrong with the ἱερὸς γάμος; that it is a 'mistranslation', for example. The latter is a questionable term in any event, on all sorts of grounds. The Holy Marriage – the KJV – was a masterful act of interpretation. In the world of the early 17th Century, it represented a wonderful, relevant, resonant and coherent interpretation of the biblical writings. To be sure, it was mandated and given the authority of the newly created 'United Kingdom', but this would not have been enough, on its own, to give it the long-standing authority it achieved; that came from its inherent quality.[2] The problem with the ἱερὸς γάμος is only that it prevents further acts of interpretation. Even that is not inevitable, but is a product of – to use the overtly religious language of Rosenzweig – an idolatrous relationship to the translation.

'What, then, shall we say to these things?' The drift of my argument, even if it is accepted, may of course be such as to lead to despair: the Holy Marriage cannot be challenged. We are all its heirs, and we must quietly

---

1   I use here the language of 'memetics', given its most definitive form by Susan Blakmore, 1999. However, another expression of the same idea can be found in Steiner, 1975 – it is the purpose of translation to 'infect' the host community with a prophetic 'word' from the other. See p.427ff.

2   The caveat we must make to this statement is that which by now will be obvious. C.S Lewis expressed 'the extreme uncertainty of our literary judgement' when approaching the KJV, precisely because the Authorised Version was so familiar, and had so many 'unfair' advantages, such as being the text used for Handel's Messiah. 'What chance has Coverdale's second rendering (in the Geneva Bible) with us, against the familiarity of the Geneva adopted by the Authorised and most unfairly backed by Handel? A man would need to unmake himself before he was an impartial critic on such a point.' (Lewis, 1954, p.211).

submit. Like all demons, though, it is much less powerful once it is named. Once we acknowledge its presence and name it, we can move on to deciding how to deal with it. One way to tackle the beast would, of course, be to simply try to produce a new translation which was not in its sway. We could, like Sir Gawain, ignore the remains of all the brave Knights who have previously come this way and arrived at the same sticky end: we could turn a blind eye to the fact that many of those who, in embarking on their work, have hubristically declared that they are going to produce a 'new' or a 'fresh' or a 'restored' translation, only to find themselves having spawned a monstrous semblance to the ἱερὸς γάμος.

The problem with such attempts is that, unless the theoretical ground of the argument is somehow shifted, the Holy Marriage is going to win, every time. It will win either by swaying the translator to produce another version of itself or, simply, by showing the translator to be 'wrong'.

Our intuitions, in other words, have been determined by the ἱερὸς γάμος. The present work seeks to escape this bind by shifting the theoretical ground of debate. Whilst we are still thinking in terms of 'equivalence', be it 'functional equivalence', 'dynamic equivalence', or some other formulation, we will find it difficult to challenge the holy marriage translation and will remain on the tramlines. Only by moving to a more hermeneutic model will it be possible to re-interpret the text and with that re-interpretation produce a genuinely new translation.

We noted earlier the problems in applying the insights of hermeneutics to translation. All of this is changing, however, with the development of Relevance Theory, to which we will now turn. The reason that Relevance Theory is so exciting in the field of translation is that it represents a fusion of approaches. Its positive engagement with contextual issues, and particularly its conception of communication as the enlargement of shared context, means that it provides a genuinely hermeneutic foundation for translation theory. At the same time, though, and because it springs explicitly from Paul Grice's pragmatics, it is expressed in terms which are readily understandable within the Anglo-Saxon tradition which is so important to English translation.

In 1990 Ernst-August Gutt published the first rigorous exposition of what we will call the Relevance Theory of Translation (RTT). His contribution has been followed by several other positive engagements, and is actively in use in some biblical translation projects.[1] The reasons why I regard this as a tremendously positive development will be apparent from the exposition of the theory which follows.

---

1   See for example, Wendland, 1996; Green and Turner, 2000; Green, 2002; Hill, 2006; Brown 2007; and especially Wendland, 2008.

Chapter Two

Challenging the Holy Marriage:
Relevance Theory and translation

What is Relevance Theory?

Relevance Theory is a development of communication theory springing from Paul Grice's notion that there must be a 'Co-operative Principle' at work in conversation. This principle underwrites Maxims of Conversation underlying our ability to communicate. One of these, the so-called Maxim of Relation, simply specifies this: Be Relevant. Grice observed that speakers in conversation seem to observe this maxim, both in speaking and in interpreting, and that it is this 'unspoken agreement' which allows communication to take place, despite the indeterminacy of reference which is characteristic of language. Two linguists, Dan Sperber and Deirdre Wilson picked up this ball in the early 1980s, identifying that the requirement to 'Be Relevant' had the potential to explain a great deal in communication theory. They have produced a theory of human communication of great elegance and wide-reaching implications, including in the field of translation theory.

Before we approach the application of the theory to translation issues, it is necessary to outline, however briefly, the main tenets of the theory itself. It is not part of my purpose to provide a detailed exposition of Relevance Theory; the approach here is to summarize the key features of Relevance Theory rather briefly, and only insofar as their exposition is necessary to the understanding of the present work. My approach is heavily informed not only by Sperber and Wilson themselves, but also by Blakemore and Gutt.

The idea in a nutshell is that the possibility of communication between human beings is guaranteed by the *Principle of Relevance* or, in the light of further reflection by Sperber and Wilson in the 2nd edition, by the two Principles of Relevance:

1. Human cognition tends to be geared to the maximization of *relevance*.
2. Every act of *ostensive* communication communicates a presumption of its own optimal relevance.

where *relevance* is defined as providing the greatest possible *contextual implications* for the hearer at the lowest *processing cost* to him. *Contextual implications* are useful modifications of a hearer's 'cognitive environment' – that is, their set of assumptions about the world. 'Processing cost' is the cost to the individual in time and energy of processing an incoming message.

In the material that follows I will refer frequently to 'the principle of relevance' or 'the presumption of relevance', by which I always mean (2). Behind the two principles is the conception of human beings (in line with the thinking of cognitive psychology) as being, or at least as having, information processors which are hard-wired with a number of optimizing capabilities, one of which is the ability to form inferences about each others' behaviour. Communication can occur between human beings because of our ability to make inferences about each others' behaviour, including the ability to infer intentions. In successful communication, a speaker has a *communicative intention* which is recognized by his hearer. The process of communication involves both code and inference: the speaker encodes her communicative intention in ostensive behaviour, often, but not always, including language; the hearer decodes this behaviour, and uses the output of this process to form hypotheses about the speaker's communicative intention. Because the hearer knows that the speaker will have formed her utterance in accordance with the principle of relevance, he knows that the interpretation which he arrives at which yields the best set of *contextual implications* for him at the *least processing cost* is the *speaker intended interpretation*. In this way, the *cognitive environment*, or *context*, of a hearer can be changed as a result of something he hears from the speaker.

Relevance Theory, then, provides an account for how communication occurs in a context. Its engagement with context is both positive and integral to the postulated processes, and in this it represents a substantial step forward from purely semiotic theories, which have to account for contextual difficulties separately. In relevance theory, mutual shared context (or cognitive environment – the terms are used almost interchangeably) determines how a communication will be formed and how it will be interpreted. The goal of communication, moreover, is defined in terms of growing the cognitive environment shared between speaker and hearer.

The dominant image of communication theory before Relevance Theory was that of 'transmission'. Earlier, this transmission was thought of in terms of 'conveying' a message, often in some kind of vehicle – and this is reflected in the very language we use: we *put our ideas into words*, and so on. Later, transmission is often thought of as a pipeline, or telephone or radio signal: *is our message getting through?* These are cases in which metaphor may come to dominate conceptualisation. One of the consequences of this set of metaphors is the negative conceptualisation of context: the pipeline (or road, telephone wire etc.) is at best a source of friction and drag on the message getting through; at worst it can prevent the message getting through, and presents itself as an obstacle. One of the features of Relevance Theory is to replace this set of images with one involving the sharing and creation of mutual context. Rather than context being seen as a negative factor in communication, it is seen as positive: communication can only occur at all if there is shared context. The imagery is reminiscent of Gadamer's 'fusion of horizons.' Perhaps one might think of a carp swimming through a series of interconnecting pools, which to the extent that they do interconnect, represent a 'shared environment.' Another appropriate metaphor, I would like to suggest, is that of a forest canopy: a monkey swings through the trees, leaping from branch to branch. Providing the trees are placed close enough to each other, and providing the monkey maintains his momentum, and his nerve does not fail, he will not fall to the forest floor. The imagery here is not only of a positive use of context to create meaning; it also replaces the idea of the completely passive, 'given' and inert message, with the notion of something living. The reasons for this will become clear later in the present work, and particularly in Chapter Six, when we revisit some central problems in translation.

The Relevance Theorists continue the long-established pragmatic methodology of building their case through the use of many examples. I will restrict myself here to just two example utterances, one to demonstrate 'descriptive use' and one for 'interpretive use.' Rather than the usual 'conversational' examples, both are from our sample text of Luke Chapters 1 and 2 – this will help establish a frame of mind for considering the text in relevance terms, as well as illustrating the principles of the theory.

In Luke 1.9 we are told of Zachariah that he goes:

εἰς τὸν ναὸν τοῦ κυρίου ('into the temple of the Lord')

In 1st Century Greek, ναός could be used to refer to the dwelling place of any god, or the inmost part of a temple, where the image of the god was placed. Additionally, κύριος could be used of any person – man or god – in a position of power or authority, or ownership. Yet Luke has no problem in communicating to his readers (and to us, if we can read Greek) that Zachariah was going into the *inner sanctuary* of *the Lord's Temple*, a very specific place in Jerusalem, and it has never occurred to any commentator to think otherwise. How is this done?

The answer in terms of Relevance Theory is that a reader or

hearer, when encountering this statement, consults her cognitive environment, also referred to as 'contextual assumptions' or sometimes simply 'context', and uses the assumptions she finds there to process it. In this case, she finds readily available assumptions to the effect that Zachariah is a priest of the line of Abia, that all this happened when Herod was king of the Jews, that Zachariah and his wife are obedient to *the Lord* (not to some other god) and so on – Luke has been careful to set the scene, and has made sure that the contextual information needed to process the statement is very readily at hand. Thus, whilst she knows that ὁ ναὸς τοῦ κυρίου *could* refer to *any* inner sanctum of *any* powerful man or god, when she processes the statement in accord with the principle of relevance, she concludes that the interpretation which yields *the best possible set of contextual implications for the least possible processing cost*, is that this is the Temple of the Lord in Jerusalem. The reason she is confident to do so, moreover, is that she recognises *Luke* as a *communication*, which therefore offers an implicit guarantee that it is relevant, or worth processing. Something is relevant when it yields adequate contextual implications for not unreasonable processing cost.

This example serves to illustrate four principles which are important to our application of Relevance Theory. First, decoding is not enough: we saw that just being able to decode the semiotic content did not ensure that communication took place – a further, inferential process was required. Second, if the audience do believe they are in a communicative situation, they will *automatically* begin to make inferences about communicative intention. Third, applying the principle of relevance is always a matter of trade-offs, or optimisation. Fourth, communicators may exploit context which already exists between them and their audience, but they also progressively *build* it.

The creation of contextual implications

The point of communication, it should be noted, is the creation of contextual implications. The relevant interpretation of an utterance involves the modification of a hearer's cognitive environment in a potentially useful way. This arises from combining assumptions conveyed in the utterance with assumptions already present in the hearer's cognitive environment. Utterances have both *analytic* and *contextual* implications, but it is the latter that constitute the 'pay-off' for communication.

For example, if we look at the full clause in which the above example occurs, we find:

κατὰ τὸ ἔθος τῆς ἱερατείας ἔλαχε τοῦ θυμιᾶσαι εἰσελθὼν
εἰς τὸν ναὸν τοῦ κυρίου,
'according to the custom of the priesthood, he was allotted to
burn incense, entering into the temple of the Lord'.

Luke 1.9

This statement has both analytic and synthetic implications. Analytic
implications are those which may be deduced purely from the statement
itself, and include such conclusions as, for example, follow from the temporal
forms – there was a moment 'before', and then 'it fell to Zacharias by lot' to
go into the Sanctuary and burn incense. Synthetic implications are those
which can be formed only by combining the information in *this* sentence
with *another* assumption. In Relevance Theory, a *contextual implication* is
a particular kind of synthetic implication, in which that other assumption
is some assumption already in the hearer's cognitive environment. So, for
example, in this case, the reader's cognitive environment may include the
knowledge that there were twenty-four orders of priests, each with a large
number of individuals, and that each order would serve for two weeks in
the year. Combining these assumptions with the new one suggested by
Luke 1.9, the reader may form completely new contextual implications,
for example:

> This was a very rare, perhaps a once-in-a-lifetime experience for
> Zacharias.

This sort of contextual implication is a potentially worthwhile modification
of a reader's cognitive environment in a way that analytic implications are
not, and Relevance Theory requires that a communicator produces an
utterance, as an interpretation of her thought, which is optimally relevant
in the given context. 'The optimal interpretive expression of a thought
should give the hearer information about that thought which is relevant
enough to be worth processing, and should require as little processing
effort as possible.' Speakers form a communicative intention. This then
has to be encoded in such a manner that hearers will be able, using the
principle of relevance, to infer that intention.

Conceptual address

Communication is ostensive, and it always consists of some behaviour
which makes manifest to a hearer the communicative intention of
the speaker. This behaviour may be non-verbal: a shrug, or a cough,
for example. However, commonly, it will be verbal; and verbal
communication is used where a greater degree of explicitness is
required. Verbal communication can be more explicit than non-

verbal, because it exploits language's ability to express concepts. A concept such as that indicated by a natural language word – let us say 'mother' – is conceived as consisting of an 'address' in the mind of that language user.

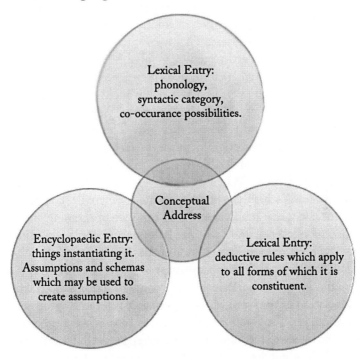

Conceptual Address in Relevance Theory

The **lexical entry** is thought of as containing 'information about the natural-language counterpart of the concept: the word or phrase of natural language which expresses it.'[1] Such information includes phonology – the sounds which allow us to identify the word and connect it with the concept, as well as the word's syntactic role and co-occurrence possibilities. The **logical entry** consists of a series of deductive logical rules which apply without exception to every instance of the concept. They can be described as 'meaning postulates' and approximate to what some traditional semantics describe as its 'denotation.'[2] These are thought of as rules essential to the concept, in the sense that anyone who did not know them could not really be said to have understood the concept. The 'logical entry' also tends to be relatively stable over time and amongst language users at a given time;

---

1   Ibid p.86.
2   Sperber and Wilson claim further that these rules are all elimination rules in the terminology of classical logic. See Sperber and Wilson 1986, p.86.

and there is a point at which it is complete. The **encyclopaedic entry**, by contrast, contains a potentially wide and open-ended range of possible uses or instantiations of the concept. The encyclopaedic entry does not contain logical rules which must be applied, but rather a wide range of possible contextual uses. It is likely that different language users will share much of this encyclopaedic information in common; however, it is not essential that they do so. Here Relevance Theory can accommodate the widely held intuition, perhaps best articulated by George Steiner, that we each of us speak our own idiolect and that we are all therefore continuously translating each other. 'Each living person draws, deliberately or in immediate habit, on two sources of linguistic supply: the current vulgate corresponding to his level of literacy, and a private thesaurus. The latter is inextricably a part of his subconscious, of his memories so far as they may be verbalized, and of the singular, irreducibly specific ensemble of his somatic and psychological identity.'[1] When we use a word, of course there is an agreed core of meaning which you share with me – otherwise, communication could not take place at all. Steiner calls this core of meaning, the vulgate, 'a statistically-based fiction',[2] whereas Relevance Theory seeks to provide a principled account in terms of logical entries.

Thus, for the case of the concept marked by the English word 'mother', we might say that the lexical entry contains information about the pronunciation of the word, about its possible roles in English sentences (as a noun, verb, or noun-modifier in this case – 'my mother mothers me on the mother-ship') and its co-occurrence possibilities (its pronoun can be 'she' but not 'he', for example). The logical entry contains a series of logical elimination rules specifying that, for example, a mother must be a female parent, that a mother must precede in some manner the thing mothered and so on. The encyclopaedic entry (a much larger entry than the other two) contains a wide variety of instantiations of the word, including metaphoric uses and so on. We will make considerable use of this model of conceptual address in the chapters which follow.

The process of communication

The three 'entries' associated with a conceptual address play different roles in human cognition. The lexical entry contains the 'handle' for the concept – the physical sounds or marks on a page whereby it is recognised (its phonology or its graphology, respectively), and is therefore the initiator of the de-coding module of the brain. The logical entry contains the logical elimination rules associated with the concept,

---

1   Steiner, 1998, p.47.
2   Ibid.

and activates deductive processes. The encyclopaedic entry contains a depository of memory which can be brought to bear to assist with the inferential processes which will complete the act of communication.[1]

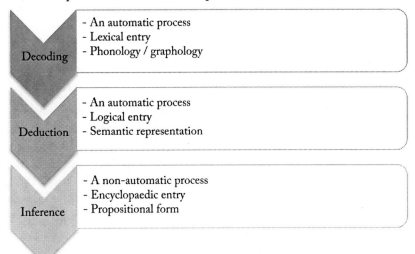

Decoding
- An automatic process
- Lexical entry
- Phonology / graphology

Deduction
- An automatic process
- Logical entry
- Semantic representation

Inference
- A non-automatic process
- Encyclopaedic entry
- Propositional form

Processes in Relevance Theory

Communication is therefore thought of as involving both semiotic and inferential processes: the relevant interpretation is the output of a series of processes involving decoding, explication and pragmatic inference in a context. Importantly, the first two processes are thought of as happening automatically, whereas the hearer/reader has some control over the last.

As we will see, this phenomenon gives a speaker a rich set of options in terms of forming an utterance which will communicate relevantly. Often, a speaker will provide *communicative clues* which guide her hearer towards the intended interpretation – for example, she may use a particular syntax or exploit the sound-qualities of certain words. Gutt makes particular use of this idea in constructing his model of 'direct translation.'[2]

Non-literal language use

We should note that the requirement here is to convey information which yields adequate contextual effects for minimal costs, not to be a *literal* interpretation. Relevance theory does not need to provide a separate account for tropes, metaphors, litotes and general 'loose talk' as Sperber and Wilson call it[3].

---

1   This, and the preceding diagram are, of course, simplifications. Readers interested in the full description of the processes involved are directed to Sperber and Wilson, 1986, pp.38–203.

2   Gutt, 1991, p.130. See particularly Chapter Five.

3   Sperber and Wilson, 1985/86, pp.153-71.

Thus for example, we read later in Luke that:

Ἔλεγεν οὖν τοῖς ἐκπορευομένοις ὄχλοις βαπτισθῆναι ὑπ'
αὐτοῦ, Γεννήματα ἐχιδνῶν, τίς ὑπέδειξεν ὑμῖν φυγεῖν ἀπὸ
τῆς μελλούσης ὀργῆς;

'So he said to the crowds coming to be baptised by him: "You
brood of vipers – Who warned you to flee from the wrath to
come?"'   Luke 3.7

Another problem case for classical Pragmatics: how do hearers
know to interpret John figuratively rather than literally? And how do
readers know that they know, in the narrative world constructed here
by Luke? The answer is again found in the principle(s) of relevance: the
hearer interprets the statement to yield the best possible implicature,
for the minimum possible processing cost. Assuming that the 'crowds'
coming out to see John are of the two-legged, rather than the no-
legged variety, the minimum cost/maximum implication solution is
going to be interpretation as a stereotypical expression, which stands
in a relation of interpretive resemblance to another more literal
utterance. Resemblance in Relevance Theory always means *interpretive*
resemblance, and utterances are thought of as resembling each other to
the extent that they, when interpreted in accordance with the principle
of relevance in the same context, will yield the same interpretation. In
this case, the text we have is in Greek, and we know that the people
coming to John were inhabitants of Judea. Our conjectures about to
what literal statement this figure bears resemblance must be governed
accordingly. ἐχιδναι ('vipers') do not appear in the LXX, but as a kind
of ὄφις ('snake') they have negative imagery, exemplified of course by
their role in Genesis 3 and Numbers 21. In this Lukan passage, it is
perhaps a context exemplified by LXX Micah 7.17 which he has in
mind: 'the peoples' are seen by the prophet as snakes squirming from
their holes on the day of retribution[1]. John is just about to tell the
crowds that they cannot rely on being children of Abraham – perhaps
they, like the nations, should be seen as squirming, in which case John's
statement is used for its interpretive resemblance to a phrase like: 'You
offspring of the unclean, no better than the gentiles – who warned
you to slither away into your holes?' Additionally, though, LXX Psalm
57.3 to 5 associates the ὄφις with the ἁμαρτωλός ('sinner') who can
speak venom, but has become *deaf* to the wise, and this would also

1   Snakes often seem to be around when judgement comes – as well as
Micah 7.17, see Amos 5.19, Jermeiah 8.17, Isaiah 14.29.

be a resonant context.[1] Communicators use figurative statements both for their brevity and for their interpretive potential. John has used a description which is both much shorter than a literal statement (and therefore prima facie lower cost to process) and much richer in terms of contextual implications. His communication is thus highly relevant – and the utility of figurative language in this respect accounts for its ubiquity.[2] As we will see, this aspect of the theory is of great importance in the establishment of a Relevance Theory of Translation.

Interpretive resemblance

Relevance Theory thus has at its core an account of the *interpretive* use of language: many utterances are *echoic* – that is, they do not seek to resemble something about the world, but rather to resemble another utterance. In fact there is a sense in which *all* utterances are interpretive: the process of communication begins and ends with an interpretive act. The speaker first 'entertains' a thought, and the act of communication then begins when she produces an utterance which *resembles* that thought in relevant respects: '. . . we want to argue that there is an . . . essential interpretive use of utterances: on a fundamental level, *every* utterance is used to represent a thought of the speakers'.[3] A speaker thus chooses her utterance for its resemblance in terms of the principle of relevance to the thought she wants to convey.[4] In Relevance Theory, this is spoken of in terms of giving it *propositional form*.

At the other end of the communication process, the hearer, too, uses the concept of interpretive resemblance: listening to the speaker's utterance, he uses the principle of relevance to infer a thought which resembles that utterance in relevant respects.

Interpretive resemblance is, then, defined as follows:

1   Nor do the options given exhaust the interpretive possibilities – snakes, for example, play important but very different roles in Greek religious discourse of which Luke was aware (the Pythia of Acts 16, for example).

2   'Cette notion d'une imagination qui produit la métaphore – c'est-à-dire tout dans le langage, hormis le verbe être. . .' Derrida, 1967, p.17. The importance of metaphor is critical to the appraisal of Relevance Theory. A critique of the approach is provided by Goatly, 1997, see pp.135-166.

3   Sperber and Wilson, 1995, p.230.

4   In fact the processes of resemblance begin even earlier, in that the thought 'entertained' in stage 1 is said to resemble either a state of affairs (ie descriptive use) or another thought (ie interpretive use). As this notion would lead us into Sperber and Wilson's epistemological assumptions, which are neither relevant to my argument here, nor essential to relevance theory, I have not focused on this stage in the account given above.

'Two propositional forms P and Q (and by extension, two thoughts or utterances with P and Q as their propositional forms) *interpretively resemble* one another in a context C to the extent that they share their analytic and contextual implications in the context C.'[1]

Resemblance is thus always a matter of interpretation within a given context, and an utterance resembles another to the extent that when processed in that context its interpretation will be the same – that is, to the extent that it yields the same analytic and contextual implications. Resemblance must also be a matter of degree. Utterances may resemble each other by virtue of their analytic implications, or of their contextual implications, or both. Speakers exploit the range of possible resemblance in, for example, reported speech and quotation.

Which of these options is chosen will depend on the communicative intention of the reporter as a new communicator, and his or her assessment of the cognitive environment (context) of her audience. Is it relevant to report the very words someone chose, or is relevance best served by a more indirect interpretation? In a police interview, the context shared by the interviewer and interviewee includes the manifest assumption: *Anything you say will be taken down and may be used in evidence against you,* and in such a context it may well be judged highly relevant to report the exact words used. In Luke, the principle characters are usually quoted exactly – in the trial of Jesus by ὁ διάβολος ('the devil') in Luke 4, as one example amongst many, care is taken to record exactly what was said. On the other hand, Jesus' opponents are sometimes only reported indirectly – for example, οἱ ἀρχιερεῖς καὶ οἱ(γραμματεῖς ('the chief priests and scribes') whose reaction to Jesus' question about John's authority is reported in Luke 20.7.

Relevance Theory of Translation (RTT)

Gutt's fundamental insight is that it is only a short step from this account of intra-lingual interpretive use of language to an account for inter-lingual translation. He poses the question: what if that which we call 'translation' were simply the interpretive use of language across linguistic boundaries? If this were so, the principle of relevance would underwrite and also define the limits of successful translation. Gutt defines translation as 'inter-lingual quotation',[2] where the choices available to the translator form essentially a range similar to the range of options in reporting speech *intra*-lingually. In what he provisionally

---

1   Sperber and Wilson, 1988a, p.138.
2   Gutt, 1991, p.105.

defines as 'Direct Translation', the translator attempts to 'directly' quote the original communicator, and seeks to provide in the target language all and only the same analytical and contextual implications as were present in the source language, assuming they are processed in the same context. In 'Indirect Translation', a looser interpretive resemblance is sought, in which analytic implications, and even some of the contextual implications, may be lost, but the key contextual implications which the translator assesses as relevant to her audience are preserved.

There is thus no especial mystery about translation: in Gutt's account it represents simply a specialized echoic use of language across linguistic boundaries. What level of interpretive resemblance a translator seeks to achieve will, as in any echoic or interpretive use of language, depend on her informative intention and her assessment of her audience's context. If she is seeking to make an interpretive utterance, the requirement is 'resemblance in relevant respects'. In this conception of translation as a special case of interpretive use, the requirement for a successful translation is that it is '(a) presumed to interpretively resemble the original . . . and (b) the resemblance it shows is to be consistent with the presumption of optimal relevance, that is, presumed to have adequate contextual effects without gratuitous processing effort . . . that is, resembles [the original] closely enough in relevant respects.'[1] As for all considerations of relevance, this is of course context-dependent. The requirement for a faithful translation is twofold: produce a target language text which 'should resemble the original – only in those respects that can be expected to make it optimally relevant to the receptor language audience' and one which is 'clear and natural in expression in the sense that it should not be unnecessarily difficult to understand.'[2] By aiming for optimal relevance, just as the original communicator did, the translator as *secondary* communicator can be faithful, and can convey to the mind of the second hearer the communicative intention of the source language speaker.

A translation, then, is intended to achieve relevance by virtue of its resemblance to another utterance. This is the theory-specific definition: rather than attempt to define translation in terms of some feature of the target-language text, or some proposed relation between it and the source text, a translation is defined by the communicative intention of its creator: if it is intended to achieve relevance by virtue of its resemblance to a source, it is a translation. (This is, as we will see, quite important in the field of biblical translation, where perpetrators of new versions often attempt to side-step criticism by declaring their offerings not to be translations at all.)

1   Ibid, p.101.
2   Ibid, p.102.

Communicative Clues

In 'direct translation', the translator has made a decision that the 'resemblance in relevant respects' must include not only *what* the speaker said but *how* she said it: in other words, that this is a situation in which resemblance must apply in (so far as possible) all respects. She will therefore attend not only to *what* its overall relevance is in the given context, but also *how* it achieves that overall relevance. Therefore such a translation will seek to produce an utterance which, when compared to the original utterance, will share all its analytic and contextual implications; and to achieve this it will pay careful attention not only to the semantics of the utterance but also to the way in which the original speaker used the stylistic value of words, syntax or other effects as 'communicative clues' for how the utterance is intended to achieve relevance. Where there is a conflict between clues – for example, where the semantics of an utterance and its poetic form cannot both be preserved in a target language utterance, the translator will use the principle of relevance as the 'gold standard' to decide what her echoic utterance will seek to preserve. Gutt cites the example of a German nonsense poem by Morgenstern (*Das aesthetische Wiesel*, 'The Aesthetic Weasel'), where the joke can be preserved in English translation only by altering the semantics[1]. In this case, the translator may decide that the form plays a greater role than the precise semantics in how the piece achieves relevance. In the field of biblical translation, the great acrostic poems in some of the Psalms and in Proverbs present a similar challenge. In Chapter Five, we will look closely at Gutt's communicative clues, in the context of biblical translation.

Why Relevance Theory?

There are some features of relevance theory which make it particularly suitable as a platform from which to tackle the Holy Marriage. Some of these will only become fully clear as we consider concrete examples in the chapters to come; others are of a more general nature. In brief, the latter are as follows.

RTT starts from where we are

If we are to challenge the ἱερὸς γάμος, we want to do so from as secure a ground as possible. In contrast to theoretical approaches which are grounded in social or cultural features,[2] Relevance Theory

---

1   Gutt, 1991, p.111ff.
2   See for example Leech, 1983, p.10.

holds the promise of a universally applicable principle underwriting all human communication, whatever the social/cultural context. Indeed it is this claim which has sparked the strongest critical response to Relevance theory: an apparently totalizing claim, such as this represents, raises the question of whether the theory can accommodate what we know about the enormous *differences* at play in reception context.[1] At times, Relevance Theory does seem to be making more or less impressionistic claims about features of communication which are grounded in 'human nature' – especially when Relevance Theorists forget to point to the very real grounding which it has in cognitive psychology. In fact, the theory is securely based in real psychological processes, and starts from the observation that people actually *are* able to communicate remarkably well: it is, in Gutt's terminology a 'competence – oriented research' approach.[2] People do form inferences from other people's behaviour – and this observation seems to apply universally to human behaviour. In the framework provided by cognitive psychology, this tendency is seen as a subset of the more general ability which we have to interpret our environment in terms of agencies which have inferable purposes. 'Inference systems make us attend to articular cues in environments and produce specific inferences from these cues . . . Skeletal versions of the(se) principles direct knowledge acquisition from infancy.'[3] A rather well known instance of this sort of ability is language acquisition itself: as Chomsky pointed out, human infants are able to infer complex rules of grammar, despite the 'poverty of the stimulus' provided to them.[4] There are many other instances, such as agency detection systems used to infer the presence of predators or prey, and in fact some theorists have postulated that human perception is subject to 'hyper-active' inferential systems which, for example, detect agency even when none is present.[5] The ability to interpret the behaviour of predator or prey has clear survival value; so does the ability to interpret the behaviour of other humans.

In Relevance Theory, the human mind is conceived as being a sort of information processor. The conception of human beings as being computers (in the technical sense – that is, as a sort of Turing

1   See Green, K, 1997, p.133, Mackay, 2002, p.169, Pilkington, MacMahon, Clark, 1997, p.139, Toolan, M, 1999, p.255.
2   'CORT' defines, for him, Competence-Oriented Research in Translation - Gutt, 200, p.205.
3   Boyer, 2002, p.132.
4   For an accessible account, see Maher and Groves, 1996.
5   Boyer, pp.106-191. Boyer draws extensively on Guthrie, 1993.

machine) is securely grounded in cognitive psychology, which has made significant progress in the last thirty years.[1] Within cognitive psychology, and following the work of Jerry Fodor,[2] the mind is understood to be just such a device, which operates in modular fashion, with some modules acting as collectors of inputs, and some acting as processors.

The idea that humans, as information processing devices, might work by seeking to *optimize* useful contextual effects and processing costs has both strong intuitive appeal and a secure scientific foundation. Theoretical psychologists are not in full agreement as to *how* this takes place: the dominant view suggests that different 'modules' of the mind perform different functions, and that there is or are further specialist modules which perform the optimizing calculations. This is the view inherent in Fodor's modular view of mind; others have a more holistic view of its functioning – however, there is no doubt that the mind is capable of making such trade-off decisions.[3]

Relevance theory simply postulates the extension of this sort of ability into the arena of communication. Thus, in ostensive communication, the hearer forms inferences about the speaker's intentions based on her verbal or other behaviour. Again, we find that this is what people do: if someone starts speaking (or waving, or gesturing in some other way), her audience immediately, and spontaneously begins to form inferences about what she 'means'.[4] In language, we use a developed sign system to allow communication to be more explicit. Semiotic systems as well as inferential systems are thus at work; but Relevance Theory does not need a separate account for language-based communication, which operates according to general principles of human behaviour which can be seen to work in many areas.

---

1   See Eysenk and Keane, 2005, p.3.
2   See Fodor, 1983.
3   Styles, 2006, pp.153-180, summarises the debate.
4   In passing it is important to remind ourselves that this conception of inference is a far cry from the pre-Wittgensteinian notion of 'intention' as some kind of shadowy internal entity or process which the hearer has to grasp – for example the kind postulated by Wimsatt and Beardsley in their famous exposé of 'the intentional fallacy'. The concept of intention used here is that developed within the pragmatic tradition, particularly by Grice himself and John Searle. The processes of inference are, as a matter of empirical observation, used by hearers to generate a construction of a speaker's 'communicative intention'; speakers exploit this behaviour in their own. None of this requires the postulation of mysterious mental objects. For a summary of the issues, see Thiselton, 1992, p.59 ff and p.558 ff.

What is true of Relevance Theory itself is also true in RTT. Put two or more people in a room who do not share a common language and they will immediately start translating each other. Translation is *of course* an every-day, quite ordinary phenomenon. When we begin to learn French or Spanish at school, we do not need to first undertake a foundation course in translation theory, just as when we first start to play football we don't need to be taught Newtonian physics. We seem to be able to undertake the *practice* of translation quite naturally, even if we have no idea what it is we are doing theoretically. We also have strong intuitions about what constitutes a good translation, and as we saw in Chapter One, when our professional translations do not meet those intuitive expectations, we *feel* the problem, even if we do not have the theoretical equipment to *explain* it. In this sense, the activity of translation feels like something of the same type as linguistic competence in general.

Translation is not sui generis

Translation turns out to be a subset of that quintessentially ordinary-yet-mysterious activity of communication. 'Any model of communication is at the same time a model of translation, of a vertical or horizontal transfer of significance. No two historical epochs, no two social classes, no two localities, use words and syntax to signify exactly the same things, to send identical signals of valuation and inference. Neither do two human beings.'[1] In Steiner's conception of language we each as individuals speak our own 'idiolect', based on our own personal lexicon, and we are therefore in ordinary discourse constantly translating ourselves and others. 'The concept of a normal or standard idiom is a statistically-based fiction.'[2] Relevance Theory provides a theoretical account for Steiner's insight that all communication is translation.

The advantages of this re-assimilation are considerable, and they do not all fall under the heading of 'Occam's Razor'. If communication theory and translation theory are held separately, they have a tendency to appear to pull in opposite directions. For example, classically, Schleirmacher placed the requirements in opposition: either the reader is moved towards the text (the requirement of translational fidelity), or the text is moved towards the reader (the requirement of communication). This kind of opposition also results in the sterile debate about literalism we discussed in Chapter One: either the text is translated 'literally' (the translation requirement) or it is translated 'idiomatically' or 'fluently' (the communicative requirement); you cannot have both. In the words of the old (and rather sexist) joke: translations are like women – they can be either beautiful, or faithful – but

1   Steiner, 1975, p.47.
2   Ibid.

not both.[1] Once translation theory is seen as part of communication theory, we are more inclined to be sceptical about these supposed oppositions: the requirement is rather, stated simply, to successfully communicate at each stage in a continuous process, from an original author, to a translator, and from her to a new audience.

A realistic account for failure and success

However, Relevance Theory also has a useful contribution to make in terms of helping define and explain the *limitations* of successful translation. In Relevance Theory, what makes communication possible is threefold:

1. Shared psychological machinery – speaker and hearer are capable of making inferences;
2. Shared sign-system – speaker and hearer use the same semiotics;
3. Shared context – speaker and hearer share cognitive environment.

Traditional accounts of translation tend to emphasise item 2. The reason for this is that it is this requirement whose absence is so palpable in inter-lingual translation situations; this in turn leads to the commonly held but false view that once 2. is solved, the essential problems of translation are over. The language of 'equivalence', we have argued, tends to exacerbate this misperception, reinforcing the commonsense (but false) idea that a sign in a given language denotes a real 'thing', so that all the translator has to do is to determine the 'thing' being denoted, and find a sign for it in the target language. Translation theorists, of course, know that this is not true – but, if their approach is rooted in the idea of equivalence, this means that their final account will have to either stretch semiotics unnaturally to cover all kinds of communication difficulty, or to invoke insights from other areas of theoretic enquiry, quite separately.

Relevance Theory allows us to see that items 1 and 3 are just as important in successful communication, and therefore in translation. The third requirement, shared context, is of major importance and we will discuss it many times in detail in the chapters which follow. Where there is insufficient shared context, communication will not occur – and this applies intra-lingually as much as in inter-lingual translation. There are some situations of attempted communication where the hearer just doesn't 'get it', and where this is not a question of the wrong words being chosen by the speaker, or of 'interference' in the process of transmission, but of the absence of enough shared context. Anyone who listened to the 'dialogue' between Union leaders and

1   Naomi Seidman gives a wonderful extended exposition of this 'joke' and its ramifications in the politics of translation. See Seidman, 2006, pp.37-72.

company bosses in the strike-torn Britain of the 1970s will understand this point. By way of contrast, when we share a lot of context (for example with a spouse or very close friend) communication can be effective even when utterances are highly abbreviated or, considered from a more distant perspective, ambiguous.

Item 1. is often passed over in silence in the literature, probably because it is so obvious. However, together with item 3., it specifies important limits to what we can expect to achieve in translation. It suggests, for example, that machine translation is impossible, or at least that it will only be possible once artificial intelligence has reached the level of sophistication at which *interpretation* can occur. Relevance Theory requires that at each 'end' of the communication process there is a mind, and that that mind is capable of inference (including the ability to infer human intentions) and of performing trade-offs, either consciously or unconsciously. This, then, would suggest the basic specification for true machine translation: it is the same blue-print as for the human mind. In practice of course, machine translation projects undertaken to-date[1] have sought to find a short-cut to achieve some sort of result without having to contemplate the wildly ambitious project of creating a human mind. Success has been achieved in machine 'translation' of highly formulaic stereotypical texts such as weather-reports.[2] In terms of a Relevance-theoretic approach, what this amounts to is a sophisticated look-up system: the computer program consists simply of a large database of matched stereotypical phrases, with look-up procedures. In this sense, it is not much more than an intelligent lexicon, and this falls a long way short of human translation in which a 'new word' is conveyed from one mind to another.

Programs such as that used by Alta-Vista's *Babel-Fish©* are more ambitious in the sense that they attempt some grammatical analysis as well as having large encyclopaedic memories. The program can therefore potentially receive a completely new input phrase and produce an output translation. As anyone who has attempted this knows, it does so with very mixed results.[3] In Relevance-theoretic terms, the problems it has are not only or perhaps mainly semiotic, but more to do with establishing context, or shared cognitive

1   See Somers, in Baker, ed., 1998, p.143ff for an excellent summary.
2   The famous example is the Meteo system, developed by the TAUM group in Montreal, which translates Canadian weather reports between English and French. It is one of only a handful of systems which work with almost no human intervention. Other examples can be found in financial markets reports, which make similar use of stereotypical phrases.
3   See Eco, 2003, pp.12-18 for an amusing series of examples.

environment, and with inferring human communicative intentions. One way of conceiving the problem is that the machine needs to share so much cognitive environment with us that it actually *becomes* human. One interesting more recent development in machine translation is the use of example-based systems, and of related statistical techniques. Example-based systems work rather like the Meteo weather reports (note 49, below), and rely on huge databases of example phrases, rather than on grammatical analysis. Interestingly, these can 'result in more stylish, less literal translations.'[1] But whilst they might be more idiomatically appealing, such 'translations' are more misleading than the gobbledegook sometimes produced by *Babel-Fish©*: the fact that the output is a well-turned phrase in the target language in no way guarantees that it shares interpretive resemblance with the source language utterance, and in some ways is more difficult to assess.

On the other hand, the presence of the three basic requirements for communication accounts for its possibility in a number of 'marginal' situations. My dog and I, for example, can communicate with each other rather well, although admittedly on a narrow range of topics. This is because (1) he has the ability to make inferences about my behaviour, and I about his, (2) he has learnt a limited range of signs ('come' and 'squirrels' and so forth), and (3) we share a lot of context when we are out on a walk together. At another extreme, though, we might speculate as to whether and how we might be able to communicate with an alien species which suddenly arrived on our planet. An almost universal fantasy of science fiction is the magical ability to 'translate' the alien (without this fantasy, plots become rather difficult); this is usually passed over in silence, but when the author does offer an account for it, it is usually in the form of some sophisticated software or organic modification to allow semiotic transfer. Relevance theory shows us that this is nonsense: unless we also share psychological machinery and cognitive environment with the aliens, no amount of semiotics will help us understand them.

Whilst the preceding paragraph might be considered frivolous speculation, this material should be salutary for a biblical translator. Any translator, setting out to understand the 'other' does so as an act of faith (Steiner called this 'initiative trust'.)[2] The translator has to have faith that there is a mind at the originating end of the process, a person with certain psychological equipment and certain elements of

1   Somers, in Baker. 1998, p.148.
2   Steiner, 1998 (1975), p.312.

context which are in common with her: without this, any attempt at understanding is futile. When there are thousands of years and a world of cultural differences between the two, this is, to say the least, a nontrivial requirement.

Translators are interpreters

Within the tradition established by Nida and Taber it became fashionable for a while to speak of 'the language helper' assisting readers of the Bible in new linguistic situations.[1] This implies a fairly humble technical role – perhaps suggesting someone familiar with the technical machinery of words, helping a reader to reach his own interpretation. Nida saw translation as a 'technology' – that is as a specific pragmatic application of scientific knowledge,[2] and thus the notion of a translator as a – no doubt highly skilled – machine-minder makes complete sense.

An even more extreme version of this is the notion of the 'invisible translator' extensively critiqued by Venuti,[3] who points out that much of the commentary on translation practice, particularly in the Anglophone tradition since Dryden, regards invisibility as a virtue: the best target language text is one which reads like an original composition, with no hint of the role which the translator has played. Perhaps we might say: the only good translator is a dead one. As Venuti points out, the desirability of the 'illusion of transparency' pushes the translator into an unduly domesticating strategy, thus preventing the receptor culture from receiving a 'new word' from the text. It also significantly underplays the role of the translator herself.

Once, however, translation is re-assimilated into hermeneutics, via Relevance Theory, we can see that the translator is an *interpreter*. As we saw earlier in this chapter, translation can only be undertaken by *someone* who has heard and interpreted an utterance, and has the requisite language skills to produce a new utterance which interpretively resembles it. The only way translation can work is for a human being to stand in the middle of the process, understand the utterance, and commence a new communication by producing an interpretation for the benefit of another human being. There is no point *within* this process at which some sort of technical intervention can produce 'translation'. This is not, of course, to deny that the interpreter can bring all sorts of technology and machinery to bear, to help her with

1   See Beekman and Callow, 1974, p.42.
2   Nida, 1964, p.68.
3   Venuti, 1995, throughout.

this work: even a lexicon is a humble example of such.

The attempt to see translation as a 'science' or (with Nida) as a technology can be seen as part of the modernist programme of identifying 'method' critiqued by Gadamer:[1] another aspect of the Enlightenment project to eliminate the vagaries of human agency from rational knowledge. A Relevance-based account returns the interpreter to the stage: a fully human figure whose art cannot be reduced to machinery. This account is therefore in full harmony with Steiner's account of translation as an 'ethical' activity, or as an 'exact art'[2] rather than as a science. As a human agent, the translator/interpreter is fully ethically accountable. Her task is creative, in that she must produce a wholly new communication for her hearers; but she also intends her communication to be relevant to those hearers by virtue of its resemblance to a source. This is why translation is, in ethical terms, a matter of delicate balance. Relevance Theory, at a deep level, entails the suggestive figure of the human translator as a figure whose role is to help people grow their shared cognitive environment. Μακάριοι οἱ εἰρηνοποιοὶ ('Blessed are the peacemakers!')

RTT engages positively with Context

All translation theories eventually have to deal with context. Theories which begin with a semiotic account of meaning transfer must then move on to deal with contextual issues, which are usually then encountered as knotty problems in which the efficient transfer of meaning is subject to irritating interference or barriers. Relevance Theory, by contrast, builds an account of context integrally and from the start. Both the goals and the mechanisms of communication are contextual: the goal of communication is the expansion of shared context, and the mechanism of communication is the exploitation of our ability to form new contextual implications, by combining an incoming assumption with an existing assumption. As we saw, speakers and hearers know that they share a 'mutual cognitive environment' – that is, a set of assumptions which they share, and which they believe that they share. This provides the set of assumptions which they may draw upon in communication.

Translators working within RTT, then, tend to have a more nuanced understanding of contextual issues. Hill, for example, seeking to translate biblical material for the Adiokrou of Cote d'Ivoire, analyses the mutual cognitive environment in terms of a four-part matrix:[3]

1   Gadamer, 1989 (1975) is the classic statement.
2   Steiner, 1992 (1975) xvi.
3   Hill, H, 2006, p.29.

In Quadrant 4, hearers just do not have the requisite assumptions to interpret the text. Hill cites the example of messianic expectation: 'most Adioukrou are unaware of the first-century Jews' expectations of the Messiah and of the dynamics of Jew-Gentile relations. These are all assumptions the biblical author expected his audience to have, and without them, understanding of the text is severely impaired.' In Quadrant 3, hearers apply assumptions which they believe they must share with the text but in fact (in the opinion of the translator) they do not share. For example, the Adioukrou apply their knowledge of the magical transmission of evil via food to the story of the last supper in John 13. Quadrant 2 consists of cases where the hearers actually do possess the required processing context, but do not realise that they do. Only in Quadrant 1, which defines the set of assumptions actually and knowingly shared, can communication proceed in a straightforward manner.

	Hearer thinks that it is shared	Hearer does not think that it is shared
Actually shared	Quadrant 1: Intended context	Quadrant 2: Unrecognized context
Not actually shared	Quadrant 3: Unintended context	Quadrant 4: Missing context

Context-Sharing Matrix

Hill regards the task of the translator as being to get as much as possible into Quadrant 1 – and this means providing the reader with a lot of 'readers' aids' – notes, commentary and other material, to point him towards the correct processing context and away from misleading context. This is an understandable response, and Hill's analysis is far more nuanced than most of the literature, which tends to talk simplistically about context being either present or absent. Yet, it may be that the true picture is more complex still. Quadrant 2, for example, may present a number of different types of problem. Hill herself states the problem as being that the hearers 'don't recognize the label (word or expression) the speaker is using.' The example she gives is one where the speaker is using 'spirit' to refer to a concept for which the natural word for the hearer is 'divinity.' However, as we will frequently observe in the present work, there is another type of 'Quadrant 2 problem' in which the hearer *does* have the required assumptions, but they are stored quite deep in memory, and are therefore not readily accessed. As we will see later, there are more remedies available for this kind of problem than simply providing footnotes: and the latter may serve paradoxically to exacerbate the problem rather than solve it.

There are also some deeper questions one may ask using this approach, particularly if one is interested in querying the ἱερὸς γάμος. Some of the problems Hill cites may be self-inflicted, and reflect the continuing dominance Holy Marriage thinking – if, for example, we are using the word 'spirit' to describe something which the language user would more naturally call a 'divinity', we will want to ask the question: why? Is it because the ἱερὸς γάμος requires that πνεῦμα is translated 'spirit'? Pursuing this clue, we may find that a lot of the material which the translator believes she needs to add to her biblical version is actually directed at making sure that the target audience arrive at the ἱερὸς γάμος interpretation of the Bible, rather than their own. It may be that a healthy dose of Steiner's initiative trust would solve more of the issues than is immediately apparent to those reared on a particular interpretation of the text: perhaps we share more context with the biblical authors than we realise.

How RTT will be used in the present work

Our interest in Relevance Theory is instrumental. We start from the puzzle of the biblical texts, and from the desire to interpret them and therefore translate them anew, away so far as possible from the Holy Marriage. Relevance Theory gives us an exploratory framework within which to pursue this goal. It is a framework which I regard as particularly suitable, mainly because it is based on an hermeneutic approach, and the account for translation to which it gives rise is therefore securely grounded as hermeneutic rather than the search for 'equivalents'. I apologise in advance to those whose first commitment is to the theory itself; if I bend Relevance Theory out of shape in my attempt to put it to this use, any shortcomings it evinces are my own. The direction I take with Relevance Theory is, for example, quite different from that of Hill or Wendland, without taking fundamental theoretical issue with them. I believe that this can be accounted for by their strong commitment to the 'holy marriage' translation: as we saw in Chapter One, the ἱερὸς γάμος is certainly strong enough to bend theory to its own purposes. It seems to me that these practitioners are interested in using Relevance Theory to support a certain translation practice, rather than to challenge it.

Utterances or Texts?

One of the first corners to negotiate is this: Relevance Theory was developed as a theory of utterances that is of gestures performed or words spoken between two or more people in a specific context. It is not immediately apparent that it can be applied to written texts, and some have questioned its application, particularly to literary texts, which are phenomena so fundamentally different from the former that the same theoretical apparatus could not ever be appropriate for both. The point about a written text (or one recorded in any other way) is that it can be separated from its context. This is why Plato, in his recounting of the Myth of Theuth, has the high god refuse man the gift of writing: the problem with a written text is that it is a 'fatherless child', which can be torn away from its author and interpreted or mis-interpreted at will. Without its parental protection, the written text is as likely to do harm as good. This view, which for Derrida is the foundation statement for the priority of the oral over the written in Western intellectual history, seems at first to be associated with a 'high' view of texts and a 'low' view of authors. The question seems to amount to this: is a text an interaction between an author and a reader, or is it something quite different? Is it, then, properly part of the domain of communication theory, or not?

This question in a sense has become easier to answer in recent decades, given the technologically driven and progressive blurring of the lines which Plato drew between oral and written texts: email, 'text', twitter, voicemail and audio-visual recordings of all kinds call into question the distinction's sustainability. One of Derrida's main points in *Signature, Event, Context*, seems to be that *any* text (written or oral) which uses a semiotic system is vulnerable to that text being repeated 'out of context' – the very iterability of the words used expose it to that risk, as he wittily showed by misquoting Searle, his opponent in the debate. He made essentially the same point by showing that 'a context is never absolutely determinable'. We will return to the question of the 'open-endedness' of context in Chapter Six, below, but in the meantime will note that there is no sustainable theoretical difference between utterances and texts, and therefore no fundamental obstacle to applying Relevance Theory to the analysis of literary (or biblical) texts.

I propose here to follow the precedent established by Gutt and others, in viewing written texts as 'recorded utterances' – that is, as essentially the same thing as utterances, but with the recognition that they are at greater 'risk' than utterances in terms of the potential for

communication failure: the context in which they are interpreted is
indeterminate. In the language of business, a written text is a 'high
risk, high return' venture: the text may be interpreted in a context far
different from that envisaged by the author – and this can lead both to
a much richer set of interpretations, and to miss-interpretation.

Relevance Theory as a diagnostic tool

The unique perspective provided by RTT is, in the chapters which
follow, mainly used as a diagnostic. Because RTT is fully integrated
with a general communication theory, we are able to use it at each level
of enquiry. Thus, faced with a source text and a translation of that text,
we will repeatedly find ourselves asking the following three questions,
or variations thereon:

    1. The interpretation of the source text: how does the source text
achieve relevance in its original context? (the hermeneutic question)

    2. The production of the target text: how does the target text
communicate relevantly in the target context? (the communicative
question)

    3. The relationship between 1 and 2: how does the target text
interpretively resemble the source text? (the translation question)

Each of these questions presents its own challenges. In order to answer
the first question, we will have to address not only linguistic issues, but
our whole understanding of the original context of communication:
in understanding the text, we recall, nothing is formally irrelevant.
Not only research, but great powers of imagination, of reconstruction,
and human sympathy are required for this task. We will repeatedly be
struck by how much more we know today about the original context
– scholarship has made extraordinary progress in so many areas, since
the early modern period, when the ἱερὸς γάμος was being formed.

In the second question, we address how an English text achieves
relevance today. This, again, requires efforts of sympathy and
imagination – no less so, for the fact that the 'context' is all around us.
It is also important to understand that this is an integral requirement
for successful translation, and not an 'optional extra'. The RTT
framework assesses a translation as an act of communication, like any
other. It can only communicate by exploiting the principle of relevance
– that is, communication will only take place if the translation delivers
worthwhile contextual implications sufficient to justify the recipients'
effort in processing. There is, therefore, no merit in producing a
translation which is 'faithful' but which does not communicate
relevantly: it in fact cannot be 'faithful' *unless* it communicates relevantly.

In the third question we ask the essential question of interpretive resemblance. A translation, we will recall, is a text which intends to achieve relevance by virtue of its resemblance to another. A text resembles another to the extent that its interpretation in the same context is the same. We are therefore looking for translations which, when processed within the same cognitive environment, allow the reader to form the same contextual implications as did the original readers as imagined in question one. Much of the material which follows amounts to a straightforward plea to translators to allow their translations to be formed by this third requirement.

A modest proposal: the Relevance Curve

It is central to the theory that relevance is always a trade-off. The hearer or reader of a communication is thought of as performing an optimising calculation, a cost-benefit analysis, based on the presumption of relevance. Any communication, we will recall, communicates the assumption of its own relevance, and this means that it is expected to yield worthwhile contextual implications for not unreasonable effort.

This statement describes a curve. I have not been able to find it expressed thus in the literature of relevance theory. However, in mathematical terms, any 'optimisation' process can be plotted on a graph, whose axes are defined by the two variables: in this case, 'contextual implications' are being weighed against 'processing cost':

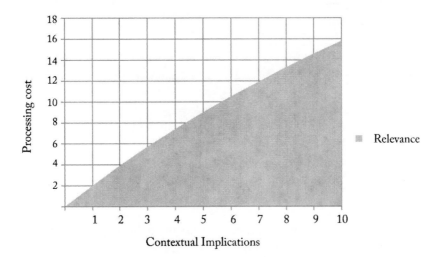

Costs and Benefits of Contextual Implications

As in any optimising process, the more 'benefit' something brings, the more one is prepared to 'pay' for it. In Relevance Theory 'benefit' means contextual effects – useful modifications of a hearer's cognitive environment. The cost to be 'paid' for these is the effort involved in processing the communication. I would like to suggest that this graph can help us in our use of Relevance Theory for diagnostic purposes. It makes clear, for example, that an utterance may achieve relevance at either end of a scale, or somewhere in-between. Thus, an utterance with only a low 'pay-off' in terms of contextual implications, might still be relevant if it has a low processing cost. This is why those humdrum communications which constitute the bulk of every-day interaction are framed in such a way as to be easy to process. The statement 'Nice day again', may have a low pay-off, but at least it is not onerous to process. If, on the other hand, we have something to communicate with a rich 'pay-off' in contextual effects, it can afford to be more difficult to process. Thus: 'Maureen says that Kay thinks Brian doesn't like her' has a much richer pay-load and can therefore be more difficult to process.

From a hearer's point of view, we might think of him processing incoming communications along the following lines:

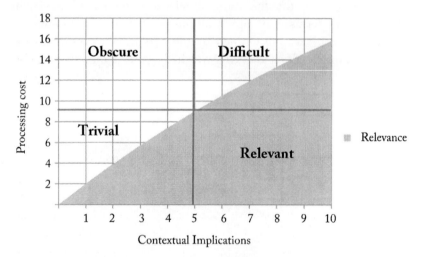

Processing for Relevance

All ostensive communications are assumed by the hearer to be relevant – that is, to fall into the golden area whose limit is described by the 'relevance curve'. A communicator exploits this behaviour by making sure that things which she wants to communicate fall within this area – and, by the same token, that things she doesn't want to communicate are left outside of it.

Multi-valent Relevance?

It is worth repeating that this feature of Relevance Theory is integral and logically necessary to it; it is not an interesting side effect, but constitutive of the theory itself. The reason this is important is to see that Relevance does not provide a key to **the** meaning of a text, but rather specifies an area within a curve, in which a reader may form any number of interpretations. This is rather important in assessing the uses to which Relevance Theory has been put by practicing biblical translators such as Harriet Hill, who is happy to talk of 'the intended meaning' of the text, and who sees part of her job as providing the necessary contextual information to allow her readership to interpret it 'correctly'. Relevance Theory cannot be pressed to the service of the Holy Marriage translation in this way.

An accommodation for multi-valency in texts is, then, integral to Relevance Theory. At the same time, though, the text does not mean just *anything*: Relevant interpretations all fall within the golden area of figure 6. This seems to me to be a useful resolution of a nagging problem in post-modern textual criticism, which wants to fully recognise the 'hyletic' nature of texts and therefore struggles to define the limits of interpretation.

The way this analysis can help us in our hermeneutic will become clear as we proceed in the following chapters. It can help us understand the behaviour both of authors (as original communicators) and of translators (as 'hearers' and as new communicators). More particularly, it provides us with a tool for analysing what we might call 'depth' of interpretation. The interpretation of a communication may legitimately fall anywhere along the relevance curve; indeed, communicators exploit this feature in order to communicate with different parts of their audience. Thus for example in the story of the boy Jesus in the Temple (Luke 2: 41 to 52), the young Jesus goes missing, and is found only after three days, sitting in the Temple precincts and discoursing with the διδάσκαλοι ('teachers') who gather there. Luke reports Mary as saying to him: Τέκνον, τί ἐποίησας ἡμῖν οὕτως; ἰδοὺ ὁ πατήρ σου κἀγὼ ὀδυνώμενοι ἐζητοῦμέν σε. ('Child, how could you do to us like this? Look, your father and I in distress searched for you'). This may be interpreted as achieving relevance at various different points along the relevance curve, and which particular point any given hearer chooses will depend both on what assumptions are already present in his cognitive environment, and how much 'processing cost' he is prepared to spend. At the most straightforward level – that is, in the bottom left-hand corner of the graph – Mary's utterance makes perfect sense in the context, as the irritated and/or reproachful rhetorical question of a mother who has been through such an experience. The quickest, lowest cost way, therefore of solving the relevance equation is to interpret it at this level. However, it is also clear that Luke is using Mary's words to speak 'over the heads' of her immediate audience, to another audience. This audience will notice that Jesus was found only after three days, and that in the meantime those who were looking for him went through agonies. This audience has, within its cognitive environment, information about the time Jesus spent in the tomb following his crucifixion, and with just a little more processing effort, can interpret accordingly. It is perhaps encouraged to do so by anomalies in the story itself – Jesus' family have just been to the Temple, for the festival; surely it would not have taken his parents three days to work out that that would be where he was?! The puzzle in the story nudges the reader up the relevance curve, to find an explanation. Further, there is perhaps yet another level of interpretation, relating to the problematic and still unresolved relationship between early Christianity and Judaism: we lost Jesus, and we searched and searched, and only found him when we returned to Jerusalem and the Temple. We found him talking to the rabbis, no less – τί ἐποίησας ἡμῖν οὕτως; how could he do this to us?! Some commentators have noted that this phrase in the LXX is a formula, always used to protest a betrayal or deception (Genesis 12.18; 20.9, 26.10, 29.25, Exodus 14.11, Numbers 23.11, Judges 15.11).

The point about these different interpretations is that they each require more processing effort, to recover more contextual assumptions; but they all of them fall along the range defined by the relevance curve. Amongst other things, they usefully illustrate the point that in Relevance Theory, communicative intention is constructed by the hearer or reader.

A further modest proposal: Attention as a variable

The foregoing analysis suggests an extension to Relevance Theory which might further expand its explanatory power. We have seen that a hearer will use the text to hypothesise about its communicative intention, arriving at an interpretation in accordance with the principle of relevance. We have also seen that this is not enough to specify a single point of interpretation: relevant interpretations lie within a curve.

The precise point along the curve at which the relevant interpretation is constructed will vary by reader. This is partly because different readers have different cognitive environments, or contexts, as we saw above. Biblical translators currently working within a relevance theoretical approach tend to emphasise this factor – if a readership fails to form what the translator believes to be the appropriate relevant interpretation, this must be because they do not have the required processing context. There must, however, be another factor at play, because as we saw earlier in our account of 'Context', context is not either simply present or absent; it may, for example, be present but stored inaccessibly. What I would like to suggest is this: in such a case, whether the reader will 'get' the relevant interpretation will depend on the amount of effort he is prepared to expend, to recover this necessary bit of context from his cognitive environment, and combine it with the communication to form the hoped for contextual effects.

In the example we used earlier, we can see that in fact there will be many readers of Luke's gospel (perhaps the great majority) who do have the information within their cognitive environment that Jesus was in the tomb for three days. However, not all of these will bring this to bear on their interpretation. Whether they recover this item of information ('assumption' in the terminology of the theory) and combine it with the assumptions conveyed by Mary's statement, will depend on how much attention they invest in understanding this text. 'Attention' is a concept from cognitive psychology, defined as 'all those aspects of human cognition that the subject can control . . . all aspects of cognition having to do with limited resources or capacity, and methods of dealing with such constraints.' Humans are limited, finite beings, and they husband the attention they offer to a task carefully. In order to attend to one thing, many other incoming stimuli must be 'screened out'. Neumann describes the processes involved as 'inhibiting' incoming signals which are irrelevant: 'all attributes of a target stimulus are fully processed, but those not required for the selection of action, or response, are inhibited.' Crucially, 'inhibitory mechanisms are goal dependent'.

Attention, therefore, represents the expenditure of the scarce resource of cognitive effort. Readers or hearers will approach a text with a willingness to 'spend' a certain amount of attention on it. It is in their interest to minimise the attention they allocate to it – but if the rewards are there, in terms of contextual implications, they may be willing to increase that allocation. Mathematically, then, we have a way of specifying a certain point on the Relevance Curve. For each reader of a text, there will be a level of attention she or he offers to it, and at that point he or she will resolve that text: all interpretations up to and including that point are available to such a reader, and none of those above it. If, for example, a certain reader of Luke 2 was represented by figure 6 above, and she was prepared to allocate processing cost of '10' to the task, she would carry on processing, and forming contextual implications, up to the '7th' level. Let us say, for the sake of argument, that this would allow her to form all three of the interpretations we

suggested earlier for the story of the *Boy Jesus in the Temple*. Another
reader, though, might be prepared to invest less attention, and only
arrive at one of them. A third reader, perhaps, might be prepared to
carry on investing processing cost up to '16', and would form a range
of further relevant interpretations not available to the other two.
This third character is interesting to us, because he or she represents
a reader pushing against the limits of interpretation. Such a reader
is likely to have moved well beyond the 'plain sense' of the text, and
is taking an interest in it as (for example) a religious practice such
as *lectio divina,* or as an exercise in deconstruction. *Lectio Divina*
and deconstruction, whilst their motives may appear to be radically
different, have much in common. As these two very different readers
apply more and more attention to the text, they proceed by parallel
routes to the same place, which one calls a Mystery, the other Aporia.
Our proposed conceptualisation of interpretation along the Relevance
Curve, allows us to accommodate such readings (which take place at
the limits of the curve in the 'difficult' quadrant of figure 6) within a
pragmatic framework. Figure 7 attempts to elucidate the similarities
between these (mis)reading styles. We will give more consideration to
such practices in Chapter Six.

This is quite an exciting finding, in terms of both communication
theory and translation. Communication is, we are saying, a kind of
bargain between a speaker and a hearer, in which useful contextual
implications are exchanged for the scarce resource of attention.
Skilled communicators produce communications rich in interpretive
possibilities within an area defined by the Relevance Curve, so that
different hearers or readers, offering different levels of attention to
the communication, can all form relevant interpretations. There is
an implied contract between communicators and their audiences:
attention must be rewarded with contextual implications. This contract
is particularly important in literary texts, and it is this contract which
some 'communicative' biblical translations breach, and which accounts
for the unsatisfying read they provide. the translator, believing that
his or her job is to provide 'the meaning', pays no attention to the
upper reaches of the Relevance Curve. This means that more attentive
readers have nothing to work on, and are left with the feeling that
something is missing – a feeling often hard to articulate, because of
course the translation in front of them is 'correct' in the sense that it
conveys 'the meaning' of the holy marriage.

This insight also suggests an alternative approach to the 'context'
problem which vexes translators: some of these contextual problems
could, perhaps, be solved by manipulating the attention required from

the reader. Consider again our earlier example. If I felt that the echo with Jesus' time in the tomb was both very important and very likely to be missed by you, I might do something to nudge you in the direction of raising the attention you are prepared to offer here (we saw that Luke did something similar, in setting up the story in such a way that it suggested a modestly puzzling timescale). If I could get you to 'pay attention' you might yourself supply the required assumptions, which are there in your cognitive environment, but perhaps buried more deeply than those of Luke's original readership. Paradoxically, this might involve me making the passage more difficult to read, rather than less. This is one way of interpreting Venuti's 'foreignization' translation strategy: those who complain that his use of 'alien' words and expressions make his translation difficult to read, are missing the point. What his approach does, is to raise the 'attention bid', so that those reading the translation are sufficiently alert to recover the required processing assumptions.[1]

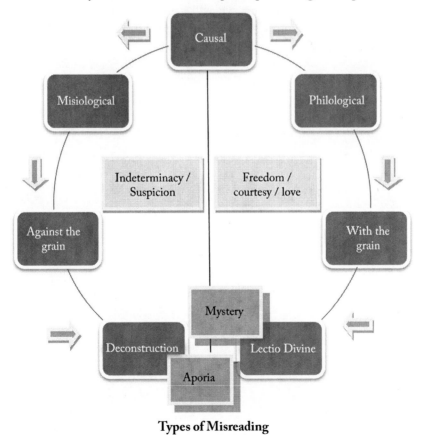

Types of Misreading

---

1   Venuti's *Passion: A Novel* (1994), a translation of Tarchetti, provides an excellent demonstration of this strategy. See also, Berman, 1992.

This finding is also highly germane to biblical translation. There is a very long and now well-established tradition of trying to make the translated text easier – we will look at this more closely in Chapter Three. This is completely understandable: there is, after all, something inherently 'democratic' about translation: one is making the text available to an audience for whom it was hitherto inaccessible. There are also sound Relevance-Theoretical grounds on which this can be argued: making a text easier is a low cost, low risk way of keeping it within the bounds of the relevance curve. But – and it is a big but – doing so may keep a text within the lower-left quadrant of the graph we have described. Further, if we attempt to solve the problem of 'missing context' by providing copious footnotes and commentary (as we will see, this is an increasingly common approach), we risk 'relaxing' our reader precisely at the point when we want him to 'pay more attention.'

In the following chapters we will seek to apply some of these insights to translation problems from the first two chapters of Luke's gospel.

Chapter Three

Start as you mean to go on?
Syntax in Luke 1.1-4

We have seen in the previous chapter that a Relevance based theory of translation (which we christened *RTT*) presents a number of attractions in forming a broadly based account for a phenomenon which plays an enormously significant role in human behaviour and culture yet has notoriously defied rigorous analysis. The attractions on which we focussed centred on the simplicity of the account, its integration with communication theory as a whole and with other aspects of human behaviour, and its potential for effecting an intellectual rapprochement with other quite different approaches to the problems of human communication, approaches which are far away from the roots of Relevance Theory in pragmatics.

We now turn to a more practical question: can RTT provide a convincing account for the ways translators actually do proceed with their work? In particular, for our purposes: can it provide a helpful account of the problems and opportunities in biblical translation which will allow us to question the ἱερὸς γάμος, the Holy Marriage translation? Could it even make positive suggestions for an *approach to* translation? Chomsky famously denied that his account of the processes of back translation into and from the 'deep structures' he detected in language could form the basis for an approach to the actual issues of translation.[1] This did not deter Nida and others attempting one; and in a strong sense Nida was right. It is surely a not unreasonable test for such a theoretical framework, to expect it to shed even a little light on actual translation practice. In this and in the following three chapters we will consider translation issues from the first chapters of Luke's gospel.[2] The passages involved have not been chosen as 'representative' of that

---

1 Chomsky, 1965, p.30.
2 Throughout the present work 'Luke' refers to whoever wrote the gospel which bears his name or to that work itself, and without meaning to conjour up the idea that we can know much about him, or that this would necessarily help in understanding the text which bears his name.

work, but rather because they provide convenient case-study material for a number of problems in biblical translation. In translation terms they are generally reckoned to be amongst the most difficult passages in the Lukan corpus, embracing as they do narrative, poetry, dialogue and several style-shifts. In the course of this study we will look at several present-day translations of these passages, mainly in English, occasionally in other modern languages. The scope of the present work does not permit a thoroughgoing diachronic approach, fascinating though this would be,[1] and the only way in which this will be touched upon is that, of course, many translations in use today have deep historical roots, and we will try to explore some of them. As for the particular translations we will consider, they have been selected for each case study for particular reasons pertaining to that study, and we will attempt to explain those reasons on each occasion. The present chapter focuses especially on a number of translations which are published alongside commentaries by the same person: we will look at translations of Luke's preface by Tom Wright, by John Nolland, by Loveday Alexander and by Walter Radl, all in the context of commentaries under those authors' names. The reason for this is that in the present chapter we will be focussing on issues surrounding the formation of the translator's communicative intention: in short, how does the translator's interpretation of a text manifest itself (or not) in the translation he or she produces? I hope to show that Relevance Theory can helpfully re-frame many of the problems identified, and that in some cases we may even see a convincing solution.

We will recall that in RTT, a translation is a text[2] intended to achieve its relevance by virtue of its interpretive resemblance to an original, or source text. Interpretive resemblance is defined in terms of similarity of interpretation of the two texts in a given context: to the extent that two texts have the same analytic implications and the same contextual implications when interpreted according to the principle of relevance in the same context, they are said to resemble one-another. A translation which aims to show *complete* interpretive resemblance to another is, in Gutt's terminology a *direct translation*, one that seeks to make an inter-lingual quotation.

There are therefore three distinct but inter-related criteria involved in assessing a given translation:

---

1   See Katz, D.S., 2004, or Daniell, D. *The Bible in English*, Yale 2003, for fascinating studies of the history of the translation of the Bible into English.
2   Strictly, an utterance in propositional form. See Gutt, 1995. Here and throughout I will not weary the reader by labouring the nuanced descriptions of texts and utterances in Relevance Theory. All references to 'texts' should be understood in the light of the comments in Chapter Two.

1. The interpretation of the source text: how does the translator understand the source text achieves its relevance in its original context?

2. The production of the target text: how does the translator produce a target text which communicates relevantly in his or her target context?

3. The relationship between 1 and 2: how does the translator ensure that the target text interpretively resembles the source text?

When a translation receives adverse criticism, one or more of these criteria is in play: either the translator has misunderstood the source text, or she has not expressed herself well in the target text, or the intended degree of interpretive resemblance between the two has not been achieved, or some combination of all of these. In what follows, we are mainly interested in 3: but to look at 3, we have to have already assessed 1 and 2. The one thing which RTT will not countenance, as we saw in Chapter Two is a 'neutral' or 'pre-interpretive' translation: a translation *always* represents an interpretation of a source text according to some criterion of relevance. Thus whilst our primary interest, as promised in the introduction, is in translation as 'performance' of an interpretation, we have to begin with understanding what that interpretation is.

The source text: relevance in its context?

Ἐπειδήπερ πολλοὶ ἐπεχείρησαν ἀνατάξασθαι διήγησιν περὶ τῶν πεπληροφορημένων ἐν ἡμῖν πραγμάτων," καθὼς παρέ δοσαν ἡμῖν οἱ ἀπ' ἀρχῆς αὐτόπται καὶ ὑπηρέται γενόμενοι τοῦ λόγου," ἔδοξε κἀμοὶ παρηκολουθηκότι ἄνωθεν πᾶσιν ἀκριβῶς καθεξῆς σοι γράψαι, κράτιστε Θεόφιλε," ἵνα ἐπιγνῷς περὶ ὧν κατηχήθης λόγων τὴν ἀσφάλειαν.

Since many have undertaken to set down an orderly account of the events which have been fulfilled among us, just as they were handed on to us by those who from the beginning were eyewitnesses and servants of the word, I too decided. After investigating everything carefully from the very first, to write an orderly account for you, most excellent Theophilus, so that you may know the truth concerning the things about which you have been instructed.   NRSV Luke 1.1-4

A text achieves relevance in a context by delivering worthwhile contextual implications to its readers, for a not unreasonable processing cost. Before attempting to determine how Luke's preface might attempt to do this, it will be useful to have in mind certain objective features of the preface, and these are set out in Figure 8.

It is not the intention of the present work to repeat the efforts of many commentators to unpick this highly compressed and rather (for the New Testament) unusual sentence. However, in order to appreciate the translation issues involved, we do need to notice some commonly acknowledged features:

Clause	Syntactical Role	Topic
Ἐπειδήπερ πολλοὶ ἐπεχείρησαν ἀνατάξασθαι διήγησιν	First subordinate clause placed before main verb	The many accounts
περὶ τῶν πεπληροφορημένων ἐν ἡμῖν πραγμάτων,	Adverbial clause dependent on first subordinate clause	The subject matter of the accounts
καθὼς παρέδοσαν ἡμῖν οἱ ἀπ᾿ ἀρχῆς αὐτόπται καὶ ὑπηρέται γενόμενοι τοῦ λόγου,	Second subordinate clause placed before the main verb	The transmission of the accounts
ἔδοξε κἀμοὶ	Main verb	The author
παρηκολουθηκότι ἄνωθεν πᾶσιν ἀκριβῶς	Participial clause dependent on the indirect object of the main verb	The qualifications of the author
καθεξῆς σοι γράψαι, κράτιστε Θεόφιλε,	First subordinate clause after the main verb	The author's addressee
ἵνα ἐπιγνῷς περὶ ὧν κατηχήθης λόγων τὴν ἀσφάλειαν.	Final subordinate clause	The author's purpose

Formal and topical features in Luke's preface

1. *A markedly different, periodic, form*

The first thing which many commentators note about Luke's preface
is its form. Nolland, for example, begins his commentary with
the remark that: 'The preface consists of a perfectly constructed
Greek period . . . which is generally judged to be the best stylized
sentence in the whole NT . . . Indeed, Luke does not devote the
same attention again to forming a sentence until Acts 28.30-31 . . .'[1]
Marshall notes that 'The preface is written in excellent Greek with
a most carefully wrought sentence structure . . . composed of one
long, periodic sentence, each of whose parts contains three matching
phrases. . . .'[2] Evans sees that 'Luke's preface is also unique among
the Gospels (indeed, among all of the writings of the NT) in that
it is written in a very sophisticated literary style that is reminiscent
of . . . Herodotus, Thucydides, and Polybius . . . [as well as]
Josephus . . .'[3] Radl notes 'Das Vorwort besteht aus einer einzigen
kunstvoll gestalten Periode . . . Die Periode ist als ganze . . . im
Rahmen des Evangeliums ungewöhnlich. ('The Preface consists of
a single, artfully crafted sentence. . . . within the whole course of
the gospel, unusual).'[4] The Greek sentence, comprising 41 words
revolving around the principal verb δοκέω ('to seem') is, it is said,
comparable with the style of Hellenistic literary prologues such as
that found in Josephus' *Against Apion*. Nolland refers to 'the balance
of Luke's sentence as it pivots around ἔδοξε κἀμοι'.[5] For Wright,
'Luke opens his gospel with a long, formal sentence, like a huge stone
entrance welcoming you impressively to a large building'.[6]

Loveday Alexander does not accept this 'high' assessment of Luke
as a stylist – his preface is instead to be seen as typical of the rather
conventional sort of introductions found in Graeco-Roman technical or
reference works.[7] The periodic style is belaboured and perhaps (though
she does not use this word herself) almost hackneyed – but of course by
virtue of this very fact it is extremely well marked: there is no mistaking
how different this opening sentence is from the paratactic material which
follows and which characterizes Luke's gospel (and Acts) as a whole.

---

1   Nolland, 1989, p.4.
2   Marshall, 1978, pp39-40.
3   Evans, 1995, p.17.
4   Radl, 2003, p.23.
5   Nolland, 1989, p.6.
6   Wright, 2001, p.1.
7   Which Alexander denotes as 'scientific' literature – covering a very wide
range from medical and mathematical treatises, to magic and astrology, to
rhetoric. Alexander, 1993, p42.

2. *Vocabulary with clear stylistic value but uncertain reference*

Commentators also find a somewhat different *vocabulary* in the preface. This one sentence contains six words which for Luke are hapax legomena (three of them hapax legomena in the NT as a whole), but which do play a role in Hellenistic and later Graeco-Roman literature, and are associated with a certain tone value. This 'high' tone is set by the opening word, 'επειδήπερ, ('inasmuch as') found in one of Josephus' introductions,[1] which Marshall describes as a 'stately opening conjunction',[2] and Nolland sees as contributing to 'the formal literary flavour of the preface'. ἀνατάσσομαι, ('I compile') is a rare word even in widely defined Hellenistic literature, but when combined with διήγησις ('account' – found in historiographical work by Lucian)[3] and αὐτόπτης ('eyewitness') it suggests that weighty matters are to be dealt with, probably in an empirical manner. The remaining two *hapax legomena*, appearing as the perfect participles πεπληροφορημέ νων ('having been fulfilled') and παρηκολουθηκότι ('having followed closely') are compounds formed by prefixing the much more humdrum πληρόω ('fill') and ακολουθέω ('follow'). This vocabulary has a portentous flavour and is certainly in extreme contrast with the Septuagintal material of the birth stories which immediately follows. Lagrange points out that the use of these extended compounds adds nothing semantically, and compares to the modern French development from *règle* to *règlement* to *règlementation*.[4] Alexander finds the choice of words to be driven not by a desire to achieve precise reference, but by a wish for a certain sonorous effect – 'Luke's language is elevated and formal in the preface; there is a certain literary flavour and the long words sound impressive . . . [and have] . . . a ponderous effect . . .'[5] Alexander further suggests that vocabulary choice may have been driven partly by an observed alliteration on the 'p' sound in the first verse.[6]

3. *Syntax which establishes under-determined relations between clauses*

The syntax of the sentence is also characterized by a certain indeterminacy, particularly in relation to the logical or causal relationships which might or might not exist between the items

---

1   Josephus, Jewish War, 1.17.
2   Marshall, p.40.
3   Lucian, How to Write History, p.55.
4   Lagrange, 1912, p.97.
5   Alexander, 1993, p.104.
6   Ibid, p.108. For a full survey of the lexis in the preface see Alexander pp.108 – 142, an excellent summary which forms an essential element of my own interpretation of the piece, but which it would not be relevant to reproduce here.

mentioned in the seven main clauses. We will approach this by looking at the key linking words (in bold in figure 4) which he uses to establish those relationships.

'Επειδήπερ is a lengthened form of 'επειδή, commonly interpreted into English as 'inasmuch as' or 'whereas'. Like the English term, it specifies background conditions which are causal but whose precise role in the causality may be left unspecified, and is commonly used in official proclamations and also, as Alexander points out, in scientific prefaces.[1] If one passes a law against carrying knives in public places, knife-crime has played a certain *causal role* in this, but at the same time cannot be said to have *caused* the law; if one writes a treatise on the treatment of syphilis, the fact that others have also attempted cures for the disease has played a part in the decision to write, but again, cannot be said to have caused one to write. Luke uses it in a similar way in 7.1: 'Επειδὴ ἐπλήρωσεν πάντα τὰ ῥήματα αὐτοῦ εἰς τὰς ἀκοὰς τοῦ λαοῦ, εἰσῆλθεν εἰς Καφαρναούμ· ('Having fulfilled all his words in the hearing of the people, he went into Capernaum'). There is some sort of temporal/causal connection between finishing speaking and going into the town, but it is not to be pressed: the former cannot really be said to cause the latter. The effect of 'επειδήπερ at the head of the preface is to establish a connection, but not to specify that connection too closely: the decision to write is connected with the fact that many have written before, and with what they wrote, but in neither a logical nor a deterministic sense.

Similarly with καθώς ('just as'), an adverb frowned on by classical rhetoricians[2] perhaps because of its vague designation as well as its clumsiness. Here, as Nolland notes, 'the point of comparison of καθώς, "(just) as" / "since" / "insofar as", is not immediately evident. καθώς is broadly used to indicate various kinds of equivalence and correspondence.'[3] It establishes a connection between the accounts, those who passed on the accounts, the initial recipient of the accounts (Luke himself) and/or the subject matter of the accounts, and even the decision to write itself - and all without being exact about what those connections might be: are the accounts passed on to us 'just as' they were compiled – implying faithful transmission? Or is the manner of transmission of the accounts produced by 'the many' being compared with that of 'those . . . becoming servants of the word'? Are these two groups, in fact, identical or quite separate? And what role does the existence of the accounts and the source of the accounts play in it

---

1   Galen links 'Επειδήπερ and δοκέω three times, as Luke does in Acts 15.24-25. Both cited by Alexander, 1993, p.108.

2   See Phrynicus.397. cited in Liddell and Scott.

3   Nolland, 1989, p.8.

seeming to Luke that he also should write, the topic of the main verb? There is ambiguity at a number of levels.[1]

The next key connector, καί ('and'), appearing in crasis with μοι ('I') is also of course quite non-committal. Its role appears to be clearly adjunctive, but is the author 'also' setting his hand to writing because of an implied inadequacy in his predecessors, or because of the fact that their accounts had come to him through those who were, after all αὐτόπται and, moreover, reliable insiders (ὑπηρέται τοῦ λόγου - 'servants of the word'?)

The participial phrase παρηκολουθηκότι ἄνωθεν πᾶσιν ἀκριβῶς ('having closely and diligently followed everything from the start') is similarly slightly under-determined in establishing causality. Did the author just happen to be someone who had followed it all closely from the start and was therefore in a good position to write a careful account, once it began to seem to him for other reasons that this was required? Or did the fact that he had followed it all closely from the start play a *causal* role in it seeming the right thing to write? Certainty of a sort only arrives with the final connective: the use of ἵνα here is the first unambiguous confirmation we have: one thing is clear, and that is the relationship the author intends to establish between the reader and the material.

4. *Compression*

A further feature of the preface is its compression, an extreme brevity which, in combination with the features already noted, gives it a very particular range of effects. Commentaries often, for example, draw attention to lexical similarities with Josephus' preface to *Contra Apionem*[2], but without pointing out that the latter is more than five times the length. Thus Josephus gives a rather clear exposition of why he is writing (in response to those who have gone before, and in order to refute them), what he hopes to achieve (to discredit those who have detracted him, and so on), his method of attack (adducing high status historic/literary Greek sources, and also introducing ones new to his readership) and the main logic of his argument (to explain why in each case the Jews are not mentioned). Luke, on the other hand, cannot possibly achieve this in his 41 words, especially given that the words he chooses are selected on grounds other than precision of reference. The effect is that Luke's preface 'touches' almost all the permissible preface topics[3] but in an almost allusive manner.

---

1   Cadbury's classic study remains the comprehensive source. See Cadbury 1922a, pp.489-510.
2   See as one of many possible examples, Evans, 1995, p.18, Marshall, 1978, p.39.
3   Omitted items include his own name (although this is not particularly unusual).

5. *Disconnection with the material which follows*

Almost the only matter pertaining to Luke's preface which is not the subject of scholarly dispute is where it ends and the following material begins. The transition at the end of verse 4 is stark, marked by all the features we have noted, and a few more: for example, hypotactic style changes to paratactic, and first person changes to third person. The change in lexis from a set of choices which can loosely be described as 'secular' to that which is often described as 'septuagintal' is also frequently noted. The transition is made particularly startling by the following pericope (Luke 1.5 – 25 – the Annunciation Narratives) beginning as it does with the paradigmatically 'biblical' phrase Ἐγέ νετο ἐν ταῖς ἡμέραις . . . ('It came to pass in those days . . .')

However, we should also note that word length shortens markedly: the average number of syllables per word drops markedly in the following pericope, and whilst the preface has two hepta-syllables, Luke does not use a hepta-syllable again in our sample text. Sentence length reduces, and the use of the more 'marked' perfect aspect reduces in frequency. The subjunctive mood of verse 4 is not found again until verse 20.

There is no attempt to avoid hiatus by using a transitional phrase, such as Josephus' ἄρξομαι δὲ νυν . . . ('I am now going to begin . . .') in *Contra Apionem*.[1] Finally, of course, the subject matter changes drastically, from the rather abstract explanatory material of the preface to straightforward narrative in 1.5-20.

Not all of these five features are noted by all of our commentators: but all do note some of them, and all are in agreement that these features are not just accidental: there seems to be a purpose behind it. Perhaps inevitably, there is somewhat less consensus about what that purpose is. For Nolland, 'Luke is evidently claiming some relationship between his own work and, especially, historical works of his day.'[2] Some have claimed that this was a professional preface for the book market. Alexander denies that Luke is writing in the 'high' literary style of a Thucydides,[3] but does see him as seeking an intelligent 'scientific' style[4] perhaps best described (although she does not herself use the word) as 'middle-brow'. Radl sees the preface as combining secular and religious characteristics in such a manner as to embrace and draw in both believing and non-believing audiences.[5] Malina and Rohrbaugh assert that 'The honorific language here ("most excellent . . .") is the language of patronage . . . Luke is thus

1   *Contra Apionem*, 2.1.
2   Nolland, 1989, p.5.
3   See for example Dibelius, *Acts*, 1953, p.104.
4   Alexander, L. 1993, p.105.
5   Radl, 2003, p.25.

writing for a benefactor whom he considers his social superior and may in fact be challenging him to continue his support for the community of which Luke is an insider . . .'[1] For Wright, 'Luke . . . constructs a grand doorway into his gospel. He invites us to come in and make ourselves at home.'[2]

Interesting though these differences are, they are not important for our present purpose. Rather, what is important to note is that all commentators agree that there is in Luke's preface a quite distinctive form and style – one which is in marked contrast to the material which immediately follows, and indeed to the rest of Luke's gospel and of Acts, perhaps one which is unique in all of the NT.[3]

A relevance theoretical account

How, then, does this passage achieve its relevance in its original context? A text achieves relevance by allowing readers to form contextual implications – that is, potentially useful modifications of their cognitive environment – at not too high a 'cost' in terms of cognitive processing. Readers form contextual implications by combining assumptions conveyed in the text itself with assumptions already present in their cognitive environment, and it is this which creates the 'pay load' of the communicative process.

As we will recall from our analysis in Chapter 2, readers are thought of as performing a cost-benefit analysis when presented with a text such as Luke's preface: how much is this going to cost me to process, and what benefit am I going to receive in the form of contextual implications? Such a formulation defines in mathematical terms a line, not a point: the writer must decide where to pitch his opening sentence such that it delivers good value, and a skilled communicator seeks always to work within the 'golden area' described by the curve in figure 6.

This requirement presents in particularly acute form in the opening words or sentences of any text: the author must quickly establish his or her credentials and gain the reader's trust that what follows is relevant. If he or she fails in this, the communication may fail completely as the reader decides not to continue. For this reason, authors are commonly particularly attentive to how their work opens.

We can now see that the analysis of Luke's preface presented above throws up quite a serious question in terms of a relevance theoretical approach. The difficulty is this: how does a sentence

1   Malina and Rohrbaugh, 2003, p.224.
2   Wright, 2001a, p.4.
3   Some of Paul's more carefully turned passages perhaps approach the stylistic effects. See for example Ephesians 1.3-10.

which is quite hard (therefore costly) to process, but which is quite vague semantically (therefore having uncertain benefits in terms of contextual implications) achieve relevance?

As we saw, Luke chose to begin his text with a sentence whose style and complexity is almost unparalleled[1] in the rest of his two volume work. We should probably not *over*-estimate the difficulty which a first century reader would have with this; presumably the periodic form would at least to a degree be familiar, and not at any rate present the same forbidding aspect as it does to a modern English speaker brought up on the merits of eiromenic style. Nonetheless, even if familiar, it is not an easy style: the deferral of sense and psychological completion to the second half of a long period requires a level of concentration and commitment which is not necessary to follow paratactic structures.

Similarly, as we saw, the lexis which Luke chooses for his preface includes no less than six hapax legomena, including unusual compounds, two hepta-syllables, and a vocabulary quite removed from his normal practice. One of the findings of Relevance Theory is that when a communicator uses unusual vocabulary, she or he puts their reader to additional processing cost: the unfamiliar word has to be recovered from deeper in their cognitive environment, or else worked out 'from scratch'.

Finally, the syntax of the sentence is under-determined: even quite a careful reader is going to find herself puzzling as to how each clause precisely relates to the others, and to find an easy flow of ideas.
Why would Luke put his readers to all this trouble?

This question becomes more pressing if, as above, we acknowledge that the actual semantics of the sentence are not all that informative.[2] Because of the extreme compression and conventional language of the preface, its primary semantic effect is to 'touch on' a number of aspects of the composition which follows, but without saying anything very much about them – having toiled through the period, we still don't know all that much about Luke and his methods or purposes. After noting the vagueness of some key terms in verse 1, for example, Alexander observes that: 'If this point in the preface represents . . . Luke's chief opportunity for explaining to prospective readers what the book is about, it cannot be described as a successful piece of communication.'[3] The problem, in relevance theoretical terms, is in forming worthwhile contextual implications from the

---

1 Perhaps the apostolic decree in Acts 15.24ff may be assessed as of similar 'full blown periodic' form, as Alexander puts it.
2 See Alexander, 1993, p.105ff, where she quotes Lagrange, van Unnik, Lagarde and others.
3 Ibid p.113.

combination of difficult vocabulary, underdetermined logical relationships and thin semantics of these verses. This could be seen as presenting grave problems for a relevance – based account: here we have an author who flagrantly flaunts the principle of relevance in the very first sentence of his text, by presenting a difficult structure with a minimal semantic payload.

At this point we should remind ourselves of the strange dance between speaker and hearer (or writer and reader, as here) which Relevance Theory specifies: the principle of relevance works both ways. Thus, every communicator is required to communicate relevantly, but by the same token every communication communicates the assumption of its own relevance, and hearers (or readers) assume that a communication *is* relevant unless and until that assumption is disproved. This means that, particularly in the case of an opening sentence, an author is in a certain sense granted the benefit of the doubt, and as we saw in Chapter 2, this can be thought of as corresponding to the first stage of comprehension in Steiner's four-fold hermeneutic motion – the stage of initiative trust. This means, somewhat paradoxically, that an author can afford to take certain liberties with a preface. In the case of Luke's preface, the reader will quickly perceive that the straightforward semantics of the piece do not justify the effort involved in reading it – that they do not deliver 'worthwhile contextual effects for no unjustifiable effort'.[1] He or she will seek to resolve this by looking for further and better contextual effects – that is, by moving up the 'relevance curve' in diagram 3. If he or she does so, she will find that the preface does provide some very worthwhile contextual effects.

Contextual implications from Luke's preface

One of these may be that this preface is a genre marker. For Nolland and Marshall, for example, it seems to indicate a history in the high classical or Hellenistic manner; for Alexander, it indicates a middle-brow reference work. Wright also notices this: 'Here, he is saying, is something solid, something you can trust. Writers in the first-century Mediterranean world quite often wrote opening sentences like this; readers would know they were beginning a serious, well-researched piece of work.'[2] Whatever its precise signification, a genre-marker is an

1   So, for example, E Hänchen, 1966, p.1ff 'If [Luke] had been willing to write the first verse in a simpler fashion, it would have read something like, 'many have told the story of the things that have happened among us", van Unnik, 1963, p.9, 'Had he spared himself the trouble of writing such a master sentence, he would have saved his later readers a nightmare of exegetical puzzles.' Both cited in Alexander, 1993, p.105
2   Wright, 2001, p.1.

extremely valuable thing in terms of relevance: all kinds of worthwhile contextual effects can be derived from knowing the genre. We will recall that contextual implications are formed by combining a decoded, explicated and analysed text with something already in the reader's cognitive environment. Thus if, with Alexander, we decide that Luke is simply using the preface to indicate that what follows should be interpreted in a context including the knowledge that it is a 'technical/ scientific' work, we can take it that he is encouraging the reader to recover those assumptions in his or her cognitive environment which are associated with such treatises, and combine them with the new communication in order to generate a range of contextual effects, including (perhaps) the implications:

- 'the author intends this to be interpreted as factual and not fanciful';
- 'the author has based his account on empirical (his own or others') experience';
- 'the author intends to make a point rather than simply recount a story';
- 'the author is warning that the material which follows will require concentration and may not be quite as simple as it first appears.'

And so on. If this is in fact the point of the preface, Luke can be congratulated – its very brevity makes it highly relevant, because it covers 'all the bases' of a 'scientific/technical' work, but in the briefest possible form. Brevity is, as we shall see, usually (not always) a virtue in relevance terms, simply because other things being equal it means that the hearer or reader has been put to the minimum trouble in return for the contextual implications he or she receives. Although Luke's preface is a relatively long and troublesome sentence, it is in fact not all *that* long for Luke, and it is after all only one sentence. If its purpose is only to indicate genre, the shorter the better once that effect has been achieved.

Another set of effects may be derived from the preface's aesthetic quality itself. As we saw when considering commentators' assessments of the preface, a common response is an appreciation of its beauty. Whilst some of these responses are undoubtedly overdone,[1] Alexander is surely a little harsh in her implied assessment of the piece as hack-work: it does have a certain pleasing symmetry, and the language is rhythmic and euphonic. The much observed 'sonority', whilst in the

---

1   Possibly some of the enthusiastic responses can be attributed to an over-familiarity with paratactic 'biblical Greek' and an under-familiarity with more classical style; however, this is not an accusation which could be levelled at, for example, Nolland or Wright.

eyes of some readers 'ponderous', does (perhaps by that very fact) lend it an almost architectural quality which makes Wright's metaphor of a 'grand doorway' seem appropriate. It is fair to say that Alexander's assessment focuses more on semantics than on structure, and that her points of comparison are drawn from the best literature from the classical period up to graeco-roman times, rather than the immediately available context of Luke's gospel itself. The latter is, of course, the only context which we *know* the original audience had, and the preface certainly is in a style which is 'heightened' in that context.

What kind of contextual implications might be derived from these features? If the context, or cognitive environment of the reader, includes assumptions about the complex relationships which can pertain between style, content, writer ability, and writing conventions, a reader might be able to recover a set of contextual implications including something like the following:

• 'the author intends to express himself as elegantly as the material will allow';
• 'the author offers reassurance that his story has a certain beauty and symmetry;
• 'if the material which follows at times appears crude, this is not because of a defect in the author's writing abilities, but a deliberate effect';

And so on. Could it be argued that the preface's euphony and rhythm prepares the reader for the challenging, luminous and also somehow charming material of the birth stories? Does the weaving of the sub-clauses into a harmonious and balanced whole prepare for the complex and yet also unified inter-woven stories of John and Jesus? The reason we do not know the answer to these questions is that we do not have a full picture of the cognitive environment of the first readers. For the moment, though, we should note that there exists in this area a potentially rich harvest of contextual implications for a reader in the original context.

A third set of contextual effects which may be derived from Luke's preface relate to its periodic form and to the question of its indeterminacy in his hands. As we observed, the periodic form requires a certain trust on the part of the reader: closure of the thought is not achieved until the end of the period. Further, Luke's 41 word period links the six main thoughts together in a way that is almost impossible to achieve in good paratactic style, and the establishment of such allusive almost-but-not-quite connections allows an experienced reader to form another set of quite worthwhile contextual implications, including for example:

• 'the author warns that parts of the story will not achieve closure until the end';

- 'the author warns that even then the story will not achieve closure by offering 'proof';
- 'the author signals that he will produce a coherent argument but that it won't be finally conclusive';

and so on.

We see then, three areas potentially rich in contextual implications for an attentive reader. It will be beneficial to pause at this point to make two observations.

The first is to remind ourselves that what we are interested in for the purposes of the present work is primarily the *method* by which a translator attempts to achieve interpretive resemblance between a source and a target text. Our main interest, therefore, is not in the truth value of such an interpretation as presented here, but rather in the sort of contextual implications which might follow from such an interpretation, and in how a translation might attempt to perform such an interpretive resemblance.

The second is to observe the process by which the reader 'gets to' these relevant contextual implications in this particular case. The reader assumes that the text she is approaching will be relevant – that is, that its interpretation will fall within the 'golden area' defined by the 'relevance curve' in figure 6 – but she cannot know exactly where on the curve it falls – particularly in the case of a preface, where there are no clues from a preceding co-text.[1] She will thus hypothesise, beginning in the bottom left-hand corner of the graph, where the minimum effort is required, as to what the speaker intended interpretation might be. Only as she absorbs or discards earlier hypotheses does she move up the relevance curve, and at some point she will arrive at an interpretation where the effort which has been expended seems to match the value of the contextual implications which can be formed.

If Luke had begun his gospel with the sentence: 'I am going to write a book about Jesus' the reader would, having explicated the simple words and syntax involved, quickly find a resolution which satisfies the criterion of relevance and move on to the narrative itself. In the case of Luke's preface, however, we might imagine the reader encountering all the features outlined above, and quickly being driven up the relevance curve, where she will be compelled to form a number of contextual implications in order to justify to herself the effort involved. This is exactly what Luke

---

1   Although of course this is the communicative purpose of codex bindings, decorative scrolls, dust jackets and the 'blurb' on the back of modern books, which can be understood as ostensive co-text.

intended her to do, and it is by this process that she has correctly inferred the writer-intended interpretation. An important part of the communicative strategy here has been the denial of easy understanding: if the reader had found an easy resolution to the semantics of the sentence, she would have stopped at that point. This would have been disastrous for the author's communicative intention, for she would have remained in the 'trivial' area of figure 6, whereas he wants her firmly in the 'difficult' area. Not only would she not be able to form the range of contextual implications we have identified, but also she would be in quite the wrong frame of mind for the material which follows: she would have no reason not to assume that the charming tales (the birth narratives) which follow can be similarly easily interpreted.

If, as we saw in Chapter Two, a writer has an interest in maximising the attention a reader will bring to his or her text, it is predictable that he or she will make as high a bid for such attention as is credible, and do so as early as possible. It is part, for example, of Alexander's observations that the writer of a scientific/technical text will pitch his preface in a 'higher' register than that demanded by the work as a whole.[1] This makes complete sense as a bid for attention: the author will err on the side of caution in flagging the attention which he or she requires from the reader.

As we saw in chapter 2, in relevance theory, a communicator may decide to use an expression by virtue of its *lack* of explicitness, in order to weakly convey a wide range of implications.[2] The examples given for such effects are often metaphorical or poetic, but the same can apply to a particular use of a grammatical structure. Here, Luke deliberately uses this convoluted style in order to withhold precise information concerning how the various factors mentioned are causally or logically connected. In doing so, he encourages the reader to put in more work – to begin to form a wide range of her own implications, and to raise the attention she is offering the text which follows.

Translating Luke's preface

Wright: 'Communicative translation'?

How have present-day translators fared with the set of translation issues presented by this passage? Our first focus will be on a translation performed by NT Wright, which appears linked to

---

1   Alexander, 1993, p.91.
2   See Sperber and Wilson, 1995, p.236 'Robert is a bulldozer.'

his own commentary in 'Luke for Everyone'.[1] Our interest in this translation derives mainly from its exemplary character: Wright's intention as a translator here is explicitly communicative. In his introduction he states: 'There are of course many translations of the New Testament available today. The one I offer here is designed for the . . . kind of reader . . . who mightn't necessarily understand the more formal, sometimes even ponderous, tones of some of the standard ones. I have of course tried to keep as close to the original as I can. But my main aim has been to be sure that the words can speak not just to some people, but to everyone.' This agenda is exemplary of a range of 'communicative' mainstream translations such as the CEV or the TEV (Good News Bible). Our interest is also, of course, driven by the fact that Wright provides a commentary alongside the translation, as well as a great deal of interpretive material elsewhere: we can have a high level of certainty as to what his interpretation of a passage actually is, independently of the translation itself.
Wright's translation of the Lukan preface is as follows:

> *Many people have undertaken to draw up an orderly account of the events that have occurred in our midst. It has been handed down to us by the original eyewitnesses and stewards of the word. So, most excellent Theophilus, since I had traced the course of all of it scrupulously from the start, I thought it a good idea to write an orderly account for you, so that you may have secure knowledge about the matters in which you have been instructed.*

The first thing we are likely to notice about this translation is that its syntax has been considerably simplified, both at the level of the whole period and for individual clauses, and that the vocabulary is relatively straightforward. The passage easily passes a Flesch-Kincaid readability test, scoring 12.9 – approximately the average adult reading age in the UK.[2] The periodic form has been abandoned, to

---

1   This is intendedly a 'popular' translation and commentary, and it might be objected that it was not intended for the kind of scrutiny to which we are about to subject it. In fact, the views expressed in the commentary are in harmony with Wright's analyses elsewhere – see for example *The New Testament and the People of God*, 1992, p.378. In any event, there is no reason to assume that there is great discontinuity between Wright's academic work and his more populist work – indeed his integrity in this regard is unquestioned. A translation is always (unless intended purely as an academic gloss) to a greater or lesser degree a 'populist' enterprise, and if it is offered by virtue of its resemblance to an original, it can only be assessed as such.
2   Dewey, 2001, p.73.

be replaced by three sentences, with an average word-count of 27 per sentence, and 4.4 characters per word. The only factor, in fact, which keeps the reading grade level this high is the use of passive sentences (2 out of 3).

Readability, of course, does, other things being equal, make a significant contribution to relevance. This is most easily seen at the extreme end of un-readability: it is possible for a text to be so hard syntactically, to use such unusual lexis and to be so unfamiliar stylistically that for a given reader it detaches from the relevance curve in figure 3 and drifts into the 'obscure' zone.[3] As we will see later, when we consider some form driven translations, Luke's preface is certainly 'at risk' in this respect. Wright has, then, been true to his word and made the preface accessible to anyone with an average reading age or higher.

How, though, would we account for this translation in terms of a relevance theory of translation (*RTT*)? We will recall the three criteria which we set out above (p 71). The first criterion relates to how the translator has interpreted the source text, and we saw in our analysis that Wright falls within the broad consensus of scholars who see that Luke 1.1-4 has a highly marked and stylized passage which has a set of implications within its original context, implications having to do with the preface form as it was used in that context. He further falls within the group (the majority) who have a high regard for its aesthetic qualities: like 'a huge stone entrance welcoming you impressively to a large building'.

The second criterion relates to how the translated text achieves its relevance in the target context, and we have already noticed how it does so: the core strategy is to make it as 'readable' as possible. The text is moved decisively down the relevance curve (figure 6), so that a present day reader can readily find a relevant interpretation.

The third criterion relates to how the translated text interpretively resembles the source text; and it is here, of course, that we can immediately see some significant problems. We have every reason to believe that Wright was aiming for what Gutt would call a 'direct translation' (to 'keep as close as possible to the original'), in which case we would predict that his translation would try to convey as many of the analytical implications as possible, together with as many of the

---

3   For a regular and enjoyable diet of examples, visit 'Pseuds Corner' in the satirical British weekly *Private Eye*. It has to be emphasised, though, that obscurity is reader-specific. Many of the examples found there will be seen as much less obscure if they are read by someone with the originally intended cognitive environment.

contextual implications as possible. In line with the 'communicative' agenda, we would expect that where difficulties are encountered, he would compromise the former to achieve the latter, which are after all the communicative pay-load of a text. In fact, when we look at the translation, we see that when interpreted in the original context, it could not possibly allow the reader to form the sort of contextual implications we identified earlier. Instead, the sort of implications which might be formed would be:

- 'the author is a child, or an adult in the early stages of literacy', or
- 'the author intends this work for children';
- 'the author offers reassurance that this story will be easy to follow';
- 'the author will present his material with no particular regard to style';

and so on.

Given this, there must be very different criteria of resemblance which have been applied.

A table like the one that follows has, of course, no significance in and of itself. A translator will always preserve some formal features of a source text and abandon others, in order to achieve an overall interpretive resemblance. A translator with a 'communicative' agenda, in particular, might be expected to sacrifice a number of formal pawns in order to capture the queen of overall interpretive resemblance. What is interesting in this case, though, is that as Wright's translation makes no attempt in terms of overall interpretive resemblance to produce the 'impressive stone entrance' to which his commentary refers, we are left asking: what, then, *are* the criteria of resemblance he is using?

This question can be answered only by looking at the texts themselves. The following table looks at formal qualities only, and suggests which of these the translator seems to have regarded as important in achieving interpretive resemblance, and which he seems to have regarded as unimportant.

To be sure, some of these items would have been different had we examined a different part of his translation. Some of the items in figure 9 deserve a little more explanation. We have already seen, for example, that in the original the periodic form and the particular choice of connectives to link clauses (features 9 and 10) play a key part in achieving the 'indeterminacy' of this sentence. In Wright's translation, the periodic form has been replaced by three sentences, and the thoughts represented by these sentences are not connected in the same way as in the original. In verses 1 and 2 they are not

Regards as Important:		Does not Regard as Important	
Formal Feature	Comment	Formal Feature	Comment
1. Preservation of verse order	*Complete resemblance*	6. Preservation of word order within clauses	Word order within clauses often changed
2. Preservation of verbal mood	*Complete resemblance (indicative for indicative, subjunctive for subjunctive)*	7. Preservation of verbal voice	Substitutes active for passive and vice versa
3. Preservation of parts of speech	*Complete resemblance (noun for noun, verb for verb, etc.)*	8. Preservation of verbal tense/aspect	Substitutes perfect for aorist, pluperfect for perfect, present for aorist, etc.
4. Preservation of clause order	*Only exception is the positioning of the main verb and the address to Theophillis*	9. Punctuation	Periodic form abandoned. Substitutes three sentences for one
5. Preservation of analytic implications of individual words	*Word for word correspondence in most cases*	10. Logical connectives between clauses	Logical connections are altered
		11. Vocabulary register	Significantly more 'accessible' vocabulary is used
		12. Vocabulary register	'preface' form not used
		13. Symmetry of form	No symmetry between clauses or sentences
		14. Rhythm	Hiatus at end of verse 1 and other punctuation prevents formation of rhythym
		15. Other aural qualities - 'sonorous' sound quality and alliteration	None

Interpretive Resemblance: Wright's translation of Luke 1.1-4

connected at all, with the latter playing a parenthetical role. In the second half of the preface, the connection of thoughts within verses 3 and 4 is preserved but made stronger than in the Greek – in Wright's translation, it is the fact that Luke has 'traced the course of all of it scrupulously' which unambiguously drives the decision to write; and, because the full stops have severed the direct connection with the first verse, weakened also is the thought that Luke is partly motivated or in his own mind justified in his endeavours by the fact that so many other accounts have been attempted.

Wright is not by any means alone in struggling to express the connections between Luke's various linked thoughts, and this is not surprising given that the kind of connections we have identified as being in play are hard to express in paratactic form in any language: they always seem to come out either too firm, or too weak. Thus the TEV:

> Many undertook to compile an account of the things accomplished amongst us. Those who from the start were eyewitnesses and became servants of the word passed them on to us. I followed it all carefully from the ground up. It seemed to me good to write it carefully for you, Theo. You would know the firm foundation of the things you have been taught.

This latter-day asyndeton avoids establishing any firm connection between five sentences which are intended to resemble Luke's one period. The result, besides being stylistically rather 'staccato' is incoherent in terms of a flow of ideas.

The CEV opts for the route of building the preface into a coherent 'case':

> *Many people have tried to tell the story of what God has done among us. They wrote what we had been told by the ones who were there in the beginning and saw what happened. So I made a careful study of everything and then decided to write and tell you exactly what took place. Honourable Theophilus, I have done this to let you know the truth about what you have heard.*

Here, there is a step-by-step building of a case for writing. Both the overall effect and the individual steps involved are not those present in the original as we have interpreted it above. In verse 1 there is the strong implication that people have tried but at least in some ways failed, and in verse 3, that this is the motivation for making 'a careful study'. Then it is the *existence* of this study which leads to the decision to write to Theophilus.

Even the NIV, which is not explicitly committed to such strong 'readability' criteria, struggles to deal with this issue:

> *Many have undertaken to draw up an account of the things that*
> *have been fulfilled among us, just as they were handed down to us by*
> *those who from the first were eyewitnesses and servants of the word.*
> *Therefore, since I myself have carefully investigated everything from*
> *the beginning, it seemed good also to me to write an orderly account for*
> *you, most excellent Theophilus, so that you may know the certainty of*
> *the things you have been taught.*

The NIV has two sentences, creating more potential for unity and
symmetry in the thought; but the use of 'therefore' at the beginning of
verse 3 establishes a strong logical link between the second half and the
first, suggesting that Luke is attempting a watertight logical argument
as to why he should write: an argument which of course makes no
sense, as the conclusion does not at all follow from the premise.

What is the effect of this translation strategy? As we saw, Wright's
translation of the Lukan preface moves it decisively 'down' the relevance
curve of figure 3. Whereas in the original source document we saw that the
reader is forced 'up' the same curve into the 'difficult' zone, where she will
work to recover some of the implications we discussed, she is kept in the
'trivial' zone by Wright's translation. The effects of this can be various, but
they are all invidious. The base level effect is to produce a communication
which appears to most readers to be unsatisfying, often in a way which
they find difficult to articulate. (We discussed an example of this in
Chapter One, where we observed David Daniell's reaction to a translation
from the Hebrew scriptures. He felt there had been a loss but could not
quite put his finger on how it had occurred.) The communication may
appear 'banal' or 'colourless', or be described as stylistically neutral. The
reason for this is that the act of communication itself has been truncated.
Whereas the original delivered a 'thin' semantic helping in order to tempt
the reader up to a much more interesting part of the table, our translation
just leaves him feeling unsatisfied – in the case of this particular passage in
Luke, 'Why doesn't he just get on with it?'

The other possibility, though, is that having performed his
translation the translator himself has an uneasy feeling that something
is wrong, and tries to do something about it. We see hints of this in
some of the translations we have so far mentioned, where there seems
to have been a felt need to 'tighten' the syntax of the piece by specifying
stronger connectives than resemblance would strictly demand. There
may also be a temptation to 'flesh out' or strengthen certain ideas, in
order to make the passage more communicative whilst remaining in
the 'easy' part of figure 3. For example in the CEV παρακολουθέω
becomes 'make a careful study', a related but somewhat different idea,

and stronger: one may closely follow the news of the terrorist attacks in Delhi without making a study of them. In self-styled idiomatic 'versions' we see this process in full flower. Consider this from *the Message:*

> So many others have tried their hand at putting together a story of the wonderful harvest of Scripture and history that took place among us, using reports handed down by the original eyewitnesses who served this Word with their very lives. Since I have investigated all the reports in close detail, starting from the story's beginning, I decided to write it all out for you, most honourable Theophilus, so you can know beyond the shadow of a doubt the reliability of what you were taught.

Or this from *Die Volxbibel*:

> *Lieber Theophilus! Viele Leute haben schon den Versuch gestartet, alles mal aufzuschreiben, was so bei uns in den letzten Jahren abgegangen ist. Als Grundlage dafür gab es ja die Berichte von den Augenzeugen, die das mitgekriegt haben, wie Gott alle seine Versprechen eingehalten hat. Ich habe diese Berichte alle genau durchgelesen und dann kam ich auf die Idee, dir diese ausführliche Zusammenfassung der wichtigsten Ereignisse mal aufzuschreiben. Du wirst bemerken: Alles, was man dir erzählt hat, hat sich tatsächlich auch so abgespielt! Es ist alles total wahr.*

The temptation to produce such things is not new. Consider the following, from 1870:

> *Since many have attempted to draw up a narrative concerning the actions and sufferings of Christ, which we have received from those who beheld Him, and ministered to Him from the beginning, and since some may be perplexed by the multitude and variety of these attempts; it seems good to me, who have been called by the Holy Ghost to write, and who have followed the course of those events from the commencement; and who from my birth and education at Antioch, the second Gentile city in the world, and in which the disciples were first called Christians . . . and from my association with Paul the Apostle of you Gentiles . . . in his travels and sufferings, as I will show in the second part of my history . . . have special qualifications and a special commission for this holy work of providing a* **written** *Gospel for you, noble Greeks and Gentiles – for you, Theophili – who by your name proclaim your love of God, and God's love for you; as written Gospels have been already provided by my brother Evangelists, for the Hebrews and Romans;*

*in order that you, who have been baptized and instructed orally
in the Creed of Christendom, may have further knowledge of the
certainty of those things wherein you have been orally instructed.*
                                          Chr. Wordsworth, London 1870

Peterson's *The Message*, Dreyer's *Die Volxbibel* and Wordsworth's
Paraphrase all meet Gutt's criterion for a translation, because they
are texts intended to achieve relevance by virtue of resemblance to
an original source.[1] What these versions do is to take a selection
from the wide range of contextual implications which the translator
believes are weakly implied in the original, and make them part of
the explicit content of the text. Because there is not space to put in
all the implications (although Wordsworth gives it a good try), there
is a selection process and this is driven by 'the message' the translator
wishes to convey ('*Es ist alles total wahr!*', perhaps?). We should notice
that one effect of this is to keep the reader from forming her own
implications further up the relevance curve. *Die Volxbibel* suffers
from the further defect of turning the dedicatee Theophilus into an
epistolatory addressee, thus triggering a set of formal expectations
which will not, of course, be met in the course of the gospel, which is
not epistolatory in form.

The difficulty in assessing these published versions is, of course,
that we do not know independently how the translator interpreted
the relevance of the original text. In the case of Wright's translation,
though, we do know, because he has told us in the commentary
and elsewhere. We know that Wright has a full and highly nuanced
interpretation of the preface; it is just that his translation does not
seem to be connected with it. We must look for the reason for the
lack of interpretive resemblance elsewhere; and we will find it in the
formation of the translator's communicative intention.

Translator's communicative intention

As we have seen, in Relevance Theory communication begins with the
formation of a communicative intention, and it is this which drives
the communicator's choices as to what she will say and how she will
say it. In RTT, the translator, having arrived at an interpretation of
the source text, begins a new act of communication by forming his

---

1   Gutt, 1993, p.106. Commonsense also will not allow that the Message
is somehow exempt from the criteria applied to translation: any book called
'The Bible in Contemporary Language' and which follows the source book by
book, verse by verse, is clearly intended to resemble its source. A paraphrase is
a translation which dare not speak its name.

own new communicative intention. In translation, the communicative intention will always include the idea that the new communication (i.e. the translated text) is to achieve its relevance by virtue of its resemblance to the original. It will further embrace what kind of interpretive resemblance he is going to seek. In the case of 'direct translation', what is desired is 'complete interpretive resemblance', and one can imagine the translator giving himself a mandate such as this:

> Produce a translated text which, when processed in the original context, so far as possible has all and only the analytical implications and all and only the contextual implications of the original source text.

The key words for the present stage of our argument are the caveat 'so far as possible'. The translator must decide what is possible. Gutt is well aware of the importance of this stage of the process, his remarks focussing mainly on the need to be realistic about what a translator can achieve.[1] In order to make a decision as to what is possible, the translator needs to have three things. First, he or she needs to have an accurate assessment of the expressive abilities and limitations of both the source and the target languages, so that (s)he can see what kind of gap has to be bridged. Secondly, (s)he needs to have the imagination to see how a bridge of the requisite strength could be built. Thirdly, (s)he needs to have what David Daniell calls 'boldness'. To see the gap, and to know how to bridge it is not enough: many practising translators have observed the need for courage,[2] and this is not surprising in terms of Relevance Theory, where all communication is 'at a hazard'.[3]

It seems that Wright has decided that the kind of interpretive resemblance we have been talking about is just not possible; or perhaps that it is possible but too risky. Alternatively, Wright may be subconsciously nervous lest his translation strays from the ἱερὸς γάμος, the Holy Marriage we identified in Chapter One as the major inhibiting factor in biblical translation. Whilst on the face of it operating to a mandate similar to the one just stated, his assessment of what is possible or desirable has led to a truncated set of objectives. If we were to assess his objectives solely on the basis of what he has actually done, we would express his self-imposed mandate as follows:

> Produce a translated text which, when processed in the original

---

1   Gutt, 2000, p.76ff, and p.175ff.
2   See for example Seamus Heaney's remarks in the preface to his Beowulf, xxv.
3   Sperber and Wilson, 1995, pp.50-54.

context, has a selection of the analytical implications and the contextual implications of the original source text, and which does not contradict the ἱερὸς γάμος.

If we were then to ask what selection criteria have been used, we might arrive at:

Select those analytic and contextual implications which can be expressed without altering the verse order or certain grammatical features of the source text, and without requiring a reading age above x.

This could be stated more strongly, because in fact Wright's translation mandate appears to allow grammatical features to actually override the earlier requirement to produce all and *only* the implications of the source text. His translation of verse 2, we will recall, reads: 'It has been handed down to us by the original eyewitnesses and stewards of the word.' 'It can only refer to the 'account' mentioned in verse 1, which in turn is a literal rendering of διήγησις. All the commentators we have mentioned interpret διήγησις here as synecdoche, and it would be surprising if Wright took a different view, particularly in view of his masterly summary of the variety of witnesses in other works.[1] The implication of Wright's translation is that many people have been working, presumably collaboratively, to produce a single account which has then been handed on to us by the original eyewitnesses (who, by further implication, are – and this is a surprise – involved in the transmission of a pre-existing report, but perhaps were not involved in producing the account itself).[2] This curious construction is, of course, the result of a combination of the 'improvements' to syntax which Wright makes and his use of a singular English word to match the singular Greek διήγησιν. It is difficult to diagnose this as anything other than a lingering intuition that the translation should use words that are somehow 'equivalent' to those of the source text.

This intuition – perhaps we could call it the ghost of equivalence – is part of the inheritance of the ἱερὸς γάμος, the idea of a Holy Marriage between English and ancient Greek which we identified in Chapter One.[3] In the theoretical vacuum left behind the collapse of Nida's project, most translators have resorted to their intuitions, and

---

1   The three magnificent volumes of *The New Testament and the People of God* series are all testament to this.
2   The only translation which comes close is the extremely literal *Elberfelder*, which has: 'Da es nun schon viele unternommen haben, einen Bericht von der Ereignissen zu verfassen, die sich unter uns zugetragen haben, wie sie uns die überliefert haben. . . .'
3   See p. 23.

these intuitions include the strong, but false, intuition that words in different languages somehow equate to one another. We will see in Chapter Six that this is linked to the equally prevalent and equally false intuition that words correspond to things in the real world.

Lest this read too much like a diatribe against 'communicative translation', let me assure the reader that that is not part of *my* communicative intention. We will now turn to a completely different translation, one produced in the context of John Nolland's masterly commentary on Luke. Our agenda, as before, is to try to diagnose what the translator's communicative intention has been, and to critique that intention.

Nolland: 'formal' translation?

Inasmuch as many have taken it in hand to arrange a narrative concerning the things that have been accomplished in our midst,₂ just as those who were, from the beginning, eyewitnesses and who became servants of the message handed it on to us, it seemed good to me also, having investigated carefully everything from way back, to write for you, most excellent Theophilus, a well-ordered account, so that you might know, concerning the reports which you have heard, the truth.

It will be clear at once that this is pitched at quite a high reading age. In fact its Flesch-Kincaid reading level is an astonishing 34.2 – right at the limit of what is generally regarded as readable for highly educated people[1]. Interestingly, the difficulty level arises mainly from the sheer length of this 81-word sentence – characters per word stand at a modest level (4.7 against Wright's 4.4) and the vocabulary is not obscure ('carefully' is a much more common and therefore in relevance terms more easily accessible word than Wright's rather academic 'scrupulously', for example.) Nolland also makes relatively modest use of the passive.

We do not have from Nolland a statement of his approach to translation, so we are at liberty to infer directly from the translation work itself and from the context in which it appears. The latter is a weighty and extremely thorough academic commentary appearing in three volumes, and a standard text for any serious student of Luke's gospel. Looking at formal features of his translation, we can observe the following:

Nolland keeps at least 10 and perhaps 11 out of 15 formal features constant (compare Wright's 5). In terms of the typology presented in chapter 1, his translation of Luke's preface is 'formal'.

As for Wright, we know from the co-text that Nolland has a highly

---

1   See Dewey, 2001, p.73.

nuanced understanding of how Luke's preface achieves relevance in its original context. Our enquiry is therefore again 'diagnostic' in nature: what kind of interpretive resemblance does Nolland's translation attempt? His strategy is essentially one of formal correspondence, and we can perhaps suggest that his self-imposed interpretation of the 'so far as possible' governing clause is:

> so far as possible means': 'providing that syntactical resemblance
> is retained except where English grammar would be violated.

In other words, Nolland is interested in resemblance in analytical and contextual implications – and we can see plenty of evidence of this in the co-text – but only insofar as they are expressible in directly equivalent formal English structures. The effect of this is that the analytical and contextual implications of individual words of the Greek are captured rather well in the English, but implications for larger structures have to take their chances, as it were: sometimes they will come through, sometimes not. Thus interpretive resemblance at word and at clause level is strong. Even the use of underdetermined connectives is done well: 'Inasmuch as' is quite an exact interpretation of Ἐπειδήπερ , and of course has a long and distinguished history in the translation of this passage.[1] The translation uses the English past participle 'having investigated' in the same way to interpret Luke's perfect participle, and so on.

At the level of words, of clauses, and of the connection between those clauses, there is a strong relationship of interpretive resemblance. Yet there may also be an intuition that there is something missing. Nolland is in the camp having a very high assessment of Luke as a stylist – this is, remember, 'the best stylized sentence in the whole NT', and for Nolland this has great significance as positioning Luke with a sophisticated readership. It is only the style and beauty of the sentence which allows the reader to form these contextual implications, and the problem is that in English the sentence has a *style* which does not allow the reader to form these implications, and, frankly, it has no *beauty* at all. The response just expressed has been registered so many times in the history of translation criticism, in relation to so many literary translations, that it has become almost a commonplace: for example, Chukovski speaking of a Russian translation of Pickwick Papers: 'although each line of the original text is reproduced with

---

1   The AV follows Tyndale in using 'Forasmuch as'. Wycliffe also uses the appropriately indeterminate Middle English: 'Forsothe for manye men enforceden to ordeyne the telling of thingis, which ben fillid in vs . . .', Luther 1545 has 'Sintemal,' the Vulgate 'Qoniam quidem.'

Regards as important:		Does not regard as important:	
Formal feature	*Comment*	**Formal feature**	*Comment*
1. Preservation of verse order	*Complete resemblance*	*11. Preservation of word order within clauses*	*Word order within clauses often changed*
2. Preservation of verbal mood	*Complete resemblance (indicative for indicative, subjunctive for subjunctive)*	*12. Preservation of verbal tense/aspect*	*Partial resemblance, but English perfect used for aorist*
3. Preservation of parts of speech	*Complete resemblance (noun for noun, verb for verb, etc.)*	*13. Vocabulary register*	*Significantly more 'accessible' vocabulary is used*
4. Preservation of clause order	*Complete resemblance*	*14. Overall stylistic marking*	*'Preface' form not used*
5. Preservation of analytic implications of individual words	*Word for word correspondance in every possible case*	*15. Other aural qualities – 'sonorous' sound quality and alliteration*	*None*
6. Preservation of verbal voice	*Active for active, passive for passive*		
7. Punctuation	*Single sentence, Periodic form retained*		
8. Logical connectives between clauses	*Logical connections are retained*		
9. Symmetry of form	*Symmetry between clauses retained*		
10. Rhythm	*Rhythm resembles that of the original*		

Interpretive Resemblance: Nolland's translation of Luke 1.1–4

mathematical precision, not a trace has survived of Dickens' youthful, sparkling, stormy hilarity.'[1] This can easily descend into a simple case of rather unproductive disagreement about style. Can RTT provide a better frame for this discussion?

We may observe several effects of Nolland's translation in Relevance terms. The first we have already noted: the reading level required is very high. This is not in itself a disaster, because we will recall that relevance is always a trade-off: providing a text carries assumptions from which a very worthwhile pay-load of contextual implications can be formed, it can be as hard to read as one likes (or perhaps, better, as hard as the communicator *dares* in the context).

Thus, and returning again to figure 3, a sentence may be pitched at the high end of processing cost, provided it yields a really interesting set of contextual implications. The challenge for Nolland is that his strict formal rendering of Luke's work has produced an English sentence which is excruciatingly hard to process, and the relevance stakes are thus raised very high. This sort of periodic style is very unusual in modern English – in relevance terms, the assumptions required to process such a sentence are either not present at all or are buried quite deep in the cognitive environment. This is not, of course, to say that the sentence is impossible in English: Nolland has produced a perfectly grammatical period.[2] Nor is it difficult to find similar examples in the English canon. Consider for example the second sentence from the translators' preface to the Authorized Version of 1611, which is of course addressed to King James:

> *For whereas it was the expectation of many, who wished not well unto our Sion, that upon the setting of that bright occidental star, Queen Elizabeth of most happy memory, some thick and palpable clouds of darkness would have overshadowed this land, that men should have been in doubt which way they were to walk, and that it should hardly be known, who was to direct the unsettled state: the appearance of your Majesty, as of the sun in his strength, instantly dispelled those supposed and surmised mists, and gave unto all that were well affected exceeding cause of comfort; especially when we beheld the government established in your Highness, and your hopeful seed, by an undoubted title, and this also accompanied with peace and tranquillity at home and abroad.*[3]

---

1   Chukovski, 1984, p.49, cited in Gutt, 2000, p.131.
2   Nor is he by any means alone – see Joel Green's translation of the same piece (Green, 1997, p.33) or The Restored New Testament, p.327.
3   CUP, 2005, xv. Edited by David Norton, who modernized spelling and

At one time, indeed, such a stylistic marking (doubtless under the influence of the Greek and Latin 'classical' authors who formed the core curriculum in the English educational system) would have been considered suitable for an introduction like this. However, as time progresses the style becomes less and less acceptable, retaining its position only by an occasional 'poetic' appearance.[1]

Late 20th Century and early 21st Century English favours a far more paratactic style, as the following sentence from the Preface to the NIV (1983) shows:

> *The first concern of the translators has been the accuracy of the translation and its fidelity to the thought of the biblical writers. They have weighed the significance of the lexical and grammatical details of the Hebrew, Aramaic and Greek texts. At the same time they have striven for more than a word-for-word translation.*

The stakes, then, are high: to succeed as communication, Nolland's rendering of the preface must pack a powerful punch in terms of contextual implications. The problem is that this periodic form does not permit this in present-day English. There is no such thing as the 'periodic preface form' in present-day English: so the assumptions conveyed in such a sentence do not lead to the kind of contextual implications in which we are interested. These implications, many of them identified by Nolland in his commentary, are, we will recall:

- 'the author intends this to be interpreted as factual and not fanciful';
- 'the author has based his account on empirical (his own or others') experience';
- 'the author intends to make a point rather than simply recount a story';
- 'the author is warning that the material which follows will require concentration and may not be quite as simple as it first appears'.

These are the assumptions which would be formed if, in line with (our hypothesis of) Luke's communicative intention, the reader was led up

---

some punctuation in the process.

1   As an example see W.H. Auden's *In praise of Limestone*:
   If it form the one landscape that we, the inconstant ones,
   Are consistently homesick for, this is chiefly
   Because it dissolves in water. Mark these rounded slopes
   With their surface fragrance of thyme . . .
Even here, we should note, the period is considerably shorter and made easier to process by the versification. Auden was, of course, of the last generation of major English poets brought up on the 'classical' educational diet.

the relevance curve by the use of the periodic form. Unfortunately instead, in Nolland's translation, the sentence has detached from the relevance curve and drifted vertically upwards into the 'obscure' zone. In this area of the graph, recall, the author loses all control over what implications the reader is forming, and communication as specified by Relevance Theory ceases to occur. The reader has been put to considerable processing cost, and therefore she *will* form some implications to justify this cost to herself; however, they are very unlikely to be the implications intended by the author. For example in this case she may form the following:

- 'The author is a pompous academic';
- 'The author does not know how to communicate clearly';
- 'The author is prepared to waste my time'.

These are very grave problems for a communicator, particularly in the first line of a work.

This set of difficulties, though, is not at all unusual in literary or scriptural translation. When Alan Williams approached his translation of the medieval Persian *Masnavi* of Rumi, he found there a 'unique musicality, not least because of the metre, or rhythm of the couplet'.[1] There also could not be any doubt that this musicality played a key role in how the *Masnavi* achieved its relevance in its original context: 'this rhythm is considered a hard metre, the most mystical one for qawwali (religious singing), in South Asian Islamic culture. It seems not to pause, tending to move the listener out of the rhythms of ordinary consciousness: it is believed to induce ecstasy in performer and listener alike . . .'[2] This metre, though, is 'the apocopated six-fold running metre', in which each couplet consists of two eleven-syllable hemistiches, each of these comprising three feet.[3] There is no precedent for this metre in English, and it would present extraordinary difficulties for translator and reader alike. Had Williams attempted to reproduce this in English, he would have produced verse in the 'obscure' zone of figure 3: the reader, presented with something so unusual and difficult to process, would begin by forming implications over which the translator has no control, and end (probably quite quickly) by abandoning the effort.[4] Instead, Williams chose to render

---

1 Williams, 2006, p.xix.

2 Ibid, xx.

3 Ibid, xix.

4 In fact, although Williams does not mention this, one of the problems is that this metre is quite similar to the English children's rhyme 'The Little Train that Could' ('I think i can, I think I can . . . I knew I could, I knew I could.')

the verse in blank iambic pentameters, and this was not because of some spurious notion that this was somehow 'equivalent' in function, or effect – there are no recorded cases of iambic pentameters inducing 'ecstasy' in English hearers. Rather, the reason he chose this verse form was that it represents a 'marked' form that has approximately the same syllabic length (therefore imposing some discipline of economy) as the Persian, and that it is 'the proven metre of English dramatic verse'. In relevance terms, the use of this form represents an aesthetically satisfying and effective route up the relevance curve into the 'significant' or 'highbrow' zone, where the reader or hearer can begin to form some of the implications which formed part of (Williams' hypothesis of) Rumi's communicative intention.

Why did Nolland not attempt such a route? There is, to be sure, a certain kind of 'academic' translation whose communicative intention is to act as a kind of gloss or aide-memoire for scholars. In such cases, the translator has formed her communicative intention around providing a set of reminders or prompts for scholars who are already familiar with the text in its original form, or who are seeking to gain such familiarity. A translation like this serves the same purpose as an inter-linear, and had Nolland chosen to perform an inter-linear translation of Luke's preface, it would presumably have appeared something like this:

One of the interesting things about this is that it is not significantly less 'communicative' than the translation as it appears in Nolland's commentary. Clearly, English grammar in terms of word-order has been violated, but presented as an inter-linear, there is no risk of confusion and the reader is not even materially slowed down. In terms of figure 3, then, it is not in a significantly 'higher processing cost' area of the graph. If, however, we turn to the other axis in figure 3, we find that it is *much more informative* than Nolland's translation: that is, that it provides many more assumptions from which the reader can (with the appropriate application of attention) form useful inferences, even if she has no knowledge of Greek yet. Overwhelmingly the most important of these are the set of implications arising from the recognition that this is not an original communication. The reader can see where word-order differs from the original; where there has been expansion or interpolation (for example in verse 3, where Nolland adds the substantive 'account'); where the same Greek word has been rendered by different English words (for example the different renderings of ἡμῖν ('to us' in verses 1 and 2); and so on. These observations, however, are not the same thing as contextual implications formed as a result of a communicative process: rather, they are just that: observations of differences between an original and an interlinear.

What has happened here is that the process of *communication* has

Ἐπειδήπερ πολλοὶ ἐπεχείρησαν   ἀνατάξασθαι διήγησιν περὶ
Inasmuch as many   have taken it in hand to compile   a narrative concerning

τῶν πεπληροφορημένων   ἐν ἡμῖν   πραγμάτων, 2 καθὼς   παρέδοσαν
the [ ] that have been accomplished   in our midst [things]   just as   they handed on

ἡμῖν   οἱ   ἀπ᾽ ἀρχῆς   αὐτόπται καὶ ὑπηρέται γενόμενοι
to us those who from the beginning   eywitnesses   and   servants   became

τοῦ λόγου,   3 ἔδοξε κἀμοὶ   παρηκολουθηκότι   ἄνωθεν
of the message   it seemed good to me   having investigated   from way back

πᾶσιν   ἀκριβῶς καθεξῆς   σοι γράψαι,   κράτιστε Θεόφιλε,
everything carefully a well-oredered account   for you to write most excellent Theophilius

4 ἵνα   ἐπιγνῷς   περὶ   ὧν κατηχήθης   λόγων τὴν ἀσφάλειαν.
so you might know concerning the which you have heard reports   the truth

in fact been suspended. By placing the English words in such close
proximity and in such clear relation to the Greek words, the writer of the
interlinear has released both the reader and himself from the dynamics of
the relevance curve. When one reads an interlinear, one does not relate to
the writer as a communicator in his own right, but only as the provider
of a gloss of an original communication. One therefore does not look for
a relevant communication, and the requirement for the communicator to
provide assumptions which permit contextual implications in proportion
to the processing cost involved simply does not apply. The reader is
thereby released to 'observe' the interlinear rather than to 'hear' it as a
communication. In Relevance Theory terms, this is what lies behind
Steiner's acute intuition that 'a rigorous interlinear is . . . a no-man's-land
in psychological and linguistic space. . . . The psychological and formal
risks are considerable. At work between his own language and that of the
source-text, the literalist exposes himself to vertigo.'

There is in the history of translation studies a long tradition of what
can only be described as a kind of paradoxical longing for a perfect interlinear, particularly in the field of scriptural translation. Jerome, whose
general rule was *sed sensum exprimere de sensu*, ('thought translate
thought') found himself profoundly uncomfortable in translating in
such a way when dealing with 'the mysteries' – where 'even the word
order is of God's doing', and reverted to *verbum e verbo* ('word for

word'). Philo Judaeus, as early as 20 BCE distinguished μετάφρασις from παράφρασις (metaphrase from paraphrase) and assured his readers that in the case of the Septuagint the former was the rule: 'each Chaldean word was exactly translated by a precise Greek equivalent, which was perfectly adapted to the thing signified.' Walter Benjamin asserts that 'The interlinear version of the scriptures is the archetype or ideal of all translation.' A.E. Knoch, in the 1930s, produces his *Concordant Version* as an interlinear working at the level of morpheme, with a 'literal' translation alongside. We even find Nida, the high priest of communicative translation, finding that 'there are certain important religious symbols which, though often obscure in their meaning, are necessarily important for the preservation of the integrity and unity of the biblical message, e.g. expressions like 'Lamb of God', 'cross' or 'sacrifice'. Such 'symbols' should be rendered 'literally' as in an interlinear, notwithstanding the precepts of dynamic or functional equivalence.

We will discuss literalism in depth in Chapter Six. However, we can already see that the desire for a 'literal' interlinear represents *the longing of the translator not to be a translator.* This feeling, which is related to but not identical with the feeling that translation is somehow a betrayal of the original text, paradoxically increases with the regard which the translator has for his source material. This longing to be excused is as good a piece of evidence as is needed that translation is, again in Steiner's terms, an ethical activity.

Returning to Nolland's translation of the Lukan preface, we can see that, of course, he does not provide an interlinear. His formal rendering of the text may be only a few steps below an interlinear in terms of 'literalness', but it does not excuse him from the process of communication, and this is why it can be judged in relevance terms, and perhaps judged to be a failure. Unlike the provider of an interlinear, a translator places himself in the role of communicator, and therefore in a relation of ethical responsibility to the original text and to his or her audience.

Before turning to some other translations of this piece, we will pause to note where we might place the two translators (and the original) on the relevance graph:

I assess *Luke* itself as being in the upper right-hand quartile, but towards the 'low' end of that quartile. His Greek period permits the formation of a very worthwhile payload of contextual implications, and his level of difficulty (which we may for present purposes equate with 'processing cost') is relatively high, although not impossibly so, for a reasonably educated reader. Wright remains on the relevance curve, but only at the cost of sliding down into the trivial quartile: his translation permits only a small sub-set of the contextual implications, but at least his text is very low cost in terms of processing. Nolland is very costly to process but also does not allow the relevant implications to be formed: it therefore comes adrift from the relevance curve and is placed in the obscure quartile.

The balance of this chapter will look at some other translations, and then consider whether an approach based explicitly on relevance theoretical considerations might provide an alternative framework.

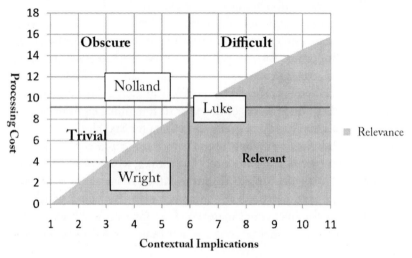

Nolland, Wright, and Luke on the Relevance Curve

Some other translations

We will glance briefly at some other translations, beginning with those whose commentaries we have mentioned above.

Walter Radl

> *1Da es schon viele unternommen haben, eine Darstellung der Ereignisse zu verfassen, die sich unter uns vollzogen haben, 2wie sie uns diejenigen überliefen haben, die von Anfang an Augenzeugen des Wortes gewesen und Diener des Wortes geworden waren, 3habe auch ich mich entschlossen, von vorne an allem genau nachzugehen und es dir, hochverehrter Theophilus, in der rechten Reihenvolge aufzuschreiben, 4damit du die Zuverlässigkeit der Lehre, in der du unterrichtet worden bist, erkennst.*   Radl, 2003

Radl's rendering of the passage shares most of the characteristics of Nolland's translation, and many of the same remarks apply generally to both. Radl does, however, also share the tendency, which we noted in the communicative translations, to 'tighten' the causal relations between clauses – it is clearly *because* many have undertaken to fashion an account (v1) that Luke made his decision (v3). Moreover, the decision is not just to write, but to *investigate* (nachgehen + dative) *and write*. More positively, another feature we might notice is that the Radl version is not quite as stylistically awful as Nolland's: contemporary German is much more at home in periodic form.

Loveday Alexander

Alexander's translation is almost unique amongst those reviewed here, in showing a lively apparent connection between the interpretation of the passage given by her commentary and that given by her translation:

> *Inasmuch as many have undertaken the task of compiling an account of the matters which have come to fruition in our midst, just as the tradition was handed down to us by the original eyewitnesses and ministers of the world,[1] it seemed good to me also, having followed everything carefully and thoroughly, to write it all up for you in an orderly fashion, most excellent Theophilus, so that you may have assured knowledge about the things in which you have been instructed.*
>
> Alexander, 1993

As we will recall, Alexander holds a somewhat dim view of Luke as a stylist: his preface is thought to be a slightly clumsy formula determined by the conventions of 'scientific' literature. Alexander consciously seeks to imitate what she sees as a 'pompous' tone, and although she only remarks on this in terms of vocabulary choices,[2] the use of a modern English period reinforces this effect. We cannot therefore argue with her translation on the grounds of formation of her overall communicative intention. However, some detailed choices hint that this impression arises only as a happy accident. For example, she chooses the word 'eyewitnesses' to render αὐτόπται, because 'it is the neatest and most obvious equivalent . . .' despite the fact that 'it has misleading associations for modern readers. For us, the word has forensic links . . . The Greek word is hardly ever used in this way, and a better translation might be, "those with personal/first-hand experience; those who know the facts at first hand."'[3] A translator who chooses an English rendering because it is 'neater' and 'obvious', even though misleading, is making a decision that merits some reflection. In terms of RTT, we would have

---

1   Printed as 'world' but it is clear from the commentary that this is a typographical error. Alexander, 1993, p.123.
2   Alexander, 1993, p.108.
3   Ibid, p.120.

to conclude that in this case the translator decided that the felicity of the English expression was sufficiently compelling to override the requirement that the translation should interpretively resemble the original – and moreover to override it so strongly that she was content for her translation not just to fall short of complete resemblance to be actively misleading.[1] This would be comprehensible if Alexander had decided that above all Luke was a great stylist, and that therefore the most relevant dimension of resemblance to be sought in her translation was that of stylistic excellence. However, given that her view of his writing style here is that it is *infelicitous,* the choice is surprising.

Jérusalem and CERF

Lest the phenomena we identify be thought to be specific to the English and German traditions, we will glance briefly at a French version and one of its predecessors. Although there are 'communicative' French versions[2] the tradition is more dominated by 'formal' renditions. The characteristics are broadly as for Nolland and Radl. Again, the result is stylistically better than the English, as modern French continues the practice of 'elevated' and (from an English perspective) convoluted construction in certain situations:

> *Puisque beaucoup ont enterpris de composer un récit des événements accomplis parmi nous, d'après ce que nous ont transmis ceux qui furent dès le début témoins oculaires et qui sont devenus serviteurs de la parole, il m'a paru bon, à moi aussi, après m'être soigneusement informé de tout à partir des origins, d'en écrire pour toi un récit ordonné, très honourable Théophile, afin que tu puisses constater la solidité des enseignements que tu as reçus.*
>
> *Alliance Biblique Universelle* – Le CERF (1996)

> *Puisque beaucoup ont enterpris de composer un récit des événements qui se sont accomplis parmi nous, d'après ce que nous ont transmis ceux qui furent dès le début témoins oculaires et serviteurs de la Parole, j'ai decide, moi aussi, après m'être informé exactement de tout depuis les origins d'en écrire pour toi l'exposé suivi, excellent Théophile, pour que tu te rendes bien compte de la sûreté des enesignements que tu as reçus.*
>
> *La Bible de Jérusalem* (1955)

---

1   At this point we should note that, embedded as it is in her full and acutely communicative commentary, there is little chance that any reader would *actually* be misled. Had Alexander decided to publish her own translation of Luke, then she would perhaps have felt compelled to address this issue, with possibly different decisions being made on lexical choices.

2   For example *Les Bonnes Nouvelles,* 1975.

One peculiarity is the increased emphasis in the French versions on the author himself: this arises from the increased use of reflexive verb forms, and the stylistic necessity to repeat the personal pronoun in verse 3.

In this brief summary we have attempted to critique the formation of communicative intention for a number of translators – and we have proceeded by looking at what they have actually done, and then (where possible) compared that with what the same translators state to be their interpretation of the passage in question. We have found a number of anomalies – for example, just as we found that self-declared 'communicative' translators are sometimes affected by the felt need to translate in terms of formal 'equivalence', so we also find that 'formal' translators feel the need to 'communicate.' Through all these cases we can perceive the same uncertainty and confusion about what 'faithfulness' in translation might mean.

Towards a relevant translation?

We saw at the beginning of the present chapter how a translator seeking to work within a Relevance-Theoretical framework might approach his or her work:

- The interpretation of the source text: how does the translator understand the source text achieves its relevance in its original context?
- The production of the target text: how does the translator produce a target text which communicates relevantly in his or her target context?
- The relationship between 1 and 2: how does the translator ensure that the target text interpretively resembles the source text?

Let us suppose, in line with our analysis presented earlier in this chapter, the following as our answer to the first question:

Luke 1:1-4 achieves its relevance in its original context by enabling the reader to identify how the author intends it to be used (as a 'source book' or reference work); by whom it is to be used (God-lovers; those who have already been told something of the story); by whom it has been written (by one who has followed those who learnt at first hand); how it has been written (with great attention to style, order and to the beauty of the story) and; what the intended reader mind-set is (concentration and commitment to reach the end – the material is challenging). These assumptions are contextual implications derived by the reader combining formal features of the piece with assumptions already in her cognitive environment. The reader is assisted by the 'markedness' of the piece in relation to the material which follows: she infers from this that the preface is to be interpreted at this meta-textual level.

As noted in the preliminaries to this chapter, our primary purpose is not to advance a particular interpretation (though the above is defensible on a number of grounds), but to see how interpretation leads to translation. In RTT, a translation *never* arrives naked at the party: a translation is *always* an interpretation according to some criterion of relevance.

If our translation is intended to be 'direct', its interpretation in context must resemble this interpretation. We saw that this is no easy matter in this case: modern English does not possess a periodic form able to bear the weight of the required assumptions, and when someone tries to produce one (as Nolland does) it drifts into the 'obscure' zone. As its translator ruefully observed, 'The *New English Bible* does not compete with the *Authorized Version*, certainly not in language and style: this is not a period of great writers equal to Spenser, Sidney, Hooker, Marlowe and Shakespeare.'[1] We also saw, though, that this is a not uncommon problem in literary or religious translation, and the solution area is to be found in seeking a form in English which can permit the formation of the required implications. One of the *obstacles* to finding such a solution is the cloudy notion of 'equivalence'– we observed above that if Alan Williams had tried to find an 'equivalent' English form for Rumi's verse form in the *Masnavi*, he would have tried in vain – whether he was searching for 'dynamic' equivalence, 'functional' equivalence, or any other kind.

The problem here is one stage worse than that faced by Williams: at least the latter had access to a range of 'tried and tested' English verse forms, and was able to choose one which served. In contemporary English there is no periodic preface form at all, and so we will have to innovate. Amongst the options we might consider is, indeed, poetry. A versification would give the text its 'markedness' and allow readers to form the implications relating to the aesthetics and complexity of Luke's work, but on the other hand would work against the 'factual' source-book implications; it would also set up a misleading accordance with later passages such as the Magnificat and Benedictus, which certainly *should* be interpreted as poetry.

The approach attempted in the Experimental Translation (see *Appendix*) is to use what might loosely be described as 'shape poetry'. The appearance of the text on the page is intended to flag the 'markedness' of the preface, and to allow the English reader to form the implication that what follows will pay close attention to aesthetics and style. It is also intended to be arresting in the sense that it is not too easy to read – the reader must slow down in order to

---

1   Grayston, K, 1979, p.288, cited in Stephen Prickett, 1986.

absorb the semantics of these verses. Additionally, the unusual lay-out and punctuation weaken the logical connections between clauses and facilitates the indeterminacy we noted in the original.

This version makes free with verse order and clause order, in contrast with all the other translations considered; nor is it, of course, a foregone conclusion that this is a step forward in relevance terms. For scholars working on the interpretation of the scriptures, the pattern of chapter and verse established by Robert Estienne in printed form in 1553[1] has provided a reliable reference grid for more than fifteen hundred years: of course it may be regarded as a relevant feature to preserve in translation (in conformity with requirement 2, above). However, it certainly cannot be regarded as contributing to how the text achieved relevance in its original context. The persistence of the chapter and verse system for lay use may be accounted for partly by referential convenience, but it also reflects a certain mistrust of the translators: we know that there has been some funny business in translation, and we want to compare any new version with the 'correct' one (probably the ἱερὸς γάμος).[2] In the present chapters (Three, Four and Five) we are exploring some ways of renewing trust between translators and readers, and if this were successful, one of the predictable benefits might be the relaxation of the 'verse for verse' requirement: if one trusts one's guide, one does not need him to reference every instruction he gives to every previous instruction.

Other formal similarities and dissimilarities may be compared in the following table, which subjects the Experimental Translation of Luke 1.1-4 to the same scrutiny as that applied to the 'communicative' and 'formal' translations we discussed earlier.

One of the interesting observations from this table is that notwithstanding its startlingly different 'feel', this translation shares almost as many formal resemblances with the original as does Nolland's, and almost twice as many as Wright's – yet it does not strike immediately as a 'literal' translation. One reason for this is that it holds a somewhat different set of variables constant: instead of verse order, clause order and the semantics of individual words, it privileges verbal voice, mood and aspect, and stylistic features such as vocabulary register and symmetry. It also makes no attempt at 'gametic literalism' (which we will define in Chapter Six).

---

1   De Hamel, Christopher, 2001, p.240.
2   The chapter and verse system is mighty persistent: all the mainstream versions retain it. *The Message*, and Andy Gaus' *The Unvarnished New Testament*, preserves chapters but not verses. Even the deeply whacky *Good as New: A Radical Retelling of Scriptures* preserves the full apparatus for its canonical sections.

Nor does it strike one as particularly 'free' – why would a 'free' translator not (like Wright) choose an easier form of expression and make himself more accessible to target readers? The traditional 'formal/ free' dichotomy is not a very helpful tool in assessing how it attempts to achieve relevence. It does so by attempting to achieve interpretive resemblance to the original, and this means that it seeks as close as possible a resemblance for all analytic implications and all synthetic implications in the original context. Where there are conflicts, choices are made according to criteria of relevance. One example of such a decision is the use of 'helping words'. Many of the translators we discussed above felt the need to to add a direct object for 'write' in verse 3: Nolland, Wright and the NIV all have 'account', *Die Volxbibel* has 'diese ausführliche Zusammenfassung der wichtigsten Ereignisse', the Jérusalem has 'l'exposé suivi'. Others (Alexander, The Message) have 'it'. This cannot be said to be driven by the needs of the target language, as modern English, French and German permit intransitive use of write/écrire/schreiben, just as Koine Greek does. Alexander provides a coherent explanation for this – whilst γράφω ('I write') can be used intransitively (especially with a dative indirect object), it is 'more natural' to see γράψαι ('to write') as referring anaphorically to the matters discussed in the first two verses.[1] A decision is therefore made to add a helping noun or pronoun to make this reference clear. This is in fact another case of the felt need, shared by many of our translators, to 'tighten' Luke's syntax. It may also be symptomatic of the wish or hope of many of his readers (not Alexander) that Luke wrote history: let us make it absolutely clear, by repeating 'account'.

In the Experimental Translation, the opposite decision is made: 'write' is left without a direct object. The reason for this is that the translator believes that part of the way that Luke achieves relevance for his preface is by its *indeterminacy*. In aiming for interpretive resemblance, therefore, it is important to follow Luke in making 'write' intransitive.

The opposite case occurs in the latter part of the preface, in line 10 of the translation, where the Experimental Translation has added a helping auxiliary verb, 'be able', working with the subjunctive 'you would . . . feel'. This clearly does not correspond to Luke's text, where the subjunctive ἐπιγνῷς ('you should recognise') appears alone. The reason the translator has added the auxiliary in his English version is aesthetic – because he regards the appearance of the text on the page as making a significant contribution to its relevance, it is important that the 10th line is a little longer than the 9th and a little shorter than the 11th. In this case, the use of 'be able' does not significantly affect

1   Alexander, 1993, p.132.

the semantics or the implications of the text: 'so that you might be able to feel' does not have very different implications from 'so that you might feel', and there is no detrimental effect on how the text achieves relevance. The decision is therefore to include the auxiliary.[1]

The same aesthetic considerations partly drive the re-ordering of words, clauses and verses.[2] A more serious objection might be raised in relation to this: as a sentence is a diachronic phenomenon, beginning at a certain point and proceeding through time to its conclusion, might not the order in which ideas are presented make a significant contribution to relevance? The answer is that sometimes this is so, and sometimes not so. In this particular case we have a long period-form sentence in which the clauses work together to create a certain overall effect: in the original there is no clear temporal or logical line. The order of presentation in fact bears little relation to a real-time ordering of events. Nor, (in my interpretation) as we have seen, is Luke here attempting to make a watertight case for his 'right to write' – had this been his intention, then the logical order of his argument *would* have been relevant, and a translation aiming for interpretive resemblance would have *prima facie* had to preserve it. In any event, our translation might be defended as representing *spatially* a structure which in the original was represented *temporally*.[3]

1　Once again flouting the precept that 'brief is best' in achieving relevance. The topic of brevity is an interesting one in translation studies. Eco puts it most forcefully, stating quite simply that, in the case of a translator who came to a publisher with a target work twice as long as the source text, 'I believe one would be entitled to fire the translator before opening his or her product.' (Eco, 2003, p.3). He makes no argument for this, though, appealing instead to 'common sense' and 'commercial reality'. Fascinatingly, he goes on in Mouse or Rat? to cite a number of exceptions to this rule, and one is left wondering whether there is any valid argument here at all. Certainly, in translating into English a Greek heptasyllabic participle, which conveys information about an action, a time reference, an aspect from which the writer is considering the action, the gender and number of the agent performing the action, and what relation that agent bears to the action, I see no reason at all to suppose that it can be done in one English word. Accepting that there are 'commercial realities' – especially in the matter of simultaneous interpretation, where one must communicate within a certain time-slot, I cannot see a principled reason why a translation should be even approximately the same length as its source – and in the Experimental Translation this is not regarded as a criterion which contributes to relevance.

2　There are other reasons, too, which will become apparent when we have considered the material in the following chapter.

3　And this, of course, is a common move in structuralism. See Derrida's critique of Foucault in *L'écriture et la différance*. Graham Ward speaks of 'the illusion of depth, the drive for immediate, theatrical impact so that the spatial order dominates the temporal' (Ward, 1997, xvi) The translation presented

Regards as important:		Does not regard as important:	
Formal feature	*Comment*	**Formal Feature**	*Comment*
1. Preservation of verbal voice	*Active for active, passive for passive*	10. Preservation of verse order	*Verse order rearranged*
2. Preservation of verbal tense/aspect	*Tense aspect treated accordantly*	11. Preservation of word order within clauses	*Word order within clauses often changed*
3. Preservation of verbal mood	*Complete resemblance (indicative for indicative, subjunctive for subjunctive)*	12. Preservation of clause order	*Only exception is the positioning of the main verb and the address to Theophilius*
4. Vocabulary register	*'middle brow' vocabulary register preserved*	13. Preservation of parts of speech	*Often varied*
5. Overall stylistic marking	*Marked as 'shape poem'*	14. Preservation of analytic implications of individual words	*Word for word correspondence in only a few cases*
6. Symmetry of form	*Symmetry preserved through shape form*	15. Punctuation	*Periodic form abandoned. Substitutes two sentences for one*
7. Rhythm	*Matching of perfects and line lengths*		
8. Other aural qualities 'sonorous' sound quality and alliteration	*Shape form slows reading speed and lends sonorous sound quality*		
9. Logical connectives between clauses	*Logical connections are altered*		

Interpretive Resemblance in Experimental Translation of Luke 1.1-4

One possible reaction to the translation as we have presented it is that it is somehow cheating: scriptural translations should be rendered either in conventional paragraphs or (for 'poetical passages') in verse form. This, however, would be hard to justify on any grounds other than conventional,[1] nor do any of the translations we have considered bear close resemblance in terms of physical appearance to the source text as it appears on the page. In order to communicate relevantly to modern readers, *all* translators deviate from the ancient practice of pagination and punctuation, which if reproduced would present significant obstacles.

'Aural quality' may be the source of a further objection: by 'spatializing' the text, are we jeopardizing its readability, especially its readability out loud? In fact, the above translation does retain some of its 'shape' when read aloud. The CEV proclaims itself 'an audio transmission in print form, crafted to be read aloud without stumbling, heard without misunderstanding, and listened to with appreciation,'[2] and we might reasonably expect it therefore to provide a model in this respect. The CEV rendering of Luke's preface (given above) does not, however, strike one as so. The repetition of 'what' (three times in the first two verses), and the construction 'They wrote what we had been told by the ones who were there . . .' may be cited in evidence.

The most serious problem which the 'shape poem' form presents is in fact to do with the seriousness of Luke's project: in our interpretation, he presents his work as a sort of source or reference book. Shape poems, on the other hand, are associated in modern languages with the charming whimsicality of a Lewis Carroll, a Morgenstern, an E.E. Cummings or a Jacques Prevert.[3] There is clearly a risk that the use of a shape poem leads to quite unintended contextual implications. This is undeniable (there is no communication which does not carry the risk of miscommunication:

---

above may be guilty as charged, but is not at any rate motivated by a desire for 'theatrical impact' but by the struggle to produce a translation interpretive of the communicative intention of the original.

1   Allowedly the conventional does have its own relevance: a convention is a pre-packaged form which allows the reader to quickly establish how something is intended to be read, thus reducing processing cost and contributing thereby to relevance. The point here is that there is no rooting of this particular convention in any practice associated with the source texts, which do not generally include any punctuation at all.

2   CEV, 2000, ix.

3   Respectively, *The Tale*, *Fisches Nachtgesang*, *Buffalo Bill*, and *Chanson du Vitrier*.

the Experimental Translation is at risk like any other). The translator in this case attempts to manage the risk in two ways. First, he uses a shape which is not fanciful and which is relevant to the thrust of Luke's gospel. The use of a cruciform is also evocative of the chiastic structure, which some interpreters see both in the preface itself and in his work as a whole. Had the preface been presented in other shapes – for example, in the form of an arch or gateway, to remind us of Wright's 'grand entrance' – the risk would have been higher. Secondly, he maintains tight control over lexical choices: the vocabulary is kept 'business-like', and whilst there is a hint of the heaviness which Alexander identified ('accomplished', 'weighed', 'substance'), there is a careful avoidance of any vocabulary which might lead to a whimsical interpretation (for example 'story' is avoided as an interpretation, either for διήγησις or λόγος).

There are, of course, many other objections which could be raised against the Experimental Translation we have considered here. Attentive readers will note a number of other apparent anomalies (the repetitions in the first and last lines; the explication of Theophilus' name, and so on), features whose rationale will become clearer in the following chapters. This translation is presented as a case study for the lively connection which should exist between the interpretation of a source text and its translation: it makes a case for the careful formation of the translator's communicative intention in this regard. There is, naturally, a lot more to producing a translation than the formation of communicative intention, and much of the content of the text we have been considering derives from these other considerations, to which we will, in the following two chapters, turn.

Chapter Four

When is a priest not a priest?
The semantics of ἱερεύς in Luke 1

In Chapter Three we considered the Preface to Luke's gospel, and found that it was a certain combination of syntactical features, rather than the semantics of the piece, which gave it its relevance. This, of course, is not the universal or perhaps even the normal state of affairs: on the contrary, the semantic properties of a text are normally very important in how it achieves relevance. Although part of the agenda of the present work is to challenge the assumption that semantics are always and everywhere the 'trump card' in interpreting a text, it has to be acknowledged that they are often of first importance. Traditionally, semantics are usually thought of as describing 'what is said' by a text as opposed to 'how it is said'; moreover this 'what' is usually regarded as self-evidently more important than the 'how'.[1] This will be much more apparent in, for example, a narrative section of our text than in what is usually acknowledged to be a preface whose styling is atypical for the work as a whole. In the present chapter we move on to the first section of narrative in Luke's gospel, in which we meet a number of characters connected with John the Baptist. The topic of the present chapter is communicative clues arising from semantics: in particular, we will be looking at the role of ἱερεύς τις ('a certain priest'), whom we meet in Luke 1.5. We will deploy the key idea of conceptual address as developed within Relevance Theory and as described in Chapter Two. Using this model, we will examine the traditional translation of ἱερεύς (pronounced 'hiereus', normally translated as 'priest') in English. We will attempt both to account for this translation within the model and to put it into question. In doing so we will touch on topics of great importance for biblical translation, topics frequently dealt with in the literature under the headings of 'context problems' or 'cultural translation',

---

1   'In transferring the message from one language to another, it is the content which must be preserved at any cost; the form, except in special cases, such as poetry, is largely secondary . . .' Nida and Taber, 1969, p.105.

'explication' and 'implication'.[1] Another way of approaching the issues is in terms of 'domestication' or 'foreignization' strategy: at least from Schleiermacher, and most particularly with Venuti, translation theorists have been wrestling with the issue of to what extent the author should be moved toward the reader, and to what extent the reader toward the author.[2] By using a completely different theoretical model, I hope to shed new light on old issues.

The case of a certain priest: ἱερεύς τις

To some readers this chapter's agenda will seem a foolish undertaking, because, naturally, there is no question as to how ἱερεύς 'should' be translated: it means 'priest', as everybody knows. The traditional English translation embodied in the Holy Marriage reaches back through Tyndale and Wycliffe (*prest*) to the Old German *Priester*, and Old French (*prēster*). Behind these is Ecclesiastical Latin *presbyter*.[3] Although (as we will see later) we will meet one or two dissenting voices, nearly every English translation produced for the last 400 years has used the word 'priest' in Luke 1.5. The programme of the present chapter involves asking *why* we feel so comfortable that 'priest' is the correct translation of ἱερεύς, and then moving on to consider some alternatives. To do so, we will deploy the idea of conceptual address, which we introduced in Chapter Two. Although our approach will be essentially synchronic, holding the traditional translation up to the light will also involve a certain amount of history.

---

1   The tradition exemplified by Nida embraces a fundamental contradiction. 'Cultural translation' is frowned upon: '. . . one is not free to make in the text any and all kinds of explanatory additions and/or expansions. . . one may make explicit in the text only what is linguistically implicit . . . one may not simply add interesting cultural information which is not actually present in the meanings of the terms used in the passage.'(Nida and Taber, 1969, p.111). This seems clear, until we learn that exceptions to this rule may be made for 'idioms', for 'figurative meanings' and for a number of other cases, including even the 'provision of contextual conditioning' such as 'classifiers, e.g. "animals called camels".' (p110). In some biblical passages the exceptions are far more numerous than the norm.

2   'Either the translator leaves the author in peace, as much as possible, and moves the reader towards him; or he leaves the reader in peace, as much as possible, and moves the author towards him.' Schleiermacher, On the different methods of translating', tr. Lefevre in *Translating Literature: The German Tradition from Luther to Rosenzweig*, p.74f.

3   As we will see, the history of transmission is nothing like as simple as this statement implies; but for the moment we should note simply that English and its predecessor languages have generally translated using this word for at least 400 years.

Achieving relevance in context

How might we approach the ἱερεύς (hiereus) we meet in Luke 1.5 using this apparatus? As we did in Chapter Three, let us begin by attempting to reconstruct how Luke 1.5 communicates relevantly in its original context; how, that is, its use allows the reader to form worthwhile contextual implications for a not-unreasonable processing cost. This is, as before, an exercise in historical imagination, informed by our understanding of the source language and culture, and by our understanding of the mental processes involved. Again it is to be emphasised that the following is not intended to be an exhaustive analysis, but to give an outline of an interpretation which could stand up to such an analysis, had we the space to pursue it.

Lexical Entry

A reader (or hearer) approaches the text, and in the course of processing the sentence in which it occurs, reads (hears) the word 'hiereus'. This activates the automatic decoding process in her brain, which accesses the lexical entry of a concept associated with that word. The concept associated with ἱερεύς has a lexical entry showing that this word is (for example) pronounced with a rough breathing, two vowels and a diphthong. It also indicates that the word is formed from two lexemes: ἱερ–, which is used in cognate adjectives, nouns and verbs dealing with sacrificial rites; and –εύς, which is used in masculine agent nouns.

Logical Entry

Having accessed the concept associated with this lexical entry, the logical entry now comes into play, by specifying what deductive rules are associated with that concept. Let us suppose (our analysis below will validate a supposition which is for the moment merely stated) that we decide that the logical entry in this case contains rules or 'meaning postulates' which specify 'male human expert in selection of victims for, and procedures of, sacrifice'. These, then, are thought of as the deductive rules the absence of which would indicate that the concept of a ἱερεύς had not really been grasped. The deductive processes of the brain use these rules to form a 'semantic representation' of the concept. A semantic representation is a set of blueprints, or hypotheses for the interpretation which will shortly emerge. It is difficult to 'catch' the semantic representation, as it is immediately taken up by the inferential part of the process, which uses the encyclopaedic entry to arrive at a propositional form. The semantic representation is like a springboard: the mind touches it for the briefest of moments, using it as a launch into encyclopaedic memory. Crucially, the logical entry's deductive rules 'apply automatically: the mere presence of a concept in semantic representation is sufficient for the hearer to apply all of its meaning postulates, regardless of context.'[1]

In Luke 1.5, then, the reader/hearer uses the deductive rules found in the concept's logical entry to generate a 'semantic representation', which is of some sort of official engaged in sacrifice, but without specifying what kind.

Encyclopaedic Entry

The reader's mind then turns to the encyclopaedic entry. Our working assumption that Luke's first audience was a mixed Greek and Jewish urban community in the Eastern Mediterranean specifies what is likely to be present in the reader or hearer's 'encyclopaedia'. There are a large number of entries for ἱερεύς, which in the world of the first century Mediterranean is a pan-religious term with multiple possible references. One set of references will certainly embrace the cultic figure presiding over traditional Greek religious practices: a figure such as we encounter in Acts 14.13. A ἱερεύς ('hiereus') was a specialist whose role was to preside over τα ἱερά – ('ta hiera') the rites of offering or dedication associated with sacrifice.[2] His precise function varied, but was not generally the actual butchering of the animal (which in public sacrifice was usually the role of a μάγειρος, or 'butcher') but the correct performance of the rites over the victim, and vetting of victims to ensure acceptability to the god or goddess involved - to ensure, that is, that the ἱερεῖον is ἱερόν (that the holy offering is holy). Usually associated with a particular ἱερόν, in the sense of a place of sacrifice, his role was to know the rites and sacred laws associated with the relevant cult, and to ensure that they were followed correctly. This often included the upkeep and maintenance of the ἱερόν, and to pay for this and to sustain him, the ἱερεύς had the right to receive a certain portion of the sacrifice. The role therefore had a political and economic dimension, and was a public appointment. In Plato's ideal republic, ἱερεῖς could only serve for one year at a time and their spiritual and temporal power was hedged about by ἐχηγήται ('exegetes' or 'interpreters') and treasurers to manage the associated revenues.[3] The particular nature of ἱερατεία ('priesthood') seems to be very closely associated with the

---

1   Gutt, 2000, p.141.
2   The description of Greek religious practice I use here is derived from Zaidman and Pantel, tr. Cartledge, 1992, pp.27-62. My description of Hebrew priesthood is drawn from a variety of sources including Jacob Milgrom, 1991, and R.S. Hendel, 1995.
3   Plato, *Laws*, 759-760.

specification and selection of the victim of the sacrifice (the ἱερεῖον) and with the offering or slaughtering (described by the verb ἱερεύω), whereas the actual enjoyment of the victim by the god in question was associated more with the verb θύω ('I sacrifice'). The agent noun ἱερεύς clearly has an etymological connection to the adjective ἱερός, which in Homer most commonly seems to denote the excellent, the outstanding or wonderful, a descriptor which by extension describes the nature of a victim which will be acceptable to a powerful god.

A second set of encyclopaedic references will embrace the βάρβαρος priest-king, a figure which some anthropological work suggests is not only involved in sacrifice, but himself may be in some traditions *the victim* of sacrifice.[1] A third set of references will provide metaphorical uses of the word, such as that suggested by Aeschylus' reference to a 'priest of pestilence' (ἱερεύς τις ἄτης)[2], and Aristophanes' comic reference to λεπτοτάτων λήρων ἱερεύς ('the priest of vacuous nonsense').[3]

Next, and most obviously for the present passage the reader's encyclopaedic memory will include references for the distinctive Hebrew priestly figure. ἱερεύς is the LXX translation for כהן (cohen), whose function and status is specified in the classical Hebrew texts, and developed in the priestly tradition through to the Second Temple period. Deuteronomy 33.10 offers one summary: 'They teach your customs to Jacob, your Law to Israel. They send incense rising to your nostrils, place the holocaust on your altar.'[4] This part of the encyclopaedia also recognises that stream of the tradition which places the authority of the כהן in question: a succession of prophets (Isaiah, Jeremiah, Amos, Hosea, Micah) declare that Yahweh is disgusted by their sacrificial rites,[5] that he only wishes for justice, for mercy. In this tradition, the moral precepts of Torah seem to be placed in opposition to its ritual requirements (ἔλεος θέλω καὶ οὐ0 θυσίαν – 'I desire mercy, not sacrifice' says Hosea LXX 6.6): it is not a question of the rites only being acceptable to Yahweh if they are authentic or sincere, but an 'either/or' issue.[6]

This part of the encyclopaedic entry may, further, include the idea of the self-sacrificing priest who enters the Holy of Holies on the Day of Atonement, and who we might identify with Jesus.[7]

---

1   See particularly Girard, 1986.
2   *Agamemnon*, 735.
3   *Clouds*, 359.
4   Tr. Jerusalem Bible, 1966.
5   See for example Isaiah 1.10-17; Jeremiah 6.20, 7:25-26; Amos 5.21-24; Hosea 6.6; Micah 6.6-8, etc.
6   See Hendel, 1995.
7   Baker, Margaret, 2003.

Finally, of course, the encyclopaedia of individual readers may include some ἱερεῖς actually known to the reader; it may include a vivid memory of a particular occasion when the reader witnessed a ἱερεύς going about his bloody sacrificial business, and so on.

These entries are all candidates for the final interpretation of ἱερεύς. What the reader's mind does, though, is to look at the context, and in accordance with the principle of relevance, infers the interpretation which yields the best possible contextual implications for the least possible processing cost. In Luke 1.5, beginning as it does with a classic 'Septuagintalism',[1] with the reference to Herod, who is described as βασιλέως τῆς Ἰουδαίας ('king of the Jews'), and with a transliterated Hebrew name, the interpretation which meets this criterion is to 'flesh out' the ἱερεύς as a *Jewish* priest, working in the Temple in Jerusalem a generation or two before its destruction. The process of communication has worked perfectly here, and almost paradigmatically from a relevance perspective: Luke has chosen a pan-religious term (ἱερεύς) whose semantic representation makes available to the reader a wide-ranging encyclopaedic entry; he has also provided the suggested context for processing this term. The end result is that he has accurately communicated his idea and put the reader to minimal processing cost.

It should be noted that a skilful communicator uses both semantic representations and encyclopaedic clues to guide his audience to the relevant interpretation. One advantage of using semantic representations is that they trigger the deductive, reasoning part of the brain – they raise the audience to a certain level of attention. If sufficient context has been given, such that processing can proceed efficiently, and quickly reach a relevant interpretation, this is also completely satisfactory for a reader or hearer. This is in contrast to the encyclopaedic part of the process, which requires the audience only to recover something from memory. We will examine this distinction more closely in Chapter Five when we consider clues arising from 'formulaic expressions', which are thought of as being stored as a chunk in encyclopaedic memory.

What Luke has done here is to open a rich seam of contextual implications. Luke 1.5a has comparable force to the following English sentence:

> *In the days when Reagan was still the Leader of the Free World, there was a certain trader working in the Twin Towers, whose name was Zack.*

In just a few words, a very exact time and geographical location is

---

1   We will examine this concept closely in Chapter 5.

specified, together with the rhetoric of the period ('the Leader of the Free World'/ βασιλεύς τῆς ᾽Ιουδαίας) and the pathos of our knowing that this is a world which was violently destroyed and is gone forever. Similarly in Luke, whatever the reader's relationship with τo ἱερόν, he or she certainly knows that it has been destroyed by the Romans in 70 CE, that the world and way of life associated with it has gone: that there are no more ἱερεῖς working there any more; that there will be no more ἱερά to the Lord in Jerusalem. The opening of his narrative is therefore pregnant with pathos and meaning.

We are also very quickly made aware in this passage of the great *significance* of Zacharias' status as ἱερεύς. This is achieved by the three uses of the root in quick succession in verses 5 to 9: here we have a priest, going about his priesting, according to the customs of the priesthood. (We will recall from Chapter Two that a relevant communicator will not put the reader to the trouble of reading such repetitions except in order to drive him up the relevance curve to look for contextual implications.) The significance of Zacharias as ἱερεύς is that here we have – perhaps for the first time since Ezekiel – a ἱερεύς who is also προφήτης: in verse 67 he opens his mouth and prophecies, bringing together the prophetic and priestly tradition; moreover, here we have a priest who fathers the last and greatest of the Hebrew prophets. It is vital for the relevance of this idea that ἱερεύς is a backward-looking concept: the ἱερεῖς are the mediators of the old covenant. It is the prophetic activity, and the fathering of John the Baptist which looks forward to the new covenant. It is also of vital interest that Zacharias is a *virtuous* ἱερεύς, and again the idea is emphasised: Zacharias and his wife walk in *all* the commandments and judgements of the Lord – they are absolutely blameless. It is tempting almost to regard this as concessive: yes he was a priest, but he was also virtuous: the opposition between priestly sacrificial ritual and the moral precepts of the law which Hosea saw is overturned at last.

ἱερεύς in translation

How can this perspective help in the task of translation? The traditional translation of ἱερεύς as 'priest' or 'prêtre' or 'Priester' can be thought of as seeking resemblance in terms of semantic representation. Like ἱερεύς, the English word 'priest' specifies a religious official with powers and functions of a certain kind. This 'blueprint' *is* contained in the *logical entry* for the concept associated with this English word, and therefore it is, it can be argued, in terms of semantic representation, a suitable translation of ἱερεύς. At the same time, of course, and in significant contrast, the *encyclopaedic* entry for the English concept is likely to be quite different from that of the Greek. Sadly for relevance theorists, dictionaries do not neatly divide their entries into 'logical' and 'encyclopaedic' sections.[1] The Oxford English Dictionary offers the following primary definition for 'priest':

1.   One whose office is to perform public religious functions: an official minister of religious worship.

2.   In hierarchical Christian churches: a clergyman of the second of the holy orders (above a deacon and below a bishop), having authority to administer the sacraments and pronounce absolution.

3.   In more general sense: A clergyman, a member of the clerical profession, a minister of religion.

4.   A sacrificing priest, a minister of the altar.

5.   An official minister of a pagan or non-Christian religion; originally implying sacrificial functions, but in later use often applied to the functionaries of any religious system, whether sacrificial or not.

This is an essentially 'encyclopaedic' entry; the 'logical' entry is an abstraction of it, and its precise delineation will always be contentious. Taken together, this OED entry does show how the word 'priest' communicates in English. Provided the context gives the reader sufficient clues as to which encyclopaedic reference might be the relevant one, the word 'priest' works well, giving the right clues from its semantic representation for the rest of the clause to work upon. Indeed the English sentence provided in the NRSV works in exactly the same way as the source Greek:

> *In the days of King Herod of Judea, there was a priest. . . .*
>
> Luke 1.5a, NRSV

If we were called upon to defend this translation within the Relevance-Theoretical framework, we would say that 'in the days of King Herod of Judea' gives ample contextual clues that the text refers to an ancient Jewish setting and therefore to an ancient Jewish priest, with all that that entails: communication has occurred.

Challenging the consensus

Should we feel any uneasiness with this account? As a matter of fact, I appreciate that most readers will not feel any unease – but this, I will argue, is the result of custom and familiarity rather than anything else. Suppose we encountered the following passage in a novel:

---

1   Perhaps it is not sad that there is no attempt to do so. The arguments would be endless.

Darkness closed in as the priest moved towards his victim, hands tightly gripping the glimmering knife. Better make it a good cut, make it clean. A candle sputtered as he raised his arm for the final blow. His victim jerked suddenly, pulling against the ropes. . . .[1]

When you read this, how did your imagination construct the scene? Was it a wicked priest about to commit a murder? Or was it a virtuous priest going about his normal everyday business of sacrifice? A reader who is familiar with the world of ancient religion, and particularly one whose cognitive environment has been conditioned by reading the present chapter up to this point, is likely to correctly infer that this is a virtuous priest going about his normal business; however a general reader usually infers a murderer.[2] Such a reader's concept of *priest* is so constructed that she is very unlikely to form an accurate idea of the figure we encounter in Luke 1.5a. We can be confident about this conclusion because of course in order to construct the image of the priest as a murderer she had to overcome any stereotypical assumptions she held about normal priestly behaviour. Had she really had any notion of a priest as one involved in sacrifice, she would have got to this before she got to the murder implication.

This exercise illustrates how encyclopaedic memory works in conjunction with semantic representations. The semantic representation gives a clue, which is used as a springboard to an encyclopaedic entry. The context provided gives the pointer as to what area of the encyclopaedia we should look. However, encyclopaedic memory is organised according to principles of 'availability.' Those items to which reference is frequently made are kept near the surface – just as a shopkeeper will keep fast-moving stock items close to hand. Slower-moving items are kept at the back of the shop. The issue with *priest* is not that the English concept does not embrace the idea of sacrifice – it does, as a glance at a dictionary or encyclopaedia will show; the issue is, rather, that *sacrifice* is kept at the back of the shop, and *as relevance is an optimising process* which seeks to reach the 'best set of implications for the least processing cost', it will rarely be recovered.

In translation terms, then, the question is: granted that *priest* is a semantically correct translation for ἱερεύς, is it a sufficiently bouncy

---

1   This passage was made up for the purpose of illustration.
2   I have tried this experiment on countless unfortunate friends and relatives. The reader is recommended to try it, preferably with individuals whose forbearance is not a result of being students of ancient religion or biblical translation.

springboard for a modern reader to leap over all the more available notions of *priest* to get to the idea of the kind of priestly figure we encounter in Luke 1.5? The NRSV translation gives the English reader exactly the same combination of a semantic representation (priest) and a suggested processing context (Herodian Judea) as did the first century version, and hopes the English reader will form the same relevant interpretation. My suggestion is that this is unlikely to succeed, because although the English reader actually does possess the relevant context, it is buried too deep and hence is very unlikely to be recovered in an optimising process. There are some very vivid and easily available encyclopaedic entries which she will reach first, and which apparently fit the bill and allow an interpretation to be formed. Reading the NRSV sentence, then, will give rise to the interpretation of the ἱερεύς we meet in Luke 1.5 as a kindly old gentleman such as our own parish priest is: there will be no smell of blood or burning flesh about him, and no association with the old covenant.

It is worth pausing here to note one or two general points. The first relates to what seems to me to be a defect in the literature of translation theory, which very frequently talks of context (or 'readers' cognitive environment' or 'frame of reference') in binary terms, as being either 'present' or 'absent'.[1] This goes against the grain of Sperber and Wilson's notion of 'manifestness' in a given context: items may be present in a cognitive environment but more or less *manifest*.[2] They may be more or less *available*, in a non-technical sense. This means that special effort may be required in some translation situations to get the reader to supply the necessary processing context. Note that this is not a question of supplying context which is absent – for example by explication. We are not saying that ἱερεύς 'implies' ritual slaughterer – at least not in the sense that Luke intended to introduce an 'implication' in his description of Zacharias but without making it explicit. An ἱερεύς in the context

---

1   See for example even Gutt, 2000, p.81. The question of whether present-day readers can appreciate the relevance of Matthew 1 (the genealogy) is discussed entirely in terms of whether they 'have' or 'don't have' the necessary background assumptions already present in their cognitive environment. My point is that very often readers do have the necessary assumptions, but they are relatively inaccessible. A moment's refelction shows that it would be nonsense to say, for example, that modern readers have no understanding of the importance of who fathered whom – it is the stuff of TV soap opera the world over. As we saw in Chapter Two, Hill (2006) has a much more nuanced account of contextual issues, but still ultimately tries to divide readers into 'haves' and 'have nots'.

2   Sperber and Wilson, 1986, pp.38-46.

described by Luke is, rather, quite *explicitly* someone whose job is the conduct of animal and other forms of sacrifice. If our translation does not allow the reader to see this, we have on this measure failed to satisfy the requirement of interpretive resemblance.

The second general point here is the admittedly paradoxical and problematic conclusion that scholars immersed in the source culture do not necessarily make very good translators. A professional biblical translator is very unlikely to see that 'priest' is not a good translation for ἱερεύς, because he of course *knows* (it is very manifest in his cognitive environment) that 'priest' incorporates the idea of sacrifice which is central to the Greek word. It is Steiner once again who provides the most richly suggestive treatment of this problem: translators must achieve a balance between 'elective affinity' and 'resistant difference' – that is, they must know the source culture so well that they feel at home in that language's expressive powers; yet they must be sufficiently alien to that culture to also feel its strangeness, to appreciate what is mysterious about it, what the target language readers will find difficult or be apt to misunderstand.[1]

The third general point I would like to note before considering some alternative translations is that it is this practice of unthinkingly translating originals with the canonically prescribed Holy Marriage 'equivalent' which is the principal cause of what can only be described as the boredom-inducing quality of most biblical versions. In Luke 1.5, do we encounter someone who is fascinatingly different from us, and yet somehow also understandable (through his sharing in childlessness, one of the forms which human misery takes)? Or do we encounter just a priest who is childless?

The persistence of the ἱερὸς γάμος tradition

The persistence of 'priest' as the translation for ἱερεύς is remarkable, showing resilience through many re-translations and and 'radical' re-tellings of scripture. *The Message*, for example, has:

> *During the rule of Herod, King of Judea, there was a priest assigned service in the regiment of Abijah.*   The Message, Luke 1.5a

It is notable that Peterson seeks to freshen his translation with the decidedly odd 'regiment' for ἐφημερία ('of the day'), and with the military idea of being 'assigned' in a situation which he knows very well is hereditary, and yet retains 'priest' for ἱερεύς. We notice the same pattern in other 'innovative' translations:

---

1   Steiner, 1998/1975, p.399.

*There was, in the days of Herod king of the Jews, a priest named
Zachariah, from the line of Abijah.*
                        The Unvarnished New Testament, Luke 1.5a

*Und zwar war das so: In der Zeit, wo Herodes noch in Judäa das
Sagen hatte, lebte ein jüdischer Priester in der Gegend, der Zacharias
hieß. Zacharias gehörte zu der Gruppe der Abija-Priester . . .*
                        Die Volxbibel 2.0, Luke 1.5a

Dreyer's *Volxbibel* innovates for the Septuaginatalism Ἐγένετο ('it
came to pass'), for the idea of kingship, and for the day-rota, but
preserves *Priester* intact, as required by the tradition.

*Au moment où Hérode le Grand est roi de Judée, il y a un prêtre appelé
Zakarie. Il fait partie de la famille d'Abia, une famille de prêtres. Sa
femme appartient au clan d'Aaron et elle s'appelle Élisabeth.*
                        La Bible Parole de Vie, Luke 1.5a

Parole de Vie expands the Herod reference and innovates with 'famille'
and 'clan' for ἐφημερία, whilst preserving *prêtre*. We could multiply
examples, but the point is sufficiently made: although (as we will see) there
are exceptions, the rule amongst translators is to accept the translation
as priest/Priester/prêtre. At a certain – not very helpful – level, we could
explain this with the obvious rhetorical statement that this is so simply
because this is the 'correct' translation! An argument could perhaps be
made that we see innovation in (for example) translating ἐφημερία, but not
in ἱερεύς, because the former is a concept unknown to our world whereas
the latter has a reference which is clear to us.[1] In fact, though, as we saw in
our analysis above, this is hard to reconcile with our recognition of the very
different 'encyclopaedic entries' associated with ἱερεύς and 'priest.' We do,
however, with this point begin to get closer to the true reason.

Let us look at the history of this translation practice. ἱερεύς
originates in the biblical tradition as the LXX translation for כהן
(cohen) Jerome translated ἱερεύς – and כהן – as *sacerdos*, a Latin
word with a logical entry and encyclopaedic range very similar to the
Greek. A *sacerdos* worked in or with *sacra* and dealt with issues to do
with the *sacer*, just as a ἱερεύς worked in a ἱερόν and dealt with the
ἱερός – hiereus; hieron; hieros). Like ἱερεύς, it was a pan-religious
term. It also nearly made it into modern English, as can be seen from
the Anglo-Saxon version of the gospels:

1   To me, it seems rather to be the other way around. The idea of a day-rota
or weekly shift is a common, everyday notion in the contemporary working
world; whereas the concept of an intermediary with the gods who makes
sacrifices and manages purity distinctions is quite alien.

On Herodes dagum, Iudéa cyninges, waes sum sacerd on naman
Zacharias, of Abian tune: his wíf waes of Aárones dohtrum, and hyre
nama waes Elizabeth.

Anglo-Saxon, c.995 CE, Ed. Thorpe

However, by the time the Wycliffite Bible appeared in the early 1380s, the *sacerd* had been replaced by a *prist*. Tyndale follows Wycliffe, and the KJV (as in so many other ways) followed Tyndale. This translation history is curiously intertwined with that of πρεσβύτερος ('presbyter'), and therein lies the clue for what happened, as may be summarized as follows:

	'The Great Tradition' in English			'The Douay Rheims Tradition'
800 BCE?	Hebrew	NhK	Nkz	-
300 BCE?	LXX	ἱερεύς	πρεσβύτερος	-
1st Century	Luke-Acts	ἱερεύς	πρεσβύτερος	-
5th Century	Vulgate	Sacerdos	senior/presbyteros	-
10th Century	Anglo-Saxon	Sacerd	ealder/préost	-
14th Century	Wycliffe	Prist	elder/Prist	-
16th Century	Tyndale	Priest	Senior	priest/ancient
17th Century	KJV	Priest	Elder	priest/ancient
19th Century	RSV	Priest	Elder	priest/ancient
20th Century	NRSV	Priest	Elder	priest/ancient

Translation history of Cohen and Zaqen

πρεσβύτερος is etymologically the source (via Latin and old German) for the English word 'priest'. It is the LXX translation for זקן (zaqen), and a word which appears in the New Testament with reference first to Jewish elders (in contradistinction to ἱερεῖς – see for example Luke 7.3), but crucially also to early leaders of the Christian church (for example Titus 1.5). From the start of the Christian translation tradition, the practice began of creating *three* categories to represent the *two* Greek words. In Jerome's Vulgate Bible, *sacerdotes* are Hebrew or heathen priests; *seniores* are Hebrew elders; and *presbyters* are early church leaders. This pattern was repeated in Old English, in the form of *sacerd*, *ealder*, and *préost*. By the time of the Wycliffite translation, the agent noun *sacerd* had fallen into disuse (perhaps because it was long since that a non-Christian *sacerd* had been encountered in England, and the word became otiose),[1] and in Luke 1.5 as elsewhere was replaced by *prist*.

So far, so uncontroversial. However, by the time Tyndale produced his first version of the New Testament in 1526, this translation had become a burning issue. The translation of πρεσβύτερος ('presbyter') with 'priest' seemed to suggest that the 'hereticall Sacrificing Priesthoode' of Rome had a firm foundation in the New Testament.[2] He therefore, and following the protestant Geneva translators, found it necessary to abandon the etymological link, and to revive the Latin *seniour* to refer to Jewish or Christian elders (eg Luke 7.3). 'Priest' now had a range including: Hebrew Priests of the Old Covenant (such as Zacharias); heathen priests (such as the priest of Zeus we meet in Acts 14); Christ as the great High Priest (particularly in Hebrews); and the priesthood of all believers (for example Revelation 1.6). In fact, Tyndale's use of 'priest' embraced every possible use *except* that specified by the etymologically related word πρεσβύτερος/presbyter! Meanwhile, the Roman-Catholic scholars in Rheims produced in 1582 a version which reinstated 'Priest' in crucial ecclesiological texts such as Titus 1.5, and used 'ancients' elsewhere.

The use or non-use of the word 'priest' was thus both a good example of how etymological roots are not necessarily good guides to use at any particular point in time, and of how word-use is political – in this case, part of the bitter controversy of the Reformation. Not for the first time, nor the last, the question of how a word was to be translated was an issue not of semantics or historical fact but one of contemporary theology and politics. The key issue was that of sacrifice. Tyndale knew (as did all his protestant contemporaries) that a central plank of the Roman heresy was the doctrine of the sacrificial mass: the idea that in the eucharist the priest repeats the sacrifice of Christ. In Tyndale's hands, the use of the word 'priest' in his translation of Luke 1.5 is part of this polemic: Zacharias, the sacrificing Hebrew priest is being identified with Tyndale's heretical, Romish contemporaries, and they with he; both are engaged in sacrifice- with the one, it is taking

---

1   Another interpretation of the evidence would be that 'sacerd' was only ever a cautious transliteration from the Latin and never achieved a foothold in West Saxon at all.

2   The quote is from Fulke's Defence, i.15, 1582. Fulke was defending the Geneva Bible, but also by implication Tyndale's translation practice, against that of the Douay-Rheims scholars, who 'corruptly translate Sacerdos and Presbyter always, as though they were all one, a Priest'.

place within the old covenant, just before the 'once-for-all' sacrifice of the cross; with the other, it is taking place within the new covenant and is therefore heretical; neither have anything to do with the 'seniours' who under the Apostles lay the foundations of the early church.

This is interesting, but what is even more interesting for our present purposes is what happened in the ensuing 400 years. 'Priest' did not, in fact, disappear from normal discourse about church governance. The extensive positive use which Tyndale and then the KJV made of the word ensured its survival, and particularly after the period of the Protectorate in England (that is, after 1660) its use began to revive, as a straightforward, non-polemical term for a clergyman, particularly in the Church of England. Crucially, its use was preserved in the Book of Common Prayer (1662). Shakespeare, for example, seemed to regard the term as synonymous with 'vicar'.[1] By 1765, Samuel Johnson's dictionary gives an essentially modern entry for the word priest, embracing first 'one who officiates in sacred offices' and secondly 'one of the second order in the hierarchy, above a deacon, below a bishop.'[2] The term has been re-instated as an unslanted descriptor. *The association with 'sacrifice' has, however, been lost along with the polemical baggage.*

The use of the word 'priest' today, then, is a strange thing. It is a word which was cemented into the tradition in the white-heat of the Reformation, a word chosen precisely because of its association with the idea of sacrifice – and an idea which it has now, in its mainstream uses in English, mainly lost.

Whether this is of concern to us relates to the issue of whether and to what extent we really want our translations to communicate. All the so-called communicative translations, of course, have this as their avowed intention, but the persistence of a certain translation tradition points to something else. Venuti states it most clearly: 'Institutions, whether academic or religious, commercial or political, show a preference for a translation ethics of sameness, translation that enables and ratifies existing discourses and canons, interpretations and pedagogies, advertising campaigns and liturgies – if only to ensure the continued and unruffled reproduction of the institution.'[3] If these translators really wished to convey to their audience who Zacharias was, they would not use the word *priest*, but would seek some other less misleading term. We will now consider some of these.

---

1   'I'll to the vicar, Bring you the maid, you shall not lack for a priest.' The Merry Wives of Windsor, usually dated to 1602.
2   Johnson, Samuel, *Dictionary,* 1765, 3rd Edition.
3   Venuti, 1998, p.82.

Alternative translations for ἱερεύς

How would we set about suggesting alternative translations for ἱερεύς? The options are defined by the relevance theoretical model of conceptual address: a translator has to decide whether interpretive resemblance is served best by seeking resemblance in the **lexical** entry, in the **logical** entry or in the **encyclopaedic** entry.

'Encyclopaedic' translation

On occasion one may observe translators wavering between the options. Consider the following, from one of Nida's 'Translator's Handbooks'. This one, covering Acts and co-authored with Barclay Newman, is intended to be used by field-translators seeking to produce versions of the scriptures for new languages. At Acts 4.1, Nida and Newman encounter a similar problem to the one we have been considering: a ἱερεύς appears. Their approach to this is worth quoting in full:

> *A number of different expressions for priest are used in various languages. The important thing is that this be a term to designate a professional religious functionary. All so-called 'world religions' have their priestly castes or groups. In so-called animistic societies there may, however, be difficulty in obtaining a satisfactory word for priest. In some instances the closest equivalent is the shaman or the medicine man. In other instances it may be important to have some type of descriptive phrase as 'the one who sacrifices' or 'the one who functions in the house of God.'*[1]

These guides are in general highly informative. One of their benefits for present purposes is that they are written, as it were, with the guard down: the translator is found *dishabille* with trusted colleagues, and a number of striking features emerge. One is that it is taken for granted throughout that what one is seeking is 'equivalence', and equivalence moreover with an English word, not with a Greek one. It is clearly self-evident to the authors that *priest* is the equivalent of ἱερεύς, and that they are for practical purposes interchangeable. What is being produced therefore is not a version of the Greek text (notwithstanding assertions in the first lines of the preface to this effect) but a version of an *English* text: the ἱερὸς γάμος, or Holy Marriage between English and Bible (ideally 'the Today's English Version, since this is a more accurate and meaningful representation of the underlying Greek text than is available in more literal translations'!).[2]

1 Nida and Newman, 1972, p.90.
2 Ibid, v.

Nida and Newman are, of course, working within the framework of 'functional equivalence', and their conscious efforts in the present passage are directed towards finding the 'functional equivalent' in the target language – ostensibly for the Greek word ἱερεύς, but really for the English word *priest*. Interpreting the passage within a relevance-theoretical framework, though, we may observe that they first of all identify 'the important thing' as being that the priest is a 'professional religious functionary' – this might be regarded as their notion of the *logical* entry associated with the English word – that is, the essential rules for using the word, the violation of which by a given user would indicate that that user had not really grasped the concept. (And their notion is of course, but incidentally, one with which we might take issue: 'professional' is a concept unknown to the overwhelming majority of human cultures, present or historic). They then consider various options from the *encyclopaedic* entry, recognising that in the target language there may be no 'word for' the English *priest*, and therefore including *shaman* or *medicine man*. These seem to be the preferred solution, and only if there is no 'equivalent' at all is the translator encouraged to consider a descriptive noun phrase, which would attempt to reproduce the semantic representation.

In following this procedure, Nida and Newman seem to favour what we might term 'encyclopaedic equivalence', even when it delivers a very rough and ready result: *shaman* is, after all, a very poor equivalent for *priest*, let alone ἱερεύς. It is interesting to speculate as to what Nida and Newman would do in an imaginary world where they were missionaries to an England in which there are no priests, and no word *priest*. Once they had disembarked and begun their translation work, would they cast around for what the English *did* have, and translate accordingly? Would the ἱερεύς in Luke 1.5 end up being described as 'a certain doctor', 'a certain teacher' or 'a certain social worker'? Wouldn't it be better to bite the bullet and, instead of invoking misleading encyclopaedic correspondences, provide a noun-phrase which gave a similar semantic representation as ἱερεύς?

The instinct to reach for an encyclopaedic equivalent is widespread – we will recall from Chapter Three, Loveday Alexander's decision to translate αὐτόπτης as 'eyewitness' because this was a 'neater' solution, even as she stated it was likely to mislead. This instinct may be related to the translator's desire to stay on the 'easy' part of the relevance curve. As we saw in Chapter Two, a reader/hearer goes to less effort to recover an encyclopaedic image from memory, rather than to use deductive processes to flesh-out a semantic representation. This is how stereotypes work: the mind lazily recovers a complete set of assumptions from encyclopaedic memory rather than puzzles out what is going on in this particular case. It is certainly easier for the reader if we describe Zacharias as 'a certain priest' – it is easier because the reader is simply given a readily available encyclopaedic image: he does not have to trouble over what kind of figure Zacharias is at all. A translator who wishes to operate at 'low risk' will instinctively reach for such a translation, particularly when it has institutional and traditional endorsement. At a deeper level, it may reflect the translator's urge to 'dominate' or control the text, and it is this domesticating tendency which has received such a powerful critique by Venuti and others.[1] However it may be explained, though, I would like to advance the argument that it is or should be the role of translation theory to call such urges into question. There will certainly be many occasions where an 'encylopaedic' translation is what is required; but it is the role of theory to make sure that this is not done unmindfully. This seems to be one of the most pernicious effects of 'functional equivalence' theory in biblical translation: rather than tempering the urge to domesticate the text, it positively encourages it, by reinforcing the notion that translation can be achieved by juxtaposing approximately 'equivalent' encyclopaedic images. The result is a blurred, fuzzy *facsimile* of the original text rather than a sharp, thought-provoking *interpretation*.

'Lexical' translations

On occasion, translators will seek to achieve translation via the lexical entry associated with a concept. We may, for example, conjecture that this is what occurred when the 10th Century Anglo-Saxon translators rendered the Vulgate 'sacerdos' as 'sacerd'. Lacking an Old-English word associated with the concept of an administrator of sacrificial rites, the translators cautiously transcribed an anglicised version of the Latin word. As we saw above, this was not a word which 'made it' into modern English, but there are plenty of examples which did: the word *angel*, which occurs only a few verses later in our passage, reached English by exactly the same route and, as we will see in chapter 5, has been very successful. It is of course the norm in the 'translation' of names: Ζαχαρίας is transliterated as Zacharias, and so on.

A 'lexical' translation for ἱερεύς would be *Hierus* or the like. Most translators would regard such a rendering as reflecting one or more of the following three considerations. The first is simply the recognition that the target language is incapable of expressing the relevance of the source word or expression. Thus, for example, if we followed the argument in the immediately preceding section, one possible conclusion might be that modern English simply cannot

1   Venuti, 1998, p.11ff.

express the concept associated with the word ἱερεύς in a form which can appear in the flow of the passage, and therefore all that can be done is to transliterate the word as Hierus or something similar, and perhaps provide a gloss of the word. Luke himself occasionally takes this approach – for example his description of the Hebrew festival of פסח (pasâch) as Πάσχα (pronounced 'pascha'), sometimes with a gloss (22.1), sometimes without (2.41). This would be a more honest approach than the increasingly prevalent present-day practice of 'glossing' in biblical translation. This practice involves 'translating' the source text with the traditionally prescribed word (in this case *priest*), and providing a note somewhere to the effect that *priest* doesn't mean what you thought it meant, but something else. My Luther Bible (a delightfully produced and genuinely pocket-sized 'Pfefferkorn' edition) commits this crime, which it compounds by not even, in the text itself, highlighting to the reader that *Priester* is being used in this unusual way, and that the *Sach- und Worterklärungen* (Subject and Word Explanations) at the end should be consulted. *La Colombe, the NIV Study Bible* and many others do the same. Would it not be more honest and more communicative, rather than using a misleading word in the main text, using hierus or something similar?

The second consideration might be that a word in the source text achieves relevance only by virtue of its unique reference to an individual – it has an *empty* logical entry, and a one-item encyclopaedic entry containing just that one individual. There is therefore no question of attempting to translate at the semantic level – in fact, in classical theory, names stand outside semantics altogether.[1] The word Ἡρῴδης might provide an example: although there are historically several Herods to worry about, for present purposes the way Herod achieves relevance is simply as a lexical marker for an individual.

The third consideration which can on occasion push a translator towards 'lexical' translation is ideological. A translator wishing, for example, to emphasise the 'foreignness' of a text as recommended by Venuti or Lecercle, may be tempted to insert a transliteration, even where this is not strictly required, as a reminder to the reader that this is an encounter with 'the other'. I would like to analyse this practice in similar terms to that suggested in Chapter Three for the 'literal inter-linear'. What the gratuitous 'lexical' translation does is to suspend for a moment the process of communication. During this momentary pause a 'meta-textual' point is made by the translator to the reader/hearer ('Don't forget this is the other! Don't domesticate this text too easily!').

---

1   Anderson, John M., 2007, p.14ff.

This accounts for both the success of this approach in skilful, sensitive hands, and for the irritation which it can cause if done badly. The reader is wearied and in the end alienated by too frequent 'foreignizations'. Such a strategy can also lapse too easily into the 'exhibitionary complex' identified by Tony Bennett, and applied to translation studies by Tarek Shamma.[1] The exhibitionary complex occurs where institutions demonstrate 'the power to command and arrange things and bodies for public display.' In translation this can occur when an extremely 'literal' and 'lexical' translation has the effect of presenting the source culture as a kind of educational display, as in an exhibition or museum. Difference may be honoured, but the effect can be to emphasise the 'quaintness' of the source, and because the implicit message of any exhibition can include the assumption: 'We are the exhibitors; you are the exhibit' (in other words a power relation) the result is very far from being the facilitation of a genuine encounter with the other. Although Shamma does not use the language of relevance theory, his insight can be expressed in these terms: the normal communicative relationship between a speaker and a hearer is distorted by a translation which suspends communication too frequently.

These criticisms (and others) may be applied to the following rendition of our passage. David Stern's 'Complete Jewish Bible' has the following:

> *In the days of Herod, King of Y'hudah, there was a cohen named Z'kharyah who belonged to the Aviyah division. His wife was a descendant of Aharon, and her name was Elisheva. Both of them were righteous before God, observing all the mitzvot and ordinances of ADONAI blamelessly. But they had no children, because Elisheva was barren; and they were both well along in years.*
>
> *One time, when Z'khariyah was fulfilling his duties as cohen during his division's period of service before God, he was chosen by lot (according to the custom among the cohanim) to enter the temple and burn incense. All the people were outside, praying, at the time of the incense burning, when there appeared to him an angel of ADONAI standing to the right of the incense altar.*
>
> Luke 1: 5 - 11, Complete Jewish Bible

Stern thus describes the ἱερεύς of Luke 1.5 as *a cohen named Z'kharyah*. The merit of this translation is, of course, that Zacharias was indeed a כֹּהֵן, and the translation provided avoids the misleading equation of ἱερεύς and priest. Unfortunately as well as this merit, there are problems, mainly arising from the fact that this translation has allowed itself to be

---

1   Shamma, Tarek, 2009, p.44ff.

completely dominated by an ideological objective. In his preface Stern states the purposes of the Complete Jewish Bible, the first two of which are: (1) . . . to restore the unified Jewishness of the Bible, and particularly, to show that the books of the New Covenant are Jewish through and through. (2) . . . to express the Word of God . . . in enjoyable modern English.'[1] So, the use of *cohen* and all the other 'reverse hebraisms' would be justified as meeting the first purpose: to remind us that the Christian faith sprang from thoroughly Jewish roots. True though this may be, and laudable though it is to remind us of this, there is a question-mark here. A translation is, as we saw in chapter 2, a text which intends to achieve its relevance by virtue of its resemblance to a source. Such a text must have resemblance to a source (however interpreted) as its number one objective. A text which presents itself as a translation is assumed to seek such resemblance; and a text which purports to do this but in practice allows another objective (perhaps an ideological one) to override it, is guilty of compromising the trust which must exist between a translator and his audience. Skopos theory notwithstanding, a translator is not let off the hook of resemblance just by stating that his translation has another purpose.

There are also, of course, other problems. In relevance theory terms, we may legitimately ask the question whether the extra effort required of the reader to process the unfamiliar *Y'huda, Z'khariyah* and so on is adequately rewarded in terms of additional contextual implications. Once we have 'got it' that the characters and milieu are 'Jewish through and through', we are at risk of being wearied and insulted by the repeated sound of the translator's own 'meta-textual' voice reminding us again and again of what we already know.[2] There is also a question of semantic accuracy. The term which Luke used was ἱερεύς, a pan-religious term, and not כֹּהֵן, a Hebrew term. Had he wished to use the latter term, he could perhaps have done so (κοήν?) but this would have been against his normal practice and unnecessary in the light of the LXX translation of כֹּהֵן as ἱερεύς . By translating as cohen, Stern misleadingly suggests that this is what Luke wrote.

Stern's translation practice generates other fascinatingly intricate problems. Consider the use of ADONAI, for example. Stern will of course be fully aware that this is an English transliteration of a Hebrew word which was *pronounced* (not written) whenever the divine name

---

1   Complete Jewish Bible, 1998, xv.
2   Barnstone's Restored *New Testament* has a similar approach, and is subject to the same criticisms. His literalism is more 'gametic' than Stern's (he uses 'priest' at Luke 1.5), but he uses Hebraisms throughout, as part of a foreignizing translation strategy.

YHWH appeared in the text, to avoid uttering the name above all names. In Stern's 'Jewish Bible' it is used to represent the Greek word κύριος (pr. Kurios) which was the LXX translation of YHWH, and is used in the New Testament in a similar way. It is thus a transliteration of a Hebrew/Aramaic word which *never* appears written in either the Hebrew or LXX, nor in the Greek New Testament. Because transliteration is the basic strategy of Stern's work, there is a serious risk that the reader of the translation will be misled as to what appears in the source text: most readers would assume that the word ADONAI must appear in the Greek text .

Transliteration has its limitations and these are recognised by most professional translators. In terms of Relevance Theory, the key problem is that of providing a worthwhile set of contextual implications in return for the reader's processing effort. The three motivations for transliteration we mentioned above each have different dynamics in terms of the relevance curve. The first case – the case where the target language cannot succinctly express the concept from the source language – is difficult because the transliteration in the target text is a lexical marker for what we might term a 'ghost' concept. It is a concept with a completely empty logical entry, and a severely attenuated encyclopaedic entry, containing only information to the effect that this is a 'loan word', for example. The reader will search in vain for worthwhile implications from processing the unfamiliar word. Chapter 5 will explore what can happen in the target language when this occurs. The second case – the case where transliteration is used because the word achieves relevance only by virtue of pointing to a unique individual – is somewhat easier, as it works in precisely the same way as the normal naming process. The only issue may be that the foreign transliteration may be slightly more difficult to process than a domestic name. This is the relevance-theoretical explanation of why transliteration is usually preferred to transcription. In transliteration, the word is mildly domesticated to the target language – *Judea*, rather than Stern's *Y'huda* , for example. This makes it easier to process and therefore more firmly placed within the relevance curve. The third case – the case where transliteration is a sign of ideological concerns – is the most difficult in terms of achieving relevance, and this is why it is used only where those concerns are allowed to overwhelm the translation project.

There is a long tradition of suspicion of transliteration amongst protestant English Bible translators. One of the main charges against the 1582 English Bible produced by Catholic scholars at Douay was that it 'veiled the word': the excessive use of transliteration meant that it fell short of a translation, and required a further interpretation by the church in order to make sense to the common reader.[1] This moral/theological outrage has modulated to sniggering in the modern era.[2] Of course, linguistic history is written by the winners: it is not immediately obvious why Douay-Rheims' decision to translate the Latin *sicera* (from the Greek σίκερα) as *sicer* is inherently more ridiculous than Wycliff's decision to translate the Latin *angelus* (from the Greek ἄγγελος – pr. 'angelos') as *angel*. The fact that it seems so to us now is a reflection of the success of the latter word in English and the failure of the former.

Alongside the suspicion it sometimes evokes, transliteration has played and continues to play a large part in biblical translation. In the first 20 verses of Luke's gospel there are 20 transliterations in the NRSV, nearly all of them names but also including ἄγγελος. The traditional approach to translating names is to render them lexically – that is, to transliterate them – unless there is very good reason not to. We will explore the merits of this approach below, but it seems at least clear that transliteration is unlikely to be the best solution to the translation of ἱερεύς. Having considered the 'encyclopaedic' option and the 'lexical' option, we turn now to the third and final possibility: attempting to translate at the level of the 'logical' entry.

'Logical' translations

If we cannot find an encyclopaedic equivalent and are not satisfied by a lexical transliteration, we may turn to the 'logical entry' associated with a concept, to see whether we can translate at the level of semantic representation. We will recall our provisional suggestion for what the logical entry for the Greek concept associated with ἱερεύς might contain: 'male human expert in selection of victims for, and procedures of, sacrifice'. This is clearly a phrase which, if inserted wholesale into our translation, would have great difficulty in being a relevant communication: the long-windedness and inelegance of the phrase would mean it was very unlikely to stay within the relevance curve, whatever implications it allowed the reader to form. The translator pursuing this strategy will have to find a more easily processed way of conveying the semantic representation required.

One recent English translation – whether wittingly or unwittingly – has made considerable use of 'logical translation'. John Henson's 'Good as New', published in 2004, offers the following:

---

1   See for example Bosworth's introduction to the Anglo-Saxon Gospels, 1865.
2   Metzger, who points out such oddities as 'odible to God' (Romans 1.30) and 'he exinaninated himself' (Phil.2.7).

Kerry lived at the time of Herod the Great. He belonged to an old family of God's helpers. His wife Lisa came from the same family. God saw that Kerry and Lisa were good people. They did their best to please God by keeping the rules of their religion. They hadn't been able to have any children and were getting on in years.

One day Kerry was at work in the central place of worship in Jerusalem. He was due to take part in the service. He was allotted the task of burning the scented crystals. To do this he had to go into the restricted area set apart to mark the presence of God. The people waited outside, holding thoughts of God in their minds. Inside Kerry got a fright. He hadn't expected to see one of God's agents standing by the table. The agent said, 'Keep calm, Kerry! God has been listening to you. Lisa is going to have a baby boy. John would be a good name for him, since it means 'gift from God.' Congratulations! He'll bring you a lot of happiness, and everyone else will be pleased too. He'll be a famous man of God. He must keep away from the drink. God's spirit will be his guide from the moment he's born. He'll bring many of your people back to God. He'll tell them God is coming. He'll be a strong character and remind them of Elijah . . .

  'Good as New: A Radical Retelling of Scripture' Luke 1.5 - 17

The reaction to such translations can be extremely emotional: 'Good as New' evokes reactions ranging from 'banal', 'vacuous', 'airport English', to 'refreshing', 'unstuffy' and 'insightful', and it is clearly to be included in the genre scathingly christened by David Daniell as 'Have-a-nice-day Bibles'.[1] Once we move beyond the emotional reaction, though, we will notice that one of the core strategies is a kind of logical translation, in which an attempt is made to convey the semantic representation associated with the source-language concept. Thus for example ὁ ναός is translated as 'the restricted area set apart to mark the presence of God', the ἄγγελος κυρίου is 'one of God's agents', and ἱερεύς is '[a member of] an old family of God's helpers.' The success or otherwise of this approach can be considered both at the tactical level and at the strategic level.

At the tactical level, how successful is '[a member of] an old family of God's helpers'? The phrase does capture the hereditary nature of the office of כהן, but, as we remarked earlier in relation to Stern's Jewish Bible, what we have in the text here is not a כהן but a ἱερεύς. The latter is a pan-religious term familiar to Luke's readership from a variety of sources, and in many of these cases the ἱερωσύνη was not an hereditary office at all. The effect is compounded by referring to 'God': what we

---

1   Daniell, in Porter, 1996, p.80.

have is the semantic representation of כֹּהֵן, not of ἱερεύς. This may be intentional: Henson does not explain his translation practice in the preface, but it may be that it involves a two-stage jump: first, there is an interpretation of the source text in terms of its encyclopaedic entries, then an attempt to 'explicate' one of those entries.

One of the charms of this translation practice, whatever its motivation, is that it makes the commitments of the translator very clear: because such extensive use is made of semantic representation, it is very clear what concepts the translator believes are associated with which Greek words. There is no hiding behind vague encyclopaedic equivalence or transliteration. So, in the case of 'Good as New' it is very clear what Henson's interpretation is. The process of expounding the logical entry, or explicitation, gives rise to many opportunities for the translator to ram his interpretation home, and whilst there is no question here of 'smuggling' ideas in (everything is, after all, explicit) the result can be misleading nonetheless: how many readers of 'Good as New' would guess that Luke uses the word Θεός ('theos' – 'god') only 3 times (and κύριος 5 times) in this passage? 'Good as New' has 'God' no less than 12 times. God is both simplified and more present in the narrative.

At the strategic level we may note another problem with this approach. The effect of repeated translation of the 'logical entry' is a quite thoroughgoing de-contextualisation. Even though we are told *when* they lived more explicitly than the other translations we have considered ('at the time of Herod *the Great*'), we are left feeling very unsure about who 'Kerry and Lisa' really are, where they lived and where exactly it was that Kerry 'got a fright'. The problem with phrases such as 'the central place of worship' is not that they are inaccurate but that they do not evoke a picture which the reader/hearer can work with: that is, the semantic representation does not provide a springboard to any given encyclopaedic reference.[1] The reason for this is not the use of translation at the logical level as such, but its *repeated* use: there are not enough grappling points for the reader/hearer to work with. The effect is that 'Good as New' is in some passages almost incomprehensible unless one holds the original or another translation alongside it, an effect surely far from

---

1   This is not quite true. The place to which I occasionally felt directed was Springfield, Illinois; even this, though, was not clear. 'Burning scented crystals' is not something Homer and Marge would get involved in, but perhaps takes place on the Starship Enterprise? The thought of the people 'waiting outside holding thoughts of God in their minds' conjures scenes from zombie movies. Although I am here (perhaps unfairly) poking fun, the point is serious: if insufficient encyclopaedic clues are given, 'some place' becomes 'no place'.

the translator's intention. This is a particularly tragic outcome when one considers the skill and economy with which Luke precisely sets the scene in time and space in Luke 1.5a. Luke's phrase works by giving clues from the lexical entry (ʿΗρῴδου and Ζαχαρίας – Herod and Zacharias), from the logical entry (ἱερεύς – 'priest') and from the encyclopaedic entry (Ἐγένετο 'it came to pass'- see chapter 5). A skilled communicator uses the full range of clues.

It is for this reason that it would be wrong to despair of finding an appropriate translation for ἱερεύς at the level of logical entry. There is a tradition in protestant French translation, beginning with *La Bible de Genéve* (1560) of rendering ἱερεύς as *sacrificateur*. Ostervald's translation of 1744, Louis Segond's of 1880, J.N. Darby's of 1859, and *La Colombe* of 1978 (which is a modernisation of Segond's 1910 revision) all use this formulation.[1]

> Au temps d'Hérode, roi de Judée, il y eut un sacrificateur, du nom de Zacharie, de la classe d'Abia.   La Colombe, Luke 1.5a

The motivation for *sacrificateur* springs, like the English reformation renderings we discussed earlier, from the sectarian divisions which have marked European history: the French-Swiss translators did not want to identify the true Christian priesthood with the sacrificial practices of the old covenant, and therefore marked a distinction between *ancien* and *sacrificateur*. The methodology, though, is translation of ἱερεύς (and כהן) at the level of logical entry. As *sacrificateur* is the only 'logical entry' translation in the phrase, it works well in Luke 1.5a, slowing the reader down just enough for him to register the key relevance of Zacharias in the text. It seems unfortunate that it was one of the things sacrificed (pardon the pun) in the no doubt difficult negotiations which led to the great ecumenical French translations of the 20th Century: *sacrificateur* does not appear in *La Bible de Jérusalem* (1955) or *Traduction oecuménique de la Bible* (1967-1975). However it has survived into contemporary usage in *La Colombe*.

Could this provide a precedent for an experimental English translation? 'Sacrificer' is, however, not quite right in English. English demonstrates the same tendency which Rosenzweig identified in German to associate 'sacrifice' with renunciation.[2] Is a *sacrificer*, then, one who sacrifices another being, or one who denies himself? Moreover, as we observed earlier, the ἱερεύς was not necessarily or

1 Henri Lasserre's translation of 1887, J.B. Glaire of 1903, Monseigneur L'Évêque de Nimes of 1903, A Crampon of 1905, Le Maistre de Sacy, 1837 are exceptions.
2 Buber, w. Rosenzweig, 1936, tr. Rosenwald, p77.

usually the individual to actually slit the animal's throat, which is what *sacrificer* perhaps suggests. Rather, he is the one who works in the place of sacrifice, vets the victim of sacrifice and ensures the rites of sacrifice are correctly observed. If, with Jacob Milgrom, we accepted a relatively 'low' view of priesthood,[1] we could almost call the ἱερεύς a Sacrifice Attendant – but in English this suggests that there was someone else who was conducting the sacrifice and the ἱερεύς was only 'in attendance' to that person. Might one hope that a logical entry translation would capture some idea of ἱερός ('holy' or perhaps 'set apart' or 'excellent'), generally thought to be the root word for ἱερεύς – that is, the idea of excellence or marvel as it is applied to the victim of the sacrifice?[2] As will be appreciated by now, once we decide to translate at the level of 'logical entry', a demanding level of precision is required. This is one of the reasons it has to be used sparingly.

It seems likely that a translation at the level of logical entry will, in this case, require a neologism. When the Vulgate gospels were translated into Anglo-Saxon (sometimes referred to as West Saxon) in the 10th Century, a variety of strategies were used. As we have seen, there was a considerable amount of 'lexical entry' translation – we have had cause to mention *sacerd, engel, sicer*. However, there was also a willingness to innovate, primarily through the use of novel compounds. Thus *centurio* was translated *hundred-man*; *discipulus* became *learning-criht* (learning-youth); the man with hydropicus (Luke 14.2) is a *waeter-seoc-man*; sabbata is *reste-daeg*; similitudo becomes *bigspel* (near-example) and so on. Might we feel ourselves permitted by such precedents to try some compounding ourselves? The problems with this strategy are of course several, and are partly illustrated in the table below. The first problem we have noted: the nature of the practice means that precision is required – we must accurately delineate the practice and perception of ἱερεῖς as we actually understand it to have been. Any mistake in this, and any subsequent advance in our knowledge, would render the translation

---

1   The priest is seen almost as having a purely supervisory role: he is a technically qualified person to whom the lay person wishing to make the sacrifice delegates. Milgrom is of course talking of the classical Hebrew tradition, but he is here pointing out that this was a tradition which was not a mystery cult or elitist in the manner of Assyrian or Mesopotamian cults, but was more similar to the Greek tradition represented by ἱερεύς. See Milgrom, Jacob, Leviticus, 1991, p.56.

2   Here we come as close as we dare to the heinous crime of 'illegitimate totality transfer', identified by James Barr as one of the etymological fallacies. The question will be considered in depth in Chapter 6 below.

inaccurate. Some readers may, for example, feel that my account gives too much emphasis to animal sacrifice – vegetal sacrifice was also common, and the burning with which Zacharias was involved in Luke 1 was certainly not a holocaust, but some sort of fragrant plant-material. Some of the neologisms below may, for such a reader, give too much emphasis to the idea of slaughter. The second problem is that any innovation can be held up to ridicule and indeed is very likely to seem ridiculous on first encounter, and this is a major obstacle to achieving relevance. The third problem is that even a compound neologism which attempts to capture the whole of the 'logical entry' meaning will emphasise one element rather than another. For example, English naturally forms endocentric compounds (small-talk, dog-house, banana-fritter) in which A + B denotes a type of B, giving prominence to B as the fundamental category.

With these three problems still in mind, here nevertheless are some suggestions:

	Emphasised	De-emphasised
Sayer-of-Rites *Ritualer* *Ritesman*	Emphasises ritual nature of role. . . .	. . . but idea of sacrifice, of victim, of the excellence of victim, is lost
Slaughter-Man *Slaughter-Ritesman* *Selector- of- Victims* *Victims-Man* *Assessor* *Sacrifice-Man*	Emphasises slaughtering role . . . Or selection/assessment of the offering	. . . but 'sensationalist'. Some of these sound like a serial murderer?
Offering-Man	'Offering' is a less sensationalist way of talking of sacrifice . . .	. . . but risk of not being understood
Fresh-Slayer *Good-Slayer*	Emphasises the adjectival sense of victim quality . . .	. . . but sensationalist and unclear
Temple-Slayer *Temple-Man*	Emphasises location of role . . .	. . . but de-emphasises role itself?

Possible translations for ἱερεύς

Summary

We have considered three sets of candidates for a 'new' translation of
ἱερεύς: we can attempt an encyclopaedic entry translation (examples:
priest; shaman; medicine-man), or a lexical entry translation (*hierus*),
or a logical entry translation (*Offering-Man; Ritesman; Assessor*). The
question of which if any of these is to be preferred remains open:
the Experimental Translation (see Appendix) suggests one possible
solution.

In Chapters Three and Four we have considered at some length
the major topics of syntax and semantics. In the next chapter, we
will consider the remainder of the 'communicative clues' identified
by Gutt as part of his description of 'direct translation.'

Chapter Five

Still looking for clues

We saw in Chapter Two that in his exposition of a Relevance Theory of Translation, Gutt introduces the idea of 'communicative clues' and 'direct translation' at a crucial point in his argument.[1] A communicative clue is a feature of an utterance or a text which guides the hearer or reader to how the communicator intends it to achieve relevance. Gutt proposes eight kinds of communicative clue, and suggests that what he names direct translation 'calls for the preservation of all communicative clues . . . [B]y preserving all the communicative clues of the original, such translation would it make it possible for the receptors to arrive at the intended interpretation of the original, provided they used the contextual assumptions envisaged by the original author.'[2] Gutt's use of this notion is as a stepping-stone to his final theory, and, as we will see, it must be used with care: there is the danger that this kind of framework may lead us back into thinking that the task of translation is to produce 'equivalence' in communicative clues. Despite this danger, the use of the concept allows us to articulate the variety of ways in which a text can communicate, and to reflect on how we might deal with this in our translation practice.

We will consider each of Gutt's communicative clues in turn, illustrating them wherever possible, as usual, with examples from the early chapters of Luke's gospel. We will repeatedly observe that, in Relevance Theory, all clues are equal: the only jury is the principle of relevance itself, and there can be no firm 'pecking order' privileging one over any of the others.

Some of the material in this chapter is summary in nature – we will draw together some of our conclusions from the first four chapters, under the headings of Gutt's communicative clues. Later in the chapter some new findings will come to light, and we will try to form some conclusions, in preparation for the final, important considerations of concordance and literalism, in Chapter Six.

---

1   Gutt, 2000, p.132.
2   Ibid, p.135.

Clues arising from semantic representations

The semantic representation of an utterance, as we saw in Chapter Two, is the basis for its truth-conditionality. It represents an assumption schema which can be inferentially developed until it produces a propositional form which can be evaluated for truth value against some state of affairs.[1] For example, Luke tells us:

Καὶ ποιμένες ἦσαν ἐν τῇ χώρᾳ τῇ αὐτῇ ἀγραυλοῦντες καὶ φυλάσσοντες φυλακὰς τῆς νυκτὸς ἐπὶ τὴν ποίμνην αὐτῶν

In that region there were shepherds living in the fields, keeping watch over their flock by night.   NRSV Luke 2.8

We naturally take up the clue provided by the semantic representation from ποιμήν – we would, *prima facie*, interpret this as referring to herdsmen of some sort, and would only consider translating it as 'hunters' or 'lumberjacks' if there were some other compelling reason to do so. We considered a similar issue rather extensively in Chapter Four, where we addressed Luke's use of the term ἱερεύς. We argued that this usage should be taken seriously in terms of its semantics. Whereas traditional translations tend, in accordance with the requirements of the KJV 'holy marriage' between English and Greek, to render ἱερεύς in terms of some rough-and-ready encyclopaedic cultural 'equivalent' such as *priest*, we argued that the semantics should in this case be regarded as relevant. We can now restate this in terms of Gutt's concept of communicative clues: in these terms, Luke's use of this particular word provides a communicative clue as to how this part of the text intends to achieve relevance, a clue which only 'works' by virtue of the semantic representation which is formed from the logical entry for the concept to which it is attached. In arguing, in the final section of Chapter Four, for a reconsideration of the ἱερὸς γάμος translation, we were defending the importance of semantics in establishing relevance.

On the face of it, the necessity for this seems surprising. First level 'intuitive' reflection on translation often leads us to believe that the norm is the production of a semantically 'equivalent' text. However, as we have seen, translation in fact has a tendency to drift into encyclopaedic equivalents, particularly where there is a Holy Marriage in place, which tends to authorise them. As we will see in the rest of the present chapter, there are many cases where translators decide that what is relevant is something other than semantics.

---

1   Ibid, p.138.

Clues arising from syntactic properties

This is the second of Gutt's communicative clues to which we have already given considerable attention: in Chapter Three we saw how the use of a certain syntax (the periodic form) worked together with other communicative clues to point the reader of Luke's preface towards its intended relevance. Gutt offers a range of other examples, including repetition, elision, word order and stress.[1] Clues from syntactic properties are in fact pervasive in our text. Consider again Luke 2.8:

Καὶ ποιμένες ἦσαν ἐν τῇ χώρᾳ τῇ αὐτῇ

ἀγραυλοῦντες καὶ φυλάσσοντες

And herdsmen there were in that country,

making-their-field-their-court,[1] and watching

φυλακὰς τῆς νυκτὸς ἐπὶ τὴν ποίμνην αὐτῶν.

the watches of the night over their herd.

The structure of this sentence is determined by the repetitions of cognate words ποιμήν/ποιμνή and φυλάσσω/φυλακή, which give it a chiastic form. Although the antimetabole in this case is not particularly pronounced (I have not been able to find any commentators who observe it), it is present as a syntactic feature, and the reader must ask herself the question whether it is a communicative clue as to how this passage achieves relevance. Is this structural repetition intended to be Septuagintal? Or does it achieve relevance by evoking the repetitive and continuing[2] pattern of the herdsmen's lives – a pattern which is about to be broken by the dramatic arrival of the Lord's δόξα ('glory')?

The ἱερὸς γάμος translation of Luke 2.8 is, of course, very familiar:

And there were in the same country shepherds abiding in the field,
keeping watch over their flock by night.   Luke 2.8 (KJV)

This Holy Marriage version is faithfully continued in most English translations:

---

1   Gutt, 2000, p.144ff.
2   The use of the imperfect h)~san and the present participles is germane here: the action may be thought of as occurring continuously through the past and into the present. See the remarks on Aspect later in the present chapter.

And there were shepherds living out in the fields nearby, keeping watch over their flocks at night. Luke 2.8 (NIV)

There were sheepherders camping in the neighbourhood. They had set night watches over their sheep. Luke 2.8 (The Message)

The KJV in this case (and it closely follows Tyndale) has decided not to attempt, in Gutt's terms to 'preserve the communicative clue' provided by the repetition and chiastic structure of the Greek sentence: it is entirely, we might almost say deliberately, lost.[1] The possible explanations for this are as follows: (1) The translators did not recognise the presence of the clue, (2) They did recognise it, but decided it could not be preserved in the translation except at the cost of compromising the preservation of a clue they deemed more important – possibly semantic representation, (3) They recognised it but felt that it could not be preserved without compromising good English style, or (4) They recognised it, valued it highly, and preserved it in some other way in their translation, possibly a way which is not now readily visible to us.[2]

If we decided that these syntactic features did constitute a communicative clue, how would we preserve them in translation?

Now there were herders living rough there, through the night's watches, watching their herds.

Or, if the translator is confident that relevance is to be achieved by emphasis on the continuous round of pastoral activity:

There were shepherds around, roughing it, as there always were – watching the night's watches, herding the herds.

This latter may be thought to be mildly expansionary ('herd' is instantiated three times, not two; and 'always' is represented only by tense forms in the original), but if the translator believes that the original sentence achieves its relevance by evoking the continuity and ordinariness of the herdsmen's lives, this may be justified in a 'direct translation'.

---

1   There are stylistic reasons why this may be deliberate: English style, with its enormous stock of vocabulary, tends to frown on simple repetition as unsophisticated or childish. The Message, in this instance, represents a move back towards the Greek, with its repetition of 'sheep'.

2   This last, intriguing possibility is suggested by the observation that part of the appeal of the KJV was its pre-packaged nostalgia – was 'abiding in the fields' already an antiquated expression in 1611? See Steiner, 1998, p.367.

Clues arising from phonetic properties

We saw in Chapter Four how transliteration reflects translators' assessment of relevance. We noted that the frequency of transliteration in biblical translation is quite high: about one word per verse, in the early part of Luke's gospel, usually representing proper names, either of people or places, but also including some 'cultural transplants' – 'angel' for example. When a translator decides to transliterate in this way, she is making an assessment that it is the word's phonetic properties (or their written, graphological counterparts) which provide the relevant communicative clue. In the case of proper names, for example, it can be argued that the relevance of a name is simply to identify a unique individual person or place; it makes reference to that individual easier and may provide clues as to nationality or historical period.[1] Thus, the reference to Καῖσαρ Αὐγουστος ('Kaiser Augustus') in Luke 2.1 provides such a marker, and when the translator produces her English version, she follows the clue from its phonetic properties, rendering it as Caesar Augustus. As we saw in Chapter Four, transliteration is much more common than purist transcription, reinforcing the point that the relevance is simply to designate an individual: if the word can be made a little easier in the target language, so much the better.[2] None of this presents any difficulty for a relevance based account, for as Gutt says: 'transcription causes no special conceptual problems because it involves genuine properties of the original that can contribute to relevance.'[3]

The problems – and they are considerable - in fact arise from the issue of conflict with other communicative clues. Phonological clues are different in this respect: whereas each of the other clues may be present or absent, words *always* have phonological/graphological properties, and so they are particularly prone to conflicts. A commonsense approach is to treat them as a 'drip tray' category, or final resort: if a word does not present any of the other communicative clues, assume that its relevance arises from the only clue which is always present, that is, from the series of sounds or marks on the page which constitute that word. Thus, in the case of Luke 2.1's

---

1   See Gutt, 2000, p.150.

2   I differentiate here between transcription (by which I mean a 'literal' transfer from one alphabet to another; so that Au)&goustoj becomes in English 'Augoustos' and Louka~j becomes 'Loukas'); and transliteration (by which I mean the common practice when making such a 'literal' transfer, of adapting the word to target language conventions, so that Au)&goustoj becomes 'Augustus' and Louka~j becomes 'Luke'.

3   Gutt, 2000, p.151.

reference to Καῖσαρ Αὐγουστος we may be reasonably happy with the 'drip pan' approach to its translation. This short phrase is itself a transliteration from the Latin – we note in passing that Luke did not choose to translate Augustus into Σεβαστός, 'revered', a perfectly respectable option for him.[1] The phrase appears in a pericope whose purpose appears to be historical scene-setting, and it seems reasonable to assume that it makes its contribution to relevance only by being a marker for a unique individual.

Somewhat more problematic is the case of Θεόφιλος ('Theophilos') who we encounter in Luke's preface. In this case, as well as the phonological/graphological clue, there is a clue arising from semantic representation: Θεόφιλος gives rise to a semantic representation which we might indicate by 'god-lover', or 'Lover of God', or 'Friend of God' or something of the like. In Luke's original context, this interpretation would be very readily available in the reader's cognitive environment – both because the Greek is obvious and clear,[2] and because the co-text refers repeatedly to God, and addressing it to a God-Lover would be a readily understandable thing to do. The reader is thus highly likely to interpret its relevance in the light of clues arising from a semantic representation, rather than the clue of the phonological/graphological properties. This would in turn suggest that a direct translation would render him not as 'Theophilus' (the ἱερὸς γάμος rendition) but as 'Friend of God' or something similar. The only sensible objection to this would come from the uncovering of historical context not currently available to us: if a real historical person of that name emerged, and if we could establish that Luke was written for a readership of which he was part, then the phonological/graphological clue would be in the foreground.

Similar considerations may apply to ὁ διάβολος ('the devil') who we meet first in Luke 4.2. In this case, Luke has used a Greek word associated with a concept whose logical entry is far from being empty: it contains elimination rules to the effect of 'accuser', or 'slanderer'. In the parallel synoptic stories, Matthew makes a similar choice (Matthew 4.1-11), whilst Mark has Σατανᾶς ('satan', Mark 1.12-13) which is a transliteration of the Hebrew.

---

1   See for example Pausanias Periegeta, 3.11.4 (cited in BDAG) for an example of this translation practice.

2   And so the case is different from that in which I, for example, make a claim that my first name means 'lover of horses'. It would possibly be accurate to say that 'Philip' is a transliteration of something which once meant 'lover of horses'; however this is not a readily available interpretation to people to whom I am introduced at parties; this explains why, when this happens, they do not usually ask me where I have tethered my horse.

How does ὁ(διάβολος achieve relevance in Luke (and Matthew)? There are three principal, related and overlapping, possibilities. The first is inter-textual: Luke (and Matthew?) are seeking to identify Jesus' trial in the wilderness with that of Job (who in the LXX was tested not by Σατανᾶς but by ὁ διάβολος), or just possibly with the ordeal of another Ἰησοῦς ('Jesus' . . . or is it 'Joshua', as the Holy Marriage prescribes?) in Zechariah.[1] The second major possibility is that he used the word precisely for its semantics, because the communicative intention in this text related to a personal opposition to, or accusation of, Jesus. The third is that he was translating from a Hebrew or Aramaic source and followed the precedent provided by some (not the majority) of LXX translators in providing a translation based on a clue arising from semantic representation, rather than a transliteration. In none of these three cases is a transliteration strategy into English likely to lead to interpretive resemblance. Both Σατανᾶς and ὁ διάβολος have made their long transition into English via a series of transliterations (for modern English 'devil', the history includes early Roman *diuvalus*, old High German *tiuval*, old English *dēofol* etc). As we saw in Chapter Four, transliterations enter the target language with an empty logical entry and a highly denuded encyclopaedic entry; however, over the course of time, this very emptiness attracts new content. Both *Satan* and *the Devil* in English have gathered content, taking slightly different paths and creating different roles for themselves, and whether this content facilitates the relevant interpretation (the one which bears interpretive resemblance to the original) will vary case by case.

The ἱερὸς γάμος translation of ὁ διάβολος is, of course *the devil*, but the point here is that what began as an innocuous transliteration has become a crude encyclopaedic 'equivalent'. A translator today, aiming at interpretive resemblance, would seek to pick up the communicative clues provided by the semantic representation of ὁ διάβολος, and at the same time honour the inter-textual references (which would be present in the encyclopaedic entry), and would translate this word in Luke 4 as 'the Accuser', 'the Prosecutor' or similar.

We have, then, found two cases of proper names where the relevance theoretical approach suggests a semantic translation, rather than a phonological/graphological transliteration. Should this approach be extended further – that is, are there other cases where there are good arguments for a semantic treatment of proper names? I would like to

---

1   The Job LXX prologue has ὁ διάβολος 13 times; and Zechariah 3.1-2 intriguingly has ὁ διάβολος and Ἰησοῦς placed in dramatic opposition. The only other places he appears – normally as a straightforward human opponent – in the LXX are 1 Ch.21.1, Esther 7.4 and 8.1-5, and Psalm 108.6.

suggest two further cases for consideration from the early chapters of Luke: the names Ἰησοῦς ('Jesus') and Ἰωάννης ('John'). Both are names given by Gabriel (Luke 1.13; 31), and both have strong semantic content which is relevant to the co-text. Nolland, in line with many commentators, suggests that 'Heaven-given names always have etymological significance',[1] and points out that not only does the Hebrew *Yohanan* mean 'the Lord has been gracious', but the cognate *tehinna*, 'prayer for grace' is translated in the LXX by δέησις, the word used in Luke 1.13 for the prayer to which Gabriel announces an answer. Similarly in Luke 1.31, the semantic content of Ἰησοῦς is thought of as corresponding to that of Yehoshua, 'the Lord delivers'. In Nolland's commentary, these observations form part of an argument for a Semitic source document underlying the birth-narratives, but this is not directly our concern: the question is, given that the only sources actually available to us are the Greek texts, how should these names be treated in translation into English?[2]

Before leaping to the conclusion that these names merit semantic rather than graphological treatment, three cautions suggest themselves. The first we have already mentioned: the clue from semantic representation relates to the Aramaic/Hebrew, not to the Greek. The question as to whether this clue would be recognised by Luke's audience is the difficult (but in the end purely empirical) question of the extent and nature of their knowledge of Hebrew language and culture. Scholarship is widely divided on this question, which cannot detain us here.[3] If, with for example Brawley, we take the view that Luke's extensive appropriation and fluent use of LXX scripture indicates a high degree of assumed familiarity, including some knowledge of the underlying Hebrew,[4] then it is reasonable to assume that the relevant interpretation of Luke 1.13 and 31 includes a recognition of the semantic potential in these names.

Our second hesitation arises from nervousness about what James Barr famously labelled 'the root fallacy.'[5] The root fallacy occurs where an interpreter assumes that what a word 'really' or 'basically' 'means' can be determined by finding its etymological root. The fallacy

1   Nolland,1989, I, p.29.
2   If there was a written Hebrew or Aramaic source for the Lucan birth stories, it has never been found. The balance of scholarly opinion is against there having been such a thing. See Chang-Wook Jung, 2004, for a good summary of the arguments.
3   See Jung, 2004, again, for a summary of the arguments.
4   Brawley, 1996, Text to Text Pours Forth Speech, Indiana University Press.
5   Barr, 1961, p.107ff, esp. pp.109-10.

arises because the etymological history of a word, although it may be
informative, is not necessarily a good guide to how a word is used by
a language group at a particular moment in time. I will have a good
deal to say about this (and about Barr's other major contribution –
'illegitimate totality transfer') in Chapter Six. For the moment,
though, we will observe merely, in Barr's own words, that 'etymological
interest plays a notable part in the minds of many religious people,
so much so that it may be said to have a fascination for them. The
reasons for this are probably numerous and diverse. In the biblical
period we find a centre of popular etymologising in personal names.
Many Hebrew names were intelligible sentences. . . .'[1] Barr wants to
cure us of such primitive behaviour, and goes on to say that often in
such cases the etymologising was not even 'correct'. The point for a
translator, though, is not whether the etymologising is 'correct', but
whether as a matter of fact it forms part of the relevant interpretation
of the text for the original audience.[2] If it does, and if we are aiming
for interpretive resemblance in our translation, then it must form part
of the interpretive possibilities of the target language text.

   The third complication is more serious, and arises from relevance
considerations themselves. The words Ἰησοῦς and Ἰωάννης , as
well as presenting clues arising from semantic representation, do
also have relevance as arbitrary markers for persons, both in this
text and in others. If we translated Ἰωάννης as 'Godisgood' or 'The
Lord is Gracious' , for example, we are at risk of losing these. This is
another case of clues pointing in different directions: should a direct
translation reproduce the phono-graphological clue, or the semantic
clue? One possible solution found for these cases (and it is useful to
note that they are not frequent) may be observed in the Experimental
Translation (see *Appendix*).

   Most of the names in our text do not possess these complications.
Although (as Barr observes) many Hebrew names have semantic
content, this does not *automatically* lead to a presumption of relevance
for this content. Where there is no other clue to this effect in the co-
text (no solemn name-giving by a heavenly messenger; no semantic
relevance in context) there is no need to preserve the semantic clue in
translation. Μαριάμ can stay as Mary, and does not need to become
'Bitter-Love', however tempting it is to draw this semantic content
to the attention of present day readers. An interesting marginal

1   Ibid, p.109.
2   And this is the point implicit in Buber and Rosenzweig's etymologising
Verdeutschung of the Hebrew scriptures. This is discussed more extensively
in Chapter Six.

case is Γαβριήλ ('Gabriel') himself: he (in his earlier discourse with
Zachariah, Luke 1.19) does in a way name himself; and the semantic
clue from his name ('Might of God') does seem to be relevant to his
sense of outrage at having his word doubted by a mere man.

We might then summarise our treatment of names as in figure 15:

Type of name	Translation treatment
Names which are fore grounded in context (eg by being 'heaven-sent'):	Translate such as to provide a similar semantic clue
Names which make a high contribution to relevance via a clue arising from semantic representation:	
Other names:	Translate such as to provide a similar phonological/ graphological clue

Relevant Translation of Proper Names

This table describes what I would hope is an observed regularity,
rather than a 'rule', in the Experimental Translation. The Relevance
Theory of Translation does not admit very readily to rules, because
really the only firm rule is the principle of relevance itself. Each case of
language use must respond to that principle, which is always capable
of overriding any rules. We saw above how Γαβριήλ represents a
marginal case; in fact all cases are marginal in the sense that they all
require the translator to make a *judgement* about how the source text
achieves relevance, given all the facts at her or his disposal, rather than
turning the handle on a sausage machine. Luke/Acts itself, of course,
repeatedly faces these problems, particularly in dealing with the multi-
cultural historical context of early Christianity in Acts. Sometimes the
text translates the semantic content of a name (examples: Βαρναβᾶς
('Barnabas') Acts 4.36; Ταβιθά ('Tabitha') Acts 9.36) but much more
frequently does not; in each case where it does, the challenge is to find
the relevance-related reason for this. Elsewhere in the New Testament,
there are other, slightly different cases. In Philemon, for example,
Paul seems to make an extended joke around the name of Ονήσιμος
('Ōnesimos') and although this may be 'merely' opportunistic punning,
it seems to meet our second criterion above: the semantics of the name

make a significant contribution to relevance. A translation aiming at
interpretive resemblance must attempt to reproduce this – particularly
as the unique individual Ὀνήσιμος plays no other part of which
we aware, and there is no serious loss to relevance by omitting the
graphological clues.

Our discussion of phonological/graphological clues has focussed on
proper names, as these are important in our text. Other texts would
raise different issues: for example the great acrostic poems in Psalms
or Proverbs. In such cases, the ἱερὸς γάμος and its successors have
allowed clues from semantic representation to trump phonological/
graphological clues every time. The foregoing discussion suggests that
at the least this should be reconsidered. The principled way to do so is,
to repeat, to consider whether and to what extent such phonological/
graphological clues contribute to relevance in original context: only if
that contribution is found to be low, then an argument can be made for
their exclusion in translation.

Clues arising from semantic constraints on relevance

There are certain words whose role in a text is neither strictly semantic,
nor contextual, but which may provide crucial communicative clues
about how a text achieves relevance. This category includes discourse
markers, also known as 'pragmatic connectives',[1] examples from our
text including such words as δέ, γέ, μεν . . . δέ, ὡς, πλήν, οὖν, ὅτι,
διότι, καί (but, indeed, though, like, rather, so, for, therefore, and . . .)
and so on. Such words represent linguistically encoded information,
but of a kind which cannot be included in the semantic representation
because not truth-conditional. Gutt calls these 'semantic constraints on
relevance', and we saw in Chapter Three, when we considered Luke's
preface how subtle a range of problems they can present to translators.
Such words, because they make no direct contribution to semantic
representation, are often ignored, or allowed to be distorted. In the
case of Luke's preface, this manifested itself in translations repeatedly
missing the 'almost-but-not-quite' logical and causal relations between
the sub-clauses. Discourse markers are important in relevance terms
because they often rather explicitly point to *how* a portion of text
achieves relevance – for example as a logical consequence of something
else, or as something which is the case in spite of something else, and
so on. A translator aiming at direct translation must preserve such
clues or the coherence of the text will be lost.

A further example of the key role such a pragmatic connective can

---

1   See for example Blakemore, 1987, Gutt, 2000, p.151.

play may be found in the discourse on John the Baptist in Luke 3.7-18. The particle οὖν ('then') is repeated five times, and serves to emphasise the inexorable logic of John's challenge to the crowd, and their response. A translation which ignores this important communicative clue is likely to miss the relevance of John's harangue – the NIV, which provides 'no English equivalent'[1] in three of the five cases, and renders one of the other two as 'and' is unsatisfactory inasmuch as it fails to preserve the communicative clues.

Clues arising from formulaic expressions

A formulaic expression is a form of words which achieves relevance by virtue of *that form of words* itself having its own encyclopaedic entry. An expression such as the English 'Hello' or 'Yours sincerely' does not achieve relevance by virtue of contributing to semantic representation – rather, it provides a short-cut, via memory, to a concept of informal greeting or letter-closing. Although both of these examples *could* be developed semantically, in practice they are interpreted as a stereotype which is easily recovered from memory and constitutes a useful clue in a communicative situation, rather than as part of a truth-conditional propositional form. As well as greetings, Gutt mentions examples of proverbial sayings and conventional formulae ('Wet paint') which contribute to relevance in this way.[2]

Luke's use of Χαίρω (pro. chairo, 'I delight') represents an interesting example. The verb Χαίρω is used in the great majority of cases in the indicative and for its semantic content – see for example Luke 1.14, 6.23, 10.20; the cognate noun Χάρις plays similar roles. However it is also clear that Luke was familiar with the use of Χαίρω in the vocative or infinitive as a greeting: in Acts 23.26, the formal letter to Felix begins, Κλαύδιος Λυσίας τῷ κρατίστῳ ἡγεμόνι Φήλικι χαίρειν ('Claudius Lusias, delighted to address the most excellent Governor Felix'). This latter represents its use in order to provide a communicative clue from a formulaic expression – the captain of the guard does not expect Felix to infer communicative intention from the semantic representation; he does not expect him 'to delight'; rather, the relevance of the expression is as a formal greeting. Similarly, when Γαβριήλ ('Gabriel') greets Mary at Luke 1.28, he uses Χαῖρε, in the vocative, as a formulaic expression. However, Γαβριήλ rather wittily adds a twist: His full greeting is Χαῖρε κεχαριτωμένη, ὁ κύριος μετὰ σοῦ. ('Hail favoured one, the Lord is with you'). The joke here

1   This is the terminology used in the Greek-English Concordance (Zondervan, 1997) which relates to the NIV.
2   Gutt, 2000, p.157.

has two dimensions: as a number of commentators note, the first part of the greeting is strongly alliterative, especially given the use of the reduplicated perfect participle of Χαριτόω.[1] The effect of alliteration, which counts as an example of Gutt's eighth communicative clue – that of Sound-Based Poetic Qualities (see below) is to establish links between words which do not admit to ready semantic resolution, or which are unexpected in some other way and therefore interpretively suggestive. However, the wit also resides in the unexpected combination of a clue from the use of a formulaic expression with a clue from semantic representation: the hearer processes Χαῖρε based on the encyclopaedic entry as a formal greeting, but straight away is given a clue from semantic representation based on the cognate Χαριτόω. It is not unlike the effect in English if one were to say: 'Goodbye, God be with you' or 'Good morning, and what a good morning it is!' The first part of Gabriel's greeting presents, in fact, at least three communicative clues: first, from the formulaic expression; secondly, from the semantic representation; and thirdly from the sound-based alliteration which creates a not easily resolved link between the first two.

Before considering how translation might approach this problem, it is important to be clear about what we are saying here, and what we are not saying. The necessity for this arises from the nervousness of commentators – particularly since Barr's withering expose of 'illegitimate totality transfer' – a nervousness lest they 'read too much' into the text,[2] perhaps attempting to make theological cases on flimsy linguistic foundations – building, for example, a Mariology based on the emphatic, double endowment of grace implied by Χαῖρε κεχαριτωμένη. My intention here is not to make any theological case, but only to note the actual features of the text and the communicative clues which they represent; to make a theological or any other case from them would be a further step.[3] What I intend us to observe here is only that Gabriel's greeting does provide the three identified communicative clues. How should this be dealt with in translation?

The Vulgate rendered the greeting 'Ave, gratia plena', and this translation selects the clues from semantic representation (gratia plena), and from formulaic expression (Ave), but without linking them with any sound-based effect. Tyndale followed this precedent, with 'Hayle full of grace', but the KJV, presumably wishing to avoid a Mariology in which Mary is thought of as being 'full' of some thing or

---

1   E.g., Nolland 1989, I, p.50.
2   See for example Radl, 2003, p.60, and Marshall, 1978, p.65.
3   For further discussion see Chapter Six.

substance which she can then endow on others,[1] substituted the rather clumsy 'Hail, thou that art highly favoured.' The NIV, NRSV, ESV, *The Unvarnished New Testament*, Nicholas King and many others follow this, faithfully preserving the idea of 'favour' which the ἱερὸς γάμος introduced. All of these versions focus on the first two communicative clues. *The Message* at this point is interesting:

> Good morning!
> You're beautiful with God's beauty,
> Beautiful inside and out!   *The Message*, Luke 1.28

The 'Good morning!' is presumably based on Strobel's argument that Χαῖρε was specifically a morning greeting[2] (an argument hard to reconcile with its use in letters). The repetition of 'beauty' can be interpreted, positively, as an attempt to preserve some echo of Gabriel's playful use of language. The juxtaposition of the very ordinary formulaic expression 'Good morning' with the extravagant statement which follows is also successful in terms of helping us understand why Mary would wonder ποταπὸς εἴη ὁ ἀσπασμὸς οὗτος ('what kind of greating is this,' v. 29). A relevance theoretical 'direct translation' is, in fact, likely to proceed along similar lines. Ideally, all three communicative clues would be, in Gutt's terminology 'preserved' in the translation. Given that it is very unlikely that they can all be preserved equally successfully, priority must be given based on overall relevance considerations from the co-text. Shortly after the greeting, Gabriel goes on to tell Mary εὗρες γὰρ χάριν παρὰ τῷ θεῷ and Nolland, amongst others, picks up the clue from the appearance of χάρις at this point: this third cognate of Χαίρω is decisive, for him because of the inter-textual echoes. 'To find grace' (מצא חן) is a frequent Hebrew idiom (Genesis 6.8 and others), but because Nolland finds considerable parallels with Judges 6.11-24, its use in Judges 6.17 (and in LXX, חן is translated χάρις) is particularly relevant. What is important, then, is the introduction of the idea of חן - of the grace of God, freely given or withheld at his sole behest. Nolland's interpretation of Gabriel's dialogue is therefore that he began with the idea of χάρις, and then chose Χαῖρε for its alliterative qualities.[3] (This is of course in contrast

---

1   See Marshall, 1978, p.65ff.

2   Strobel, A, Untersuchungen zum eschatologischen Verzögerungsproblem, Leiden 1961.

3   Nolland, I, p.50. There is something strange about Nolland's argument here, given his conviction that Luke is based on a Semitic source. (Ibid, 57). Presumably in that source, the visitant angel used MOLw. Nolland's recognition of the alliteration in Luke 1.28 is a recognition of the artistry of Luke himself.

with the other way of proceeding, which would be to begin with Χαῖρε and try to find something which provides an alliterative possibility to go with it.) We have, then, a starting point for the relevant translation: begin with the semantic clue provided by Χαῖρε, and then find a conventional greeting which can be linked by alliteration (or by some other clue) to it.

The clue from semantic representation represented by χάρις presents a range of options, including (to give the major options in Liddell and Scott) the ideas of: I. outward charm or beauty, II. A felt grace or favour, including gratitude, kindness, goodwill, III. a favour or boon, IV. a gratification, delight or gift, V. 'for the sake of', or VI. the mythological Graces. The following then, in addition to the rendering in the Experimental Translation, would represent relevant direct translations:

> *'Greetings, gorgeous girl'* (in verse 30, Gabriel would go on to say *'It's the Lord who finds you gorgeous'*)
> *'Joy to you, joy-filled girl'* (In verse 30, Gabriel would go on to say, *'The Lord en-joys you.'*)
> *'Good to see you, girl; you're good as gold'* (In verse 30, *'You're good for the Lord'*)
> *'Delighted to see you, delightful woman'* (In verse 30, *'The Lord finds you delightful'*)
> *'Fare ye well, favoured lady'* (in verse 30, *'for the Lord favours you'*)
> *'A favour for you, favoured female'* (In verse 30, *'for you are a favourite of the Lord'*)
> *'Kind greetings; you're touched by kindness'* (in verse 30) *'for you have touched the Lord's kind heart'*

We have seen in this example how a word can move between a primarily semantic role and that of a formulaic expression: Χαίρω with its full range of semantic possibilities becomes Χαῖρε, indicating a conventionalised greeting. Most examples of the latter include this feature: what begins as a 'normal' use of a word, exploiting the potential of its logical entry to produce a semantic representation, moves to become a stereotypical expression, exploiting part of the encyclopaedic entry to facilitate a very low cost clue to relevance. As Gutt points out, it is this feature which makes formulaic expressions useful in situations where what the communicator wants to do is straightforward: marking the beginning or ending of a communication, for example.[1] Further examples in the dialogue between Mary and

---

1   Gutt, 2000, p.155.

Gabriel include the formulaic expression ἰδοὺ ('behold'), used by both participants in the conversation, an expression which began life as the present imperative of ὁράω ('I look'). Some commentators would also include Μὴ φοβου, ('Fear not') which has arguably by this period become a completely conventionalised way for a heavenly messenger to begin the delivery of his message.[1] By the same token, though, the use of formulaic expressions in other situations is often felt to be poor communication practice. Recovery of a stereotype from memory is a very low cost activity for a hearer, and can be accomplished with a much lower level of attention than, say, producing a semantic representation and filling it out into propositional form. It is low cost, but also low benefit: no new contextual implications are formed, and this can leave the hearer feeling dissatisfied. In terms of the 'relevance curve' depicted in figure 6, we remain resolutely in the bottom left 'trivial' quadrant of the graph.

Steiner, famously, talked of how a newly translated text can beneficently 'infect' a target language.[2] The issue with some stereotypes is that we – the target language audience – have become, in terms of the same metaphor, 'immune': what was once a means of communicating new contextual implications becomes simply a stereotype stored in memory. I would like to propose that this is a particular danger in biblical translation, specifically 'retranslation' under the influence of the ἱερὸς γάμος. The problem is that the authoritative earlier translation dictates a certain set of 'equivalents' which, even if semantically correct, become so familiar to a readership that they assume the status of stereotypes. This means that when the hearer or reader encounters the word, she fails to form any contextual implications. The birth stories we have been considering are soaked in this phenomenon: it is the very familiarity of the story, which creates this effect. Mary keeps saying in version after version, some variant of 'Behold, the handmaiden of the Lord', and each time she says it, it means less. This is an argument for innovation for its own sake: at least versions like *The Message* or *Die Volxbibel* wake us up enough to attempt to form some contextual implications from the text.

Clues arising from onomatopoeia

Gutt's sixth communicative clue arises in a similar way from the possibility of there being a concept of an expression or word itself, and it therefore having its own encyclopaedic entry. For example the

---

1   Nolland, I, p.52.
2   Steiner, 1998, p.315.

word 'quack' is the English lexical sign for a concept which has its own encyclopaedic entry, containing references to the sound which a duck makes. This kind of onomatopoeia is differentiated from what Levý calls 'sound-imitating sequences . . . created ad-hoc'[1] in that it has acquired conceptual status, so that, unlike the phonological/graphological transcriptions we considered above, it can be translated directly as a clue arising from semantic representation. Thus in French, *quack quack* becomes *coin-coin*. It is usually clear whether an author intends a certain expression to achieve relevance by means of an onomatopoeic clue or a phonological one. βρεκεκεκέξ κοάξ κοάξ ('brecc-eccex, co-ax, co-ax') in Aristophanes' Βάτροχοι ('Frogs') seems to be what Levý would call an ad-hoc sequence, and is usually transcribed in translation rather than rendered by English onomatopoeia such as 'ribbet' or 'rivet'.[2] On the other hand, the verbs ὀλολύζω, or Βοάω (Luke 3.4), which have acquired conceptual value in Greek, are usually translated ('howl' or 'wail', and 'cry' or 'shout' respectively).[3]

Difficulties in translation from ancient languages can, however, arise, especially where the evidence for how a word is intended to achieve relevance is slight or ambiguous. In undertaking a new translation of the 'Eighth Book of Moses',[4] a magical text dating probably to the 4th Century CE, Todd Klutz had to consider the translation of a wide range of animal noises. πόπ ('pop') a word which seems in the text to indicate the sound made by a κροκόδειλος ('crocodile') is a case in point. The authoritative English translation by Morton Smith had rendered this as 'pop', whereas the German translation by Preisendanz used *schnalzen*, what one would describe in English as 'smacking one's lips'. Smith, then, understood the word as an 'ad-hoc sound-imitating sequence' whereas Preisendanz took it to be onomatopoeia. The evidence in favour of the former treatment is from the co-text: we are told that: 'the "pop, pop, pop" is the first element in its name' (in Klutz' translation: 'the snapping noise is the first syllable of the name'). Now 'pop' is closer than 'snap' to 'croc'; Smith is picking up on the clue to relevance provided by the rather explicit word-play in the text. Preisendanz, on the other hand, takes his clue from the *semantics* implied by πόπ, which in all probability arise from the onomatopoeic word ποππύζω, which like the German *schnalzen* indicates a lip-smacking sound used for calling horses. Now, as anyone who has observed crocodiles in their natural state will confirm, they

1   Levy, 1969, p.91, cited in Gutt, 2000, p.160.
2   See for example Dudley Fitts' 1955 translation, 'The Frogs.'
3   For example in Lattimore's Iliad.
4   Klutz, in Balcombe and Davila, ed.s, 2011 forthcoming.

make both snapping and popping noises: the 'snap' noise arises when their jaws actually make contact with prey; the 'pop' noise is when they miss and their jaws close on empty air. Klutz' decision between the two is in the end determined by relevance considerations arising from the whole text: he feels that rendering the noise as 'pop' was part of a general strategy by Smith to make an absurdity of this unfamiliar text. Klutz' general criticism is perhaps similar to the point Tarek Shamma makes in his study of the translation history of *The Arabian Nights*: the phonological transcription of 'pop' looks on the surface like the quintessence of translational faithfulness, and might even satisfy the desire, recommended by Venuti, to preserve the 'foreignness' of a text. However, underlying this 'foreignizing' strategy is 'the exhibitionary complex' whereby the foreign is put on display in order (as Shamma puts it) 'to underline the difference of those "non-civilized" peoples.'[1]

Clues arising from the stylistic value of words

A word or expression may provide a communicative clue based on its stylistic value. This again exploits the existence of concepts of words, which can have their own encyclopaedic information associated with them. Gutt encompasses 'register' and 'connotation' within the idea of clues arising from stylistic value. For example the words 'policeman' and 'copper' have the same logical entries, and make the same contribution to the truth conditions of an utterance; the difference between them is accounted for by the fact that the words themselves have their own encyclopaedic entries, containing information about register and appropriate contextual usage.[2]

This kind of communicative clue may be exemplified by Luke's use of the deponent verb γίνομαι – (pr. 'ginomai', 'I become'). This verb occurs twenty six times in the first four chapters of Luke. In the majority (about two thirds) of cases γίνομαι presents clues arising from semantic representation: related to γένεσις, γένος, γένημα, and also found in compounds, it refers to processes of birth, generation, becoming and existence. In the other cases, though, its contribution to semantic representation seems meagre – perhaps non-existent, to the point that a number of major translations ignore it entirely: the NIV, NRSV, ESV all translate as if the verb were not present. These are the familiar 'And it came to pass' occurrences, and are all cases where it is widely accepted that Luke is using a Greek 'equivalent' for the frequently occurring Hebrew construction, וַיְהִי , either as a

---

1   Shamma, 2009, 47. See also Goodwin, 2010, forthcoming.
2   Gutt, 2000, p.162.

direct translation from a Semitic source, or in imitation of the LXX.[1]
They are distinguishable from other instances of γίνομαι by a number
of common features: the occurrences are in the aorist indicative, and
in conjunction with καί or δέ together with an indication of a time
reference: articular infinitive and/or an accusative, or adverbial clause.
The construction is so frequent in Luke (39 times in all) that it lends
a distinctive stylistic flavour to the whole text – particularly if it is read
alongside another, like John's Gospel, which does not use it. Although
the construction with δε represents acceptable, if unusual, Hellenistic
Greek, the construction with και has no precedent outside the LXX.
Thus, to take just one example Luke 2.46 has:

καὶ ἐγένετο μετὰ ἡμέρας τρεῖς εὗρον αὐτὸν ἐν τῷ ἱερω

which the Holy Marriage translation renders as:

> And it came to pass that after three days they found him in the
> temple   Luke 2.46, KJV

Now, this is one of those cases where some of the inheritors of the holy
marriage translation felt able to depart a little from the authoritative
translation. From the 1952 RSV onwards, the construction 'and it
came to pass' was dropped, two reasons being commonly given, both at
the time and subsequently. The first was that this construction was 'not
entirely natural English, but something we might term *biblis*. . . Such
phrases may be precious and entirely understandable to a believer
steeped in the Bible over decades, but they will strike others as being
something other than the English of everyday use.'[2] The second major
reason to drop this construction was that it doesn't 'mean' anything.[3]
This latter point may be re-expressed in relevance theoretical terms
as the assertion that it makes no contribution to truth conditions – it
does not play a role in semantic representation.

Neither of these reasons make much sense. The second point is, of
course, true, but it would lead to dropping the phrase in translation
only if we believed that our task was to translate just the semantics
of the text – ignoring, for example, the other seven categories of
communicative clue identified by Gutt. The first point is also true, but
seems to be an argument for including the phrase, not for excluding
it. Luke's use of the καὶ ἐγένετο construction can only be explained

---

1   Nolland, Marshall and a number of other major commentaries observe
this. For an older conception of the matter see for example Büchsel in TDNT,
1964, I, p.681.
2   Dewey, 2004, p.79, emphasis in original.
3   Ibid.

in relevance terms by the fact that he was deliberately imitating a (Hebrew or Septuagintal) 'biblical' style – precisely what Dewey calls *biblish*. A translation aiming for interpretive resemblance would have to recognise this communicative clue from the stylistic value of words, and represent it somehow in the target language text.

A number of contemporary translations have felt this problem, and produced variants on the time-honoured KJV:

> Now so it was that after three days they found Him in the temple
> NKJV

> *And it turned out that after three days they found him in the temple*
> The Unvarnished New Testament

> And after three days it so happened that they found him in the temple area   The Five Gospels

Some German examples may be of interest, because Luther's phrase, 'es begab sich' is more natural German than is the English 'it came to pass', and the phrase survives into the current (1984) Lutherbibel. Fridolin Stier uses a literally arresting rendition:

> Und es geschah: Nach drei Tagen fanden sie ihn im Heilgtum
> Stier, 1989

Die Bibel in gerechter Sprache, however, drops it:

> Nach drei Tagen fanden sie ihn im Tempel
> Die Bibel in gerechter Sprache, 2007

In assessing these various efforts, it is well to remember that when γίνομαι is used in this way, it presents two kinds of communicative clue: the first is semantic, and is undeniably present even if playing second fiddle to the stylistic clue we have identified. Like the formulaic expressions we discussed earlier, it has made a transition from a semantic origin to a specialised use in which semantics are not foregrounded, but not entirely absent either. This is particularly noticeable where the two kinds of use are juxtaposed – for example in Luke 2.15, where 'it came to pass' (καὶ ἐγένετο) that the angels departed, leaving the herdsmen talking about going to see 'this thing which is come to pass' (τὸ ῥῆμα τοῦτο τὸ γεγονὸς). A direct translation would aim to represent both communicative clues, although giving precedent to the stylistic one, which seems (in the καὶ ἐγένετο constructions) to make the largest contribution to relevance. In this respect, the least satisfactory translation above is that of *The Five Gospels* (which is also the approach adopted by Barnstone's *Restored New Testament*).

The reason for this is that the English phrase 'it so happened that' implies an element of chance or happenstance which is far away from the world view suggested by the organic imagery of γίνομαι. Things in Luke don't 'just happen': a thing is born and grows to fulfilment in accordance with the Lord's purposes. For similar reasons, *The Unvarnished New Testament* is not much better. Stier is rather good semantically: *geschehen* has a slight echo of *Geschlecht*, gender or sex. The stylistic clue is also well represented – if anything, too much so, in that the use of the colon as a kind of hiatus makes it somewhat more highly marked than in the Greek. The recently released Zürcher Bibel perhaps represents an optimum solution:

> Und es geschah nach drei Tagen, dass sie ihn fanden, wie er im
> Tempel . . . sass   Die Zürcher Bibel

The NKJV, finally, begs the question: why bother? It seems to avoid the KJV phrase purely for the sake of it. The KJV 'It came to pass' is better semantically, as *came* faintly echoes *became*. There is an argument, in fact, for reinstating the KJV rendition of καὶ ἐγένετο (and the waw-consecutive וַיְהִי) in contemporary translations, precisely for this reason – it marks a stylistic clue in an appropriate, echoic way. The Experimental Translation (see Appendix) suggests another solution along these lines. Readers will form their own judgement as to how successful it has been.

Clues from sound-based poetic qualities

Gutt observes that sound-based poetic effects such as rhythm and rhyme have the effect of disrupting 'normal' prosodic syntax, creating new connections between words which cut across semantic clues, thus opening up new interpretive possibilities. Such effects constitute powerful communicative clues, which hearers or readers use to make inferences regarding communicative intention. There is a tradition of translation of the Hebrew Scriptures which pays great attention to this area. For Buber and Rosenzweig, for example, the establishment of the text's *rhythmus* was of first importance. Methodologically, they began by establishing the 'natural punctuation', which arises phenomenologically from the drawing of breath, 'the natural segmenting of speech.'[1] Their motives for doing so, though, were entirely in accord with Gutt's observation, as Rosenwald elsewhere asserts: 'We must free from beneath the logical punctuation which is sometimes its ally and sometimes its foe the fundamental principle

---

1   Rosenzweig, Arbeitspapiere, p. 3-4, cited in Rosenwald, 1994, xlvi.

of natural, oral punctuation: the act of breathing.'[1] Rosenzweig here makes explicit his intention to allow the rhythm of a text to disrupt its syntax and semantics. Meschonnic, similarly, 'defines the rhythm of a text as the organization of meaning in time.'[2] Interestingly, Buber and Rosenzweig did not seek to naively reproduce this clue, in their *Verdeutschung* ('Germaning') of the Hebrew Bible. Rather, they allowed it to inform the syntax but above all the physical appearance on the page of the German text. One reader commented, in fact, that their version does not have an aural quality, choosing rather to represent it by means of 'typographically articulated analytical clarity'.[3] The experience of *reading* the text establishes the 'natural punctuation' which they had observed.

Examples of rhythm or rhyme from our text are meagre and questionable: although the four Lukan canticles are usually identified as 'poetic' and indented on the page accordingly, they do not obviously use either rhythm or rhyme, and this perhaps reflects their status as translations from Semitic sources. The alliteration we noticed in Luke 1.28 would perhaps fall under this category. It is also true that Luke's Jesus occasionally seems to be exploiting the rhythmic possibilities of the language.[4] More research in this area would perhaps be fruitful.

Are there other clues?

Gutt makes it clear that his list of communicative clues is not meant to be definitive.[5] At the risk of wearying by repetition: *any* feature of a text might be relevant. Examples of clues which are not explicitly discussed by Gutt, or not easily captured under the eight headings above, are discussed below, and in Chapter Six.

---

1   Rosenzweig, Die Schrift und das Wort, in Die Kreatur, 1925, tr. Rosenwald with Fox, 1994.
2   Rosenwald, 1994, xiii.
3   Ibid, xiv.
4   Εὖγε, ἀγαθὲ δοῦλε, for example in the story of the Pounds (Luke 19.17). Is it fanciful to imagine the extended 'oral' version of the story, repeating this ringing phrase for each 'worthy' servant? What we are imagining, in this case, is of course the transmission history, once the text has made it into Greek. Whether Jesus as a historical person used rhyme or rhythm is a different, and much more conjectural question, the first step for which would be the reconstruction of the (presumed) Aramaic original. Nolland suggests that John the Baptist uses a word play exploiting the similarities between 'stones' and children' in Aramaic (Luke 3.8. See Nolland commentary at that point).
5   Gutt, 2000, p.167.

Redundancy

The application of discourse analysis to literary texts over the last twenty years or so has led to an increased appreciation of how a text may be analysed in terms of planes of discourse, in which 'points of emphasis or peaks . . . may be indicated.'[1] We have touched upon a number of these in the discussion above – for example the use of word order or particular syntactic forms to indicate prominence. Other prominence indicators may also provide important communicative clues: the use of redundant pronouns is an example. When Gabriel's word is questioned by Zachariah, he responds Ἐγώ εἰμι Γαβριὴλ ('I am Gabriel' Luke 1.19). All Greek verbs are monolectic, and the verb form εἰμι already indicates the first person singular subject: there is no semantic requirement to include Ἐγω, which is best interpreted as a communicative clue to how Gabriel intends his statement to achieve relevance. In this case, this is as an ironic echo of Zachariah's preceding statement (ἐγὼ γάρ εἰμι πρεσβύτης – 'I am an old man') an echo which serves to emphasise the ontological distance between the two speakers – that is, between a feeble old man who is incapable of conceiving a child, and one whose name suggests enormous power, and who stands in the very presence of God. In a direct translation, this relevance is unlikely to be established by the simple repetition of 'I am', which has no particular prominence in English, and some other clue must be found. This kind of prominence marker may perhaps be dealt with under Gutt's heading of syntax; yet the clue provided here is more than a simple syntactic repetition. The Experimental Translation suggests one possible approach to this.

Noun inflection

Other prominence indicators are still more difficult to capture under Gutt's eight headings. Mikeal Parsons, for example, shows that noun inflection (κλίσις) may be used to draw attention to the main topic of a discourse, and that this was one of the elementary rhetorical exercises specified by the 1st Century rhetoricians Theon, and (in Latin) Quintillian.[2] By 'ringing the changes' on noun inflection, the student 'lends both charm and force to the thought'[3] and in terms of our relevance-theoretical approach, provides a vital communicative clue as to how his text is intended to achieve relevance. In Luke 15.11-32 (*The Prodigal Son)*, πατήρ ('father') occurs 12 times and in all five cases

1   Porter, 1992, p.302.
2   Parsons, 2007, p.28.
3   Quintillian, 9.3.28, LCL, cited in ibid.

(including the vocative, a rarity in Luke), whereas υἱός ('son') appears 8 times in only two cases, and for Parsons this is a communicative clue: the topic of this parable is a prodigal father, not a prodigal son. The fact that the story has come down to us in the tradition under the latter name could perhaps, then, be attributed to difficulties in translation: the problem is failure to recognise or adequately translate the communicative clue.

In Luke 1, λαός ('people') is used four times in each of the main cases (excluding vocative), and Parsons suggests that this indicates the importance of the popular Jewish setting.[1] We might go further, and observe that all four instances are in the Johannine sections, not in the interweaving Jesus sections. Moreover, perhaps the slight awkwardness of expression in verse 10 is attributable to Luke's wish to use a genitive (the nominative, accusative and dative in the other instances are more rigidly determined by the context or citation)? The identification of such a communicative clue might assist in source criticism and in other ways;[2] however our primary concern here is with translation. If we accepted the existence of this communicative clue, we would need to think carefully about how to represent it in a direct translation. Because English nouns do not (except in the genitive and simple plural) inflect, the translator into English must not only recognise the clue but make special efforts to 'represent' it in his target-language text. The Experimental Translation attempts to achieve this with careful use of the 'helping words' (of, for) which English normally uses, but the effect is weak, and if Parsons is right, a better attempt is called for – perhaps achieving prominence for 'people' by another means.

Tense morphology

A related issue, which also arises from morphology, is the question of the role Greek tense forms in marking prominence. The ability of tense-forms to provide *stylistic* communicative clues is very familiar from modern languages: in German, for example, the perfect tense is generally reserved for informal, conversational use, and the relevant interpretation of a story told in the perfect would be somewhat different from the same story related in the imperfect. Similarly in modern French, the passé simple is preferred over the passé composé for formal writing. In ancient Greek, a case is sometimes made for the pluperfect having

1   Parsons, 2007, π΄.. λαός is with one exception always used in Luke and Acts to refer to the Jewish people.
2   Such an observation might, for example, play a part on the continuing debate over whether the Lukan infancy narratives are translations from a Semitic source.

'highbrow' stylistic connotations, or for the so-called historic present being 'lowbrow'.[1] These phenomena should make us alert to the general possibility that the use of certain tenses may constitute communicative clues beyond their semantic content. It should also make us wary of the assumption that the communicative clues provided by the use of a certain Greek tense can be adequately represented by an 'equivalent' tense in a modern language. The clue I would like to focus on here, though, is that arising from relative prominence. This, unlike other issues[2] relating to the Greek tense system, is a matter of reasonable consensus: the majority of grammarians recognise that the different tense forms have differing levels of prominence, and can contribute to establishing planes of discourse in a text.[3] They are able to do this by virtue of certain features of the morphological forms. One of the most obvious of these is distributive variance: some tense forms are more common than others, and within particular texts, the pattern of distribution can vary widely.

1   See Wallace, 1996, p.506/7. One wonders, though, whether Xenophon can really be regarded as a low-brow writer – see Anabasis 1.
2   I refer mainly to the current scholarly debate about whether the tense system has any time significance at all, or is purely aspectual. See Porter, 1989, for the definitive treatment. Porter, 1992, Chapters 1 and 21 provide a simplified distillation of the same area. Fanning, written contemporaneously with Porter rather than in response to him, provides a contrary view. At issue is whether the tense system has any time-related significance at all, in addition to its aspect-related significance. For Porter, rather than indicating time values, the tense forms only grammaticalize 'the author/ speaker's reasoned subjective choice of conception of a process.' (1989, p.1.) Thus the aorist grammaticalizes the 'perfective aspect' in which an action is conceived as undifferentiated and complete; the present (and imperfect) grammaticalize the 'imperfective aspect', in which an action is conceived as being in progress or unfolding; and the perfect (and imperfect) grammaticalizes the 'stative' aspect, in which the action is conceived as reflecting a given (often complex) state of affairs. This is in contrast to more traditional grammars, which assume that the tense forms are used to grammaticalize objective time, or the *objective nature* of an action in time (*Aktionsart*). It is Porter's contention that, on the contrary, time is usually shown in Greek by deictic indicators, leaving the morphological tense system free to do other work. Porter's proposals, whilst solving some problems, create others – Why, for example, is there such a thing as the Greek Imperfect, if it does not have any time significance? According to Porter, its aspectual significance is the same as the Present, and therefore there seems no reason for a language user to choose between the two. This is a fundamental flaw in the theory, from the perspective of structural linguistics. The other main problem is the unresolved status of the Future, which Porter cannot decisively place as either a tense or a mood. If Porter's views do gain credibility, they raise interesting translation issues. However, the present work takes the view that any attempt to discuss these here would be premature.
3   See for example, Wallace, Comrie, Robertson, Goodwin, Porter.

Within our sample text (Luke 1-2), it can be seen that the aorist is the most common tense form, followed by the imperfect, and then the future (all of which occurs in the prophetic announcements made by the angel and inspired human characters). The present is relatively much less common, and is dominated by participles used periphrastically to form other tenses. The perfect is rarer still, and contributes only a handful of participles and finite verbs in the whole text.

One of the findings of relevance theory which we discussed in Chapter 1, is that processing cost varies inversely with frequency of use: if a form is used only rarely, it will be more difficult for a hearer/reader to process, and accordingly will have more prominence in the text.

Thus, in a pericope such as that telling the story of Mary's visit to Elizabeth (Luke 1.39-56), the entire narrative (as well as most of the dialogue) is carried by aorists: 30 in all, including participles, tending to support the idea of the aorist as the 'background' or 'default' tense. There are 4 Present forms (three of which are participles, and only one indicative: μεγαλύνει, at the beginning of Mary's song). The perfect occurs three times, interestingly only on the lips of Elizabeth, in the form of the perfect participles εὐλογημένος, εὐλογημένη, λελαλημένοις. This pattern of distribution may be interpreted, independently of any semantic content, as establishing planes of discourse within this text: the present and perfect forms serve to highlight those parts of the text, and as such constitute a communicative clue which a direct translation will seek to recognise.

The second feature often mentioned by grammarians is morphological bulk or markedness. The evidence is complicated in this area, but it is observable that in many cases, morphology displays the same dynamic as distribution. For example, for the verb ἀναβαίνω ('I go up', used in Luke 3.42) we may observe how the aorist ἀνέβην is (even with the incorporation of the augment) the least marked form, and the perfect ἀναβέβηκα the most marked, with the present falling somewhere in between. It is common for present stems to show additional marking, when compared with the root: the addition of ι or ισκ, reduplication (in the case of μι verbs), and so on. Reduplication in the perfect tends to add further to bulk. The correlation is far from universal or straightforward, and in part depends on the interpretation of the augment, which some scholars see as originating in an adverbial particle. However, it can add to a sense of different levels of prominence – we noted, for example, in Chapter Three, that part of the way Luke's Preface achieves relevance is through the use of two rather grand heptasyllabic perfect participles: πεπληροφορημένων and παρηκολουθηκότι, which contrast with the 7 aorists and particularly with the morphologically modest aorist ἔδοξε ('it seemed') about which the whole structure pivots.

Thirdly, the tenses can be thought of as conveying semantic clues based on their *aspect*. Porter proposes three aspects: the perfective (encompassing the Aorist); the imperfective (the present and imperfect) and the stative (the perfect and pluperfect).[1] The aorist is often thought of as the least marked way of describing something – it simply asserts that an action took place, and (as the name implies) does not attempt to delineate, define or describe it more closely. The present (and imperfect), on the other hand, describes an action from within the occurrence, as an unfolding event, and is frequently thought of as a more vivid, lively mode of description. Finally the perfect (and pluperfect) seeks to describe the action as an accomplished, often complex, state of affairs, and is sometimes thought of as being the most encompassing.[2]

The precise delineation of these features, and their full import, are of course matters for discussion amongst grammarians: however, that there are distributive, morphological and semantic differences amongst the tenses, and that these can serve to establish planes of discourse in a text is well established. In the terminology of relevance theory, the existence and interaction of different tense forms in a text can provide important communicative clues as to how that text is intended to achieve relevance. We have considered several examples of this, but let us glance at one or two more which will be helpful when considering the question of how this has been dealt with in translation.

Luke 2.39-52 presents an interesting case study in the establishment of planes of discourse. The three aspects are clearly present in the form of the aorist (21 times), the present and imperfect (together, 20 times) and the perfect (once).[3] The aorists carry the basics of the story – it happened, they finished the days of the feast, they turned back home, Jesus stayed behind, the parents didn't know . . . and so on. The Imperfects and the presents – together, the imperfective aspect – perform two slightly different functions. The first one is to provide the principal narration with a certain pictorial quality – they were going up to Jerusalem, the parents were looking for him in the caravan, they were looking for him in Jerusalem . . . Jesus was sitting with the teachers, he was asking questions, everyone was expressing surprise . . . and so on. In addition, though, the imperfective establishes the iterative context

---

1   Porter, 1992, p.21.

2   Wallace, 1996, p.500.

3   This arithmetic excludes the three cases of εἰμι, which I agree with Porter are 'aspectually vague' – in brief, although they are morphologically present and imperfect tenses, they cannot be regarded as having aspect, because, there being no 'stative' or 'perfective' forms, the verb system does not present the language-user with a choice.

of the story – this was something the family did every year, and it took place in the context of Jesus' growing up (ηὔξανεν), gaining strength (ἐκραταιοῦτο), being filled with wisdom (πληρούμενον σοφία), being guided by his parents (ἦν ὑποτασσόμενος αὐτοῖς) and (again in v52) forging ahead in wisdom (προέκοπτεν [ἐν τῇ] σοφία). All of these are expressed in imperfective forms, in verses 40 and 51/52, as the top and tail of the story. Finally, the only instance of the stative aspect (ἤδειτε – the pluperfect of οἶδα. 'I know') occurs at the climax of the story and in the mouth of Jesus – who addresses his parents using only stative and imperfective aspect – Τί ὅτι ἐζητεῖτέ με; οὐκ ἤδειτε ὅτι ἐν τοῖς τοῦ πατρός μου δεῖ εἶναί με; (Why were you looking for me thus? Didn't you know I had to be amongst my father's?') This story, then, seems to clearly establish three planes of discourse, in which the basic narrative forms the background, the actions and reactions of the participants are the foreground, and Jesus' words are the frontground.

How might this be dealt with in translation? If we look first at Tyndale and the KJV, we will be struck by the fact that the Holy Marriage, if not quite 'tense-blind' is quite relaxed about how it translates tense. The passage we have been considering appears as follows:

And the child grew, and waxed strong in spirit, filled with wisdom: and the grace of God was upon him. Now his parents went to Jerusalem every year at the feast of the Passover. And when he was twelve years old, they went up to Jerusalem after the custom of the feast. And when they had fulfilled the days, as they returned, the child Jesus tarried behind in Jerusalem; and Joseph and his mother knew not of it. But they, supposing him to have been in the company, went a day's journey; and they sought him among their kinsfolk and acquaintance And when they found him not, they turned back again to Jerusalem, seeking him And it came to pass, that after three days they found him in the temple, sitting in the midst of the doctors, both hearing them, and asking them questions And all that heard him were astonished at his understanding and answers. And when they saw him, they were amazed: and his mother said unto him, Son, why hast thou thus dealt with us? behold, thy father and I have sought thee sorrowing. And he said unto them, How is it that ye sought me? wist ye not that I must be about my Father's business? And they understood not the saying which he spake unto them And he went down with them, and came to Nazareth, and was subject unto them: but his mother kept all these sayings in her heart And Jesus increased in wisdom and stature, and in favour with God and man.

Luke 2.40-52, KJV

In the KJV, then, there is no distinguishing between the imperfect and the aorist, indicative verbs of both types being translated with the English simple past, except for verse 48b, where the imperfect is translated by an English perfect. The Greek pluperfect ἤδειτε is rendered by 'wist', which can serve as either the past tense or the past participle of the archaic verb 'wit', but in this case must be (because of the absence of an auxiliary 'have' or 'is') the simple past. What is lost in the KJV of this passage is not the semantic clues, which are probably well enough indicated, but the clues from relative prominence, or planes of discourse. Now if it is true, as Longacre waggishly pointed out, that 'Discourse without prominence would be like pointing to a piece of black cardboard and insisting that it was a picture of black camels crossing black sands at midnight',[1] that loss is severe. It is also a loss which has been faithfully transcribed to the successors of the holy marriage translation, so that the NIV, for example, appears as follows:

> *And the child grew and became strong; he was filled with wisdom, and the grace of God was upon him. Every year his parents went to Jerusalem for the Feast of the Passover. When he was twelve years old, they went up to the Feast, according to the custom. After the Feast was over, while his parents were returning home, the boy Jesus stayed behind in Jerusalem, but they were unaware of it. Thinking he was in their company, they travelled on for a day. Then they began looking for him among their relatives and friends When they did not find him, they went back to Jerusalem to look for him. After three days they found him in the temple courts, sitting among the teachers, listening to them and asking them questions Everyone who heard him was amazed at his understanding and his answers. When his parents saw him, they were astonished. His mother said to him, Son, why have you treated us like this? Your father and I have been anxiously searching for you. Why were you searching for me? he asked. Didn't you know I had to be in my Father's house? But they did not understand what he was saying to them. Then he went down to Nazareth with them and was obedient to them. But his mother treasured all these things in her heart. And Jesus grew in wisdom and stature, and in favour with God and men.*

> Luke 2.39-52, NIV

What was understandable as a translation performed in the 17th Century with limited resources and linguistic know-how, is ridiculous when reproduced in the late 20th Century, particularly when the planes

1   Longacre, 1985, cited in Porter 1992, p.302.

of discourse can, as in this case, be saved at very little cost to the reader. Gaus' *Unvarnished New Testament* manages to conserve the clues from prominence rather well, at least in the main body of the story,[1] and he does so without straining English grammar or wearying the reader with unfamiliar forms:

> And his parents used to make an annual trip to Jerusalem for the feast of Passover. And when he was twelve, after they came up as usual and finished out the day, as the rest of them were going back, the boy Jesus stayed behind in Jerusalem, and his parents didn't know that. Thinking he was somewhere in the caravan they went several days' journey and kept looking for him among their relatives and family friends . . .
>
> Luke 2.41-44, The Unvarnished New Testament

What of a case where the use of aspect is much less clear? Consider the use of the imperfective λέγω and the perfective in the account of John the Baptist's harangue in Luke 3.7-14:

> Ἔλεγεν οὖν τοῖς ἐκπορευομένοις ὄχλοις βαπτισθῆναι ὑπ' αὐτοῦ, Γεννήματα ἐχιδνῶν, τίς ὑπέδειξεν ὑμῖν φυγεῖν ἀπὸ τῆς μελλούσης ὀργῆς; 8 ποιήσατε οὖν καρποὺς ἀξίους τῆς μετανοίας· καὶ μὴ ἄρξησθε λέγειν ἐν ἑαυτοῖς, Πατέρα ἔχομεν τὸν Ἀβραάμ, λέγω γὰρ ὑμῖν ὅτι δύναται ὁ θεὸς ἐκ τῶν λίθων τούτων ἐγεῖραι τέκνα τῷ Ἀβραάμ. 9 ἤδη δὲ καὶ ἡ ἀξίνη πρὸς τὴν ῥίζαν τῶν δένδρων κεῖται· πᾶν οὖν δένδρον μὴ ποιοῦν καρπὸν καλὸν ἐκκόπτεται καὶ εἰς πῦρ βάλλεται. 10 Καὶ ἐπηρώτων αὐτὸν οἱ ὄχλοι λέγοντες, Τί οὖν ποιήσωμεν; 11 ἀποκριθεὶς δὲ ἔλεγεν αὐτοῖς, Ὁ ἔχων δύο χιτῶνας μεταδότω τῷ μὴ ἔχοντι, καὶ ὁ ἔχων βρώματα ὁμοίως ποιείτω. 12 ἦλθον δὲ καὶ τελῶναι βαπτισθῆναι καὶ πρὸς αὐτόν, Διδάσκαλε, τί ποιήσωμεν; 13 ὁ δὲ πρὸς αὐτούς, Μηδὲν πλέον παρὰ τὸ διατεταγμένον ὑμῖν πράσσετε. 14 ἐπηρώτων δὲ αὐτὸν καὶ στρατευόμενοι λέγοντες, Τί ποιήσωμεν καὶ ἡμεῖς; καὶ αὐτοῖς, Μηδένα διασείσητε μηδὲ συκοφαντήσητε, καὶ ἀρκεῖσθε τοῖς ὀψωνίοις ὑμῶν. Προσδοκῶντος δὲ τοῦ λαοῦ καὶ διαλογιζομένων πάντων ἐν ταῖς καρδίαις αὐτῶν περὶ τοῦ Ἰωάννου, μήποτε αὐτὸς εἴη ὁ Χριστός, 16 ἀπεκρίνατο λέγων πᾶσιν ὁ Ἰωάννης, Ἐγὼ μὲν ὕδατι βαπτίζω ὑμᾶς· ἔρχεται δὲ ὁ ἰσχυρότερός μου, οὗ οὐκ εἰμὶ ἱκανὸς λῦσαι τὸν ἱμάντα τῶν ὑποδημάτων αὐτοῦ·

---

1 The 'frame' imperfectives are somewhat more difficult, as a glance at the Experimental Translation will confirm.

The verb is used seven times in the Present and Imperfect (Porter's 'imperfective aspect'),[1] and three times in the aorist ('perfective aspect'). In the indicative, it is used twice in the imperfect, twice in the aorist (and once in the present, in the mouth of John). It is hard to discern any pattern in terms of the semantic clues: clearly all the actions take place in the 'past' established by the narrator (and this is quite elaborately done with all the historical information in Luke 3.1-2); moreover the kind of action seems very similar. The questions from the crowd are introduced sometimes with the present/imperfect, and sometimes with the aorist; and John's answers are sometimes introduced with the aorist and sometimes with present/imperfect, with no correlation, either, between the tense introducing the question and the tense introducing the answer.

The ἱερὸς γάμος and its successors have, as we saw in our previous example, taken a relaxed view of the different tense forms, freely interchanging between English tense-forms, depending on what feels like natural English in each case.[2] Tyndale's account of John the Baptist's preaching makes no differentiation between the Aorist and the Imperfect, for example:

> Then sayde he to the people that were come . . . And begyn not to say to yourselves . . . For I say unto you . . . And the people asked him, saying . . . He answered and sayde . . . Then came there publicans to be baptised, and sayde unto him . . .
>
>   From Luke 3.7-14, Tyndale 1526

The KJV continued this approach, and the RSV and NRSV, the NIV and NKJV have followed. There is even a recognised grammatical category for this kind of phenomenon, so that Wallace talks of 'the Instantaneous Imperfect (aka Aoristic or Punctiliar Imperfect)', commenting that 'this usage is virtually restricted to ἔλεγεν in narrative literature.'[3] Interestingly, Wallace does not have an 'Imperfective Aorist' to match this, perhaps on the logic that the less marked aorist is more likely to accommodate the Imperfect than vice-versa. Although he gives a number of examples, there is only an explanation offered for

---

1   To be precise: three times as a present participle, once as a present infinitive, once as a present indicative, twice in the imperfect indicative.

2   These comments apply particularly to the 'past tenses' – in English, the simple past, the past continuous and the past perfect. In general, the future tense has been reproduced more rigorously. In some passages, the KJV may have been influenced by a desire to harmonise tense forms with synoptic parallels.

3   Wallace, 1996, p.542.

one of them – Luke 23.42, where 'the imperfect is used to introduce a vivid, emotionally-charged statement. As such it may be called a *dramatic* imperfect.'[1] This seems a very unlikely explanation for the two instances of ἔλεγεν in our passage above, and the rule itself appears to be a case of believing that one has solved a problem by giving it a label.[2]

In fact it *is* possible to see a pattern in the sample text above. The pattern is quite simple: it begins with 5 uses of λέγω in its imperfective aspect (three of which are part of the narrative content, introducing speech), and only then does it allow some alternation with aorists (perfective aspect), before its final reversion to imperfective aspect in verse 16. This is reinforced at the end of the co-text, by summarising John's teaching using the imperfective εὐηγγελίζετο ('he was telling the good news'). Luke is laying down communicative clues but he does not want to weary us by their laboured repetition: once he has set the scene as one which is to be understood from the imperfective aspect – as if we were there, in the action, hearing John's repeated challenges – he can safely revert to using some less marked, aorist verb forms. The passage reverts to imperfective aspect as it closes, to make sure that we have not forgotten this. It is also reasonable to assume that this formed an important part of the overall relevance of this pericope – it is quite important to Luke to establish that, until Herod put paid to him, John presented a continuing, repeated prophetic challenge to the people, but one which also repeatedly denied that he was the Messiah: ἀπεκρίνατο λέγων πᾶσιν ὁ Ἰωάννης, Ἐγὼ μὲν ὕδατι βαπτίζω ὑμᾶς· ἔρχεται δὲ ὁ ἰσχυρότερός μου ... Πολλὰ μὲν οὖν καὶ ἕτερα παρακαλῶν εὐηγγελίζετο τὸν λαόν ('John again responded, saying 'I wash you with blood – one stronger than me is coming . . . ' With much like this and different encouraging them, telling the people the good news' (Luke 3. 16-18). We should note, in passing, that this is a somewhat different usage from the converse case: suppose Luke had started the passage with 5 aorists, and then had 3 imperfects, before reverting to the aorist. In such a case, we would interpret the passage quite differently, by seeking to understand why the text foregrounds the 3 words in its central part.

---

1 Ibid.
2 One suspects that this is a not infrequent practice. What are the multitude of labels (the epistolary Aorist, the Gnomic Present, the Proleptic Perfect and so on) other than just that – names for unsolved puzzles? It would be an interesting study, to examine the question of whether and to what extent grammatical categories are invented in the service of the ἱερὸς γάμος· the grammatical analysis then becomes part of the apparatus of justification for the holy marriage translation.

In translation, it seems to me that contemporary English is not completely lacking in resources to represent clues based on planes of discourse, even picking up some of the semantics of aspect. We saw, above, how Gaus used forms of the Past Continuous in English ('used to . . .', 'kept . . .') to establish an imperfective aspectual flavour. Nicholas King renders the Greek 'historic Present' in Mark with his own modern 'historic Present' in English.[1] The NASB attempts to represent the different tense forms, and whilst this sometimes results in a clumsy English text, it at least indicates that something is possible here.

The same sort of thing can be done in the Present tense, by using Continuous Present forms – 'I'm saying to you . . . ' rather than 'I say to you . . . ' In using this, the translator will do well to observe and imitate Luke's own practice, as just discussed, of not wearying the reader by undue repetition of certain word forms – there is a particular danger in English with '-ing' forms, especially if they are frequently used to translate participles as well. Once aspectual framework has been established, the clue is present in the target language text, and need not be slavishly repeated.

The perfect represents particular difficulties. A modern English perfect does show some resemblances to a Greek one – its reference to past time and continuing present significance, and its morphological bulk, for example (compare 'I have eaten' and 'I ate'). However, its stylistic value, distribution, and aspectual nuances are different, so that it is not always a good, or sufficient, way to represent the communicative clue which is provided by its presence in a Greek text, for example by establishing different planes of discourse. To do this, some special efforts may be required, and in the Experimental Translation I have sought to do this by simple repetition: where a Greek Perfect seems to provide a communicative clue based on prominence, I have duplicated the verb in the English translation. This has the effect of foregrounding that particular word without offending against acceptable English style.[2]

---

1   Interestingly, he does so for Mark, and in places for John, but not for Luke where 'the effect is different'. (King, 2004, p.9). This seeming inconsistency is completely acceptable in terms of a relevance theoretical approach, and may be taken as an illustration of the impossibility of establishing universal rules. King does not use the language of relevance theory, but his intuitions are consistent with it: although there may be a good case that the use of the 'historic present' is a communicative clue which is *prima facie* worth preserving, there may also be many other clues in play, and these may result in a different translation decision in each case.

2   The reader will, of course, judge. I take refuge in the precedent of Paul Celan's translations from Shakespeare, which make extraordinary use of

Uses and abuses of communicative clues

The idea of communicative clues has provided us with a useful check-list of things to look for when we are pursuing what I have called the hermeneutic question: how does this passage achieve relevance? However, as Gutt is careful to tell us, the concept of 'direct translation' of which communicative clues forms a part is only a step on the road towards a final unified theory of translation, not that theory itself.[1] In the final theory, the only arbiter of a translation is interpretive resemblance, driven by the assumption of relevance itself: there is no question of mechanically reproducing communicative clues. The reason it is important to emphasise this, is that it is easy to begin to reify the communicative clues, and to revert to the habit of mind whereby we believe that the task of the translator is to reproduce 'equivalent' clues in the target language texts. No: the task of the translator is to identify the communicative clues in the source text; then to form the relevant interpretation; then to produce a new text whose interpretation in the same context resembles that of the source. In doing so, the translator will of course use her or his *own* communicative clues, which may or may not be the same as those used by the original communicator. So, for example, a phonological/graphological clue in the original may be 'represented' by onomatopoeia, or by some other clue entirely; or a clue from tense morphology might be represented by repetition. In Buber and Rosenzweig's translation of the Hebrew scriptures, the clue from the 'natural punctuation' represented by breathing, is 'represented' not by any oral quality, but by the appearance of the German text on the page. In Chapter Three, we argued for the clues arising from the peculiar syntax of Luke's preface to be 'represented' by a shape-poem. To say that any of these clues are 'equivalent' to another carries no meaning within relevance theory.

It is also important to note that arbitration between clues can only be undertaken using the test of relevance itself: the clues cannot be arranged in a hierarchy, but must always be weighed by the translator in terms of their contribution to how the text achieves relevance. An example may be given from the remarks I made above about how

---

'free repetition', and from Steiner's statement that 'Repetition is the purest concentrate of translation. . . In a manner which entirely negates paraphrase it expresses the hermeneutic of compensation, the ways in which a true translation restores to the original . . . what was its own. . . . There could be no denser statement of reciprocity at close quarters.' (Steiner, 1998, pp.410-411)

1   Gutt, 2000, pp.170-171.

the Greek perfect, by virtue of its 'prominence' contributes to the establishment of planes of discourse. I made the suggestion that this clue may be represented in the English translation by use of repetition. There are many places in the Experimental Translation where this technique has been used, because it was felt that prominence was an important clue to relevance, and the repetitions appropriately provided a similar clue. Equally, though, there are places where a Perfect tense form has been used in the Greek, but it does not seem to be performing this role. Examples include some cases of perfect participles, where the word seems to have been chosen purely for the semantic clue it provides, where word choice has perhaps been constrained, or where the contribution to relevance seems to arise from a formulaic expression. Thus, for example προβεβηκυῖα ('well advanced in age') in Luke 2.36 could be interpreted as a formulaic expression; a translator may in this case not to re-duplicate the verb in English, notwithstanding that it is a clear case of the Perfect. (The Experimental Translation does re-duplicate it – partly because one of its objectives is to see how far the idea of 'direct translation' can be pushed.)

The other danger to be aware of, we have already mentioned: Gutt's list is not to be thought of as definitive. Nor, of course, is my own. I have suggested some additional areas to look for communicative clues, areas which are likely to be overlooked because the ἱερὸς γάμος, the Holy Marriage, did not know about them or did not take them seriously. However, there could be many more. The physical medium or appearance of a text is one: most authors take a keen interest in the physical 'accidentals' of their work – the typography, illustration, binding and so on, and this is of acknowledged importance in Bible translation.[1] The reasons for this interest are not narrowly aesthetic: they include a recognition that how a text will be interpreted will, in part, be determined by its physical appearance.[2] What is the relevance of a text being written on a copper scroll, for example, and how could this be represented in translation?[3] Another

---

1   As can be seen from the many 'Youth' Bibles, for example, which often only differ from their 'parent' (pun intended) by virtue of different 'accidentals'.

2   Nida mentions an interesting example. The book of Amos was published in Buenos Aires during a time of political unrest, and its student publishers 'wanted the text to be mimeographed on very poor paper and with the kind of smudges characteristic of revolutionary propoganda' (Nida, 1981, p.7). The text thus published had quite a different communicative effect.

3   The 'copper scroll' 3Q15 found at Qumran – perhaps an understanding of this might even lead to finding the treasure which seems to form its subject-matter!

interesting area is the question of omissions: not only what is in the text, but what is not in the text, may constitute a communicative clue. Consider the following:

> Enfettered, these sentences repress free speech. The text deletes selected letters. We see the revered exegete reject metred verse: the sestet, the tercet – even *les scènes élevées en grec.* He rebels. He sets new precedents. He lets cleverness exceed decent levels. He eschews the esteemed genres, the expected themes . . . [1]

Any translator who ignored the communicative clue provided by the vocalisation of this text would be doomed to missing their relevance.

There is a final communicative clue, though, which we cannot ignore in the present work. This is the clue provided by repetitive texture.[2] It is a major topic, and will be the subject of the next chapter.

---

1 Christian Bök, 2001, p.31.
2 ἀγραυλέω is here interpreted as making the ἀγρός one's αὐλή. See Marshall 1978, p.108.

Chapter Six

Repetitive texture and four kinds of literalism

We ended the last chapter with the potentially disruptive finding that *any* feature of a text may be a communicative clue, and may indeed turn out to be the most important clue to how a given text achieves relevance for a particular reader. As we have seen repeatedly, there is a long-standing practice in biblical translation of attending to only some of the clues to relevance, and this arises because the translator's mind is clouded by the idea of 'equivalence'. Because she or he thinks that her task is to produce a target text which is somehow equivalent (however that is defined) to a source, when the translator comes across a text feature for which there is no equivalent in the target language, there is a problem. This problem is often dealt with by accepting that this is regrettably but unavoidably part of what is lost in translation; so that even when the translator has an acute understanding of the relevant clue, it does not appear to influence the progress of the work. In the translation of Luke's Preface for example, as we saw in Chapter Three, the symmetry of the piece and its allusive, underdetermined logic, were recognised by all of our translator-commentators, but not represented in their translations.

There is, however, one feature of a text which is always present, and which is so thoroughly implicated in the very idea of a text, that it is easy to overlook it. This feature is the topic of the present chapter, and it is dealt with here because, although conceptually it belongs comfortably within the area of communicative clues itself, it raises a number of puzzling issues which require their own chapter if they are to be dealt with adequately. It is also a neglected topic, almost a non-topic, within the literature, for reasons we will presently examine.

Repetitive texture

The topic in view is repetitive texture, a term which Robbins introduced as part of his conception of the inner texture of a text. 'Repetitive texture resides in the occurrence of words and phrases more than once in a unit. When the same word occurs at least twice in a text, the result is repetition . . . . Repetition does not . . . exhibit inner meanings in the sequences. But repetitive texture introduces interpreters to the overall forest, if you will, so they know where they are as they look at individual trees . . . an overarching view of the texture of the language that invites the interpreter to move yet closer to the details of the text.' In the present chapter, I propose (and taking the clues from Robbins' term) to consider text as tapestry. Repetitive texture is the pattern of the tapestry considered overall, and is formed by threads of different colour, which are constituted by the repetitions of certain words, phrases, or larger textual units.

Gutt's second communicative clue – syntax – embraces the notion of repetition as a clue to relevance, in so far as it can be observed at small scale, through the microscope as it were. The idea of repetitive texture is related to this, but it operates at any level of a text. It also operates outside the boundaries of any given text, in the form of intertextuality, and it is this 'iterability' of words which allow us to talk of their having 'meaning' at all. The notion of a text which does *not* use words under iterability in this sense, is an impossible one: words can only be said to be signs insofar as they can be repeated.

Many of the communicative clues we have already examined rely for their effect on repetition. For example, we decided that the phrase καὶ ἐ γένετο ('and it came to pass' – Luke's rendering of the Hebrew waw-consecutive) achieves relevance in the text by virtue of its stylistic marking, indicating Septuagintal style. There are, as we saw, good grounds for this, but they all rely on the repetition of the phrase: if it had occurred as a *hapax legomenon*, we would have been just as likely to seek the relevant interpretation elsewhere. The same applies to communicative clues arising from syntax, and even from phonological qualities.

For Robbins, the main interest in noticing the inner texture of a text is to see how it establishes and develops its theme, or topic. Although he provides good examples of this from Mark's gospel, it is also possible to see that repetitive texture can be a rather poor, or at least not straightforward, guide to the 'theme' of a text. For example, the topic of Luke Chapters 1 and 2 is not καί ('and' – which appears 181 times) but something else – perhaps the birth and infancy of Ἰωάννης ('John' – occurring 3 times) and Ἰησοῦς ('Jesus' – 5 times). The theme of a text cannot be read off from its repetitive texture in a straightforward way, and Robbins uses a number of other kinds of 'texture' to support it, including *narrational texture, argumentative texture*, and several other categories which need not detain us for the purposes of the present argument.

The 'theme' of a text is part of its most straightforward interpretation.

Another very obvious function of repetition is the establishment of coherence: a communicator's consistent use of certain words through the course of a document is what, after all, holds it together as a coherent story, or argument, or description as the case may be. Names, for example, are only effective if they are repeated consistently. We know that *Luke* is about Ἰησοῦς because his name is repeated consistently throughout. We also know that Luke's Jesus, when he spoke to people, talked again and again about the Βασιλεία, ('the kingdom') because he consistently repeated this word (more than 40 times, in Luke). However, repetitive texture becomes very important indeed, in many kinds of textual interpretation which move beyond the straightforward noticing of 'the plain sense'. For example, in Chapter Two, we discussed the relevant interpretation of the story known as *The Boy Jesus in the Temple* (Luke 2. 41 to 52), observing that the relevant interpretation could be formed at at least three levels of attention: first, as a straightforward Hellenistic 'hero' story showing Jesus' piety, precocity and perspicacity; second as a prefiguring of his death and resurrection; and third as a foreshadowing of the uneasy relationship between the developing early Christian church and its roots in the Jewish Temple in Jerusalem. Each of these is a 'relevant interpretation' – that is, falling on or within the area prescribed by the relevance curve. However, the latter two interpretations are formed only at increased levels of reader attention. The interpretations formed at these levels of attention rely, in turn, on features of the inner texture of Luke-Acts – firstly in terms of what Robbins calls *narrational texture*, but also in terms of verbal *repetitive texture*. The former is, of course, to some degree built from the latter; only by iterating certain words can a narrative be constructed. However, even independently of their role in narrative construction, it is clear that the iteration of certain words is one of the textual features which permits and invites such interpretation. Luke repeatedly, throughout the gospel, uses the word ὑποστρέφω, for example, to describe the 'turning back' of Jesus and his disciples between Jerusalem and other places; Luke's uses of the word are particularly noticeable, because it is not used elsewhere in the canonical gospels, and in fact has only 3 non-Lukan instances in the New Testament. In Luke-Acts, the word is very often used for a movement towards or occasionally from Jerusalem after a significant event. It is the word used after the crucifixion (Luke 23.65), after the empty tomb (Luke 24.9), after the Emmaus experience (Luke 24.33), after the resurrection appearance, and after the ascension (Acts 1.12), and six times in Acts for followers' movements to and from Jerusalem. Its first two appearances are in the story of The Boy Jesus in the Temple.

Now, Luke's use of the verb ὑποστρέφω is not generally cited by commentators as being particularly marked: like other words appearing in the passage – Ἰερουσαλήμ ('Jerusalem') and ἱερόν ('temple'), for example – it appears there perhaps simply as part of the narrative building process. In the absence of compelling evidence to the contrary, we will simply note that it is a word of which *Luke* is particularly fond, or that it is habituated to using it. Perhaps we might go so far as to say that it seems to be especially prone to use it in connection with Jerusalem – perhaps there are subconscious factors at work, such as being conditioned by a certain text (now unknown – certainly not Mark or 'Q') which used it in this way. In citing its repetition, I am advancing no claim for it to be treated otherwise, but what I *am* hoping to convey, is that its presence *objectively* forms part of the repetitive texture of Luke-Acts. If Luke-Acts was a tapestry, the verb ὑποστρέφω would be a certain thread of colour which was objectively present. Whether a given interpreter of the tapestry notices it, and what use (s)he makes of it to form contextual implications, is part of that reader's subjectivity. However, it is the presence of this thread which permits a particular interpreter (in this case, me) to form a relevant interpretation higher up the relevance curve. It thus forms part of this reader's motivation for reading *attentively*, as we defined it in Chapter Two; if it was not present, both the motivation for, and the reward for, an attentive reading would diminish, and this part of the relevance curve would become inaccessible. These remarks are equally applicable, whatever *kind* of attentive reading is in mind, and would apply just as much to a *deconstructive* reading, for example, as to a traditional close academic reading, or even a 'holy reading' practice such as *lectio divina*.

Exactly the same could be said of the words Ἰερουσαλὴμ or ἱερόν, or εὑρίσκω ('I find'), or any other word which appears in the text. Every word used in the text objectively forms part of its repetitive texture, and is therefore potentially a communicative clue – its iteration through the text forms a 'strand of colour' in the overall tapestry, which the reader's subjectivity then uses to form relevant interpretations.

Repetitive texture in translation

It is in this feature that there can be a significant problem in translation, and it goes to the heart of the translation problem. Gutt, in fact, defines translation as 'inter-lingual quotation', and in what he calls 'direct quotation', the secondary communicator attempts 'the preservation of all linguistic qualities'. As we saw in Chapter Three, there is a strong tradition in translation where the translator longs to simply quote his source text: to stand aside from the role of interpreter and 'let the text speak for itself'. We have also seen, however, that this is an impossible dream: the text can only be mediated, in a secondary situation, by interpretation. The phenomenon of repetitive texture presents this problem in particularly acute form. It seems to mean that the reiteration of *every* word used in a text represents a communicative clue. The effect, for a translator, is almost maddening: here, after all, is one of the very few features of a source text which is objectively present: the words of a text, arranged in a certain pattern, are the only thing which we can be certain is present: all else is a matter (to a lesser or greater extent) of interpretation, of what we have named 'reader subjectivity'. How is it, then, that even this, phenomenologically incontrovertible feature eludes us? In each case, the use of a particular word gestures in some way towards every *other* use in the same text; it also gestures towards every word which is *not* used in the same position: words which were rejected, for whatever reason. The repetitive texture in a text is a rich source of contextual implications, and if it is lost or distorted, there will be very significant loss for any reader who wishes to read it attentively.

Concordance: a non-topic?

How a translator attempts to preserve repetitive texture has, in certain translation traditions, been dealt with under the heading of 'concordance.' This attempts to measure to what degree a translation and a source text exhibit 'harmony', or are 'concordant' in the sense that a given word or expression in the source text is always translated by the same target language or expression. For example, in the NIV, the word θεός is always and without exception translated 'God', and this pair of words exhibit complete concordance. On the other hand, the word καί is translated variously as *and, though, but, also, even, besides, so*, and many more, and exhibits only partial concordance. This simple example illustrates a number of notable features of concordance: first, that complete concordance is not possible. A translation which is completely concordant with its source text is a variety of interlinear or gloss, and represents, as we saw in Chapter Three, the abdication of the translator from the communicative process. Second, concordance is to a degree a matter of pragmatics. The non-concordant translation of καί, in all English versions, arises more from its practical impossibility than from any theoretical or even theological considerations. Third, though, all translations exhibit *some* degree of concordance. This is because all translators have at least some notion of the importance of repetitive texture, in its functional roles as guardian of the coherence of a text, and as the facilitator of a variety of special effects. Coherence, as we saw, above, may be illustrated by the use of names or titles: the simple repetition of the name holds the narrative together. Rhetorical effects from repetition are particularly easy to see on a small scale. For example, consider this possible translation of Luke 6.20-22:

> *Blessed are you who are poor, for yours is the kingdom of God,*
> *Congratulations you hungry!*
> *You will have a feast.*
> *You who are crying now are in luck,*
> *Because you will laugh.*

Each of the three different renderings of μακάριοι as it appears in Luke, is legitimate. (In fact, the first is from the NIV, the second from *The Five Gospels*, and the third from TUNT.) But there is no translation of Luke's beatitudes which looks like this combination, and this kind of switching between renderings, in such close proximity, is in fact very unusual, because for most translators it violates their sense of the rhetorical effects involved. On a larger scale, though, there is much greater variation between different translation practices. For example, the NRSV renders μακάριος as 'blessed' in Luke 1.45, and as 'fortunate' in Acts 26.2. There is no doubt that an argument could be made for this, on relevance grounds: 'blessed' clearly sounded to the translators as a natural thing for Elisabeth to say, in the atmosphere of intense Jewish piety of the opening chapter of the gospel, but an unnatural thing for Paul to say in his defence speech before Agrippa. In the latter case, collocated with the other words of his defence, his use of the term perhaps achieved relevance differently. Nonetheless, something is lost here, and it is the thread of colour represented by the repetition of μακάριος through Luke-Acts: its use by Elisabeth, then in the beatitudes, in the parables, in Jesus' eschatological speeches, and finally in Paul's trials before the temporal power of Agrippa. When it is not translated concordantly, a certain set of possible contextual implications are lost, and although the loss in the case of an individual word may be almost imperceptibly small, when it is repeated across a large proportion of the word-stock in a given text, the loss becomes very palpable.

Because all texts have repetitive texture, the obverse case also applies, when a translation establishes a concordance which was not present in the source text. For example, the NRSV for Luke 1.42 to 45 reads:

> . . . exclaimed with a loud cry, 'Blessed are you among women, and
> blessed is the fruit of your womb. 43And why has this happened

to me that the mother of my Lord comes to me? ₄₄For as soon as
I heard the sound of your greeting, the child in my womb leapt
for joy. ₄₅And blessed is she who believed that there would be a
fulfilment of what was spoken to her by the Lord.

The first 'bless' is a translation of εὐλογημένη, the third is of μακαρία.
In the English NRSV, then, there is a thread of colour representing a
connection between Elisabeth's greeting of Mary, and her assessment
of Mary's state of mind, a thread which does not exist in the source
text. A coherence in Elisabeth's discourse is established, which was
absent from the original. Again, in the case of a single word, the effect
is perhaps not very noticeable, but when it is repeated, it can have a
significant effect on the relevant interpretation of the whole text.

    This brings us to the fourth universal feature of concordance, which
is that it always has an ideological component. The reason for this
will already be apparent. Because every word in the text (apart from
the occasional *hapax legomenon* – and even here, morphemes forming
part of the word are often iterated) represents part of a thread, and
therefore makes a contribution to the overall repetitive texture, and
because not all threads can be represented in the translated text, a
decision must be made as to which threads in the tapestry are relevant,
and which are going to be sacrificed. Although the threads themselves
are objectively present, it is not possible to determine which of them
to reproduce on objective grounds: we have seen, for example, that the
number of iterations is not a reliable guide. The implication of my
remarks about Βασιλεία ('kingdom') above, for example, is that this
word represents an important thread in the overall repetitive texture
of Luke, and one therefore which 'should' be translated concordantly.
This view (which I do hold) is shared by others, but certainly not by
all, including mainstream Bible translations – and I don't think I could
prove it, on any grounds.

Concordance and literalism

Proponents of 'literal' or 'essentially literal' biblical translation do
not invariably specify exactly what they mean by the term, but they
usually seem to be thinking of a translation practice which combines
two quite different features. The first is an overall *hermeneutic* style
in which the 'plain sense' of the text is thought of as being the only
concern of the interpreter/translator; the second is a *performance* style
in which communicative clues from repetitive texture are valued very
highly, such that if the target text is not entirely 'word-for-word' in
relation to the source text, then it is 'essentially' so. These two features

are such accustomed bed-fellows that it is easy to forget that each arises from different considerations, that there is no logical connection between them, and that indeed there is some tension between these two requirements. This tension, I will argue, tends to lead to something like Nida and Taber's early doctrine of 'dynamic equivalence', in which the first requirement to 'convey the meaning' is carefully balanced against the second 'to preserve back-translatability'. The relationship between literalism and concordance is thus not straightforward; and it is in fact more complicated even than this tension suggests, as we will shortly see.

I remarked earlier that concordance has become a 'non-topic' in translation studies. Partly, it has been displaced by the 'theory of semantic domains', in which the coherence of a text is underwritten not by a repetitive texture arising from *verbal* phenomena, but by one arising from *conceptual* repetition. It has also become almost taken for granted that a concern for verbal concordance is inextricably associated with a certain kind of epistemology which many would now seek to question, and that it leads to the etymological fallacies so ruthlessly exposed as long ago as 1961 by James Barr.

Four motivations for literalism

In order to show that this is not the case, we must unpick the arguments of the literalists, particularly as they relate to concordance, and identify four very different kinds of motivation for a literal (or 'essentially literal') approach to translation, producing four rather different kinds of literalism. The labels I give these types are just that – they are simply intended to identify a species; 'neo-Platonic literalism', for example, might just as well be called 'Patristic' or even (with Seidman) 'Christian' literalism, whilst 'neo-Cabbalistic' might be termed 'Rabbinic' and so on.

I talk here of 'motivations' for literalism, rather than 'arguments', because these considerations very rarely surface as explicit arguments for literal translation. Nonetheless, they can be shown clearly to underlie those arguments, and often show their faces in the form of the imagery or metaphors chosen by the theorist or commentator involved. It is helpful to unpick the strands of motivation, as only then are we able to consider which, if any, are after all important to us. This is especially so because of the intuitive, almost emotional appeal of literalism; if the motivations are left unexamined, it will remain 'obvious' to many that literalism is the most faithful kind of translation, just as it is obvious that 'free' translation is the most interpretive, and that apples fall downwards.

Neo-Platonic literalism

Sed quasi captives sensus in suam linguam victoris jure transposuit. In this famous image, Jerome talks of how the translator 'captures' the meaning of the text (or fails to do so) in his own tongue. What is at stake for the translator is the spiritual essence or soul of the source text – a certain reading of St Paul, in which πνεῦμα (spiritus) is opposed to γράμμα (littera) in much the same way as 'soul' relates to 'body'. The soul of the source text must be liberated from its literal body, and quickly recaptured in a new one, so that readers of the target language may apprehend it. This imagery, which remains to the present day an entirely natural way of looking at the matter, a way which is woven into the very fabric of our language, seems on the face of it to mandate great freedom in translation practice: the words we use are corruptible, ephemeral, whereas the spirit is incorruptible and eternal. What is important then, is surely the latter and not the former. As Jerome himself appreciated, though, the matter is not so straightforward as this. Complications begin to arise because the task of the translator is not only to 'capture the spirit' (the *penetration*, or conquest which Steiner talks about) but also to build it a suitable new home in the target language (Steiner's *incarnation*). The translator must build a *suitable* container for this valuable commodity, from the materials (words) available to him in the target language. Here the imagery modulates from the violence of expedition and conquest, to a more homely scene: the spirit is brought home. It is valuable, it must not be damaged, it must have a *suitable* home. Steiner (following Jerome) talks of capturing a slave girl and bringing her home; perhaps we may offend fewer readers by visualising the 'spirit' as Keats' brave young man, who must be enticed into a dwelling by *la belle dame sans merci*. His entry into her *elfin grot* represents in a way his 'capture' by her; yet it is clear that this is in some sense also willed by him. It is also clear that the dwelling is a comfortable, even a wonderful place, in which all his needs are met by the woman who draws him there (who, incidentally, in Keats' version of the story, 'speaks in language strange'). The spirit is secure, in both senses of the English word.

What metaphor of translation is being invoked, when we read the following, under the heading of 'Standards of Excellence in Translation'?

> *The best translation should be accurate, clear, natural and audience-appropriate. . . . By accurate we mean that the translation reflects the meaning of the original text as closely as possible . . . A second*

> *important criterion . . . is clarity. While a Bible translation should transport the reader to a different time and place, it should do so with language that is clear and understandable . . .*

The point of all this talk of 'reflection' and 'clarity' it seems, is that the text may act like a window on 'the meaning', so that it may be discerned 'accurately'. I would like to suggest that the relevant metaphor here is that of the dwelling constructed by the translator, to house and display 'the message' which is the soul of the source text. Choosing the right words to do so thus becomes very important – we must have clear windows, clean and polished, so that the reader of today can look through them, almost as if they weren't there, to see the λόγος ('logos', or 'word'), the transcendent signified within. *Dei Verbum*, for example, which remains one of the definitive Roman Catholic statements of Biblical Inspiration, puts it thus:

> *Those divinely revealed realities which are contained and presented in Sacred Scripture have been committed to writing under the inspiration of the Holy Spirit. . . . However, since God speaks in Sacred Scripture through men in human fashion, . . . the interpreter of Sacred Scripture, in order to see clearly what God wanted to communicate to us, should carefully investigate what meaning the sacred writers really intended, and what God wanted to manifest by means of their words.*

This seems on the face of it relatively clear: what is important is 'the divinely revealed *realities* which are *contained* and *presented* in Sacred Scripture' (my emphasis). The words, then, are mere windows on these 'realities'.

However, it is an easy step from here to the conclusion that we should be careful to arrange our windows so that the faithful reader can easily see through them, and perhaps even that there should be one for each important concept within. This imagery is even more apparent in the appeal to 'transparency' which is one of the commonplaces of essentially literal translation. Thus the Preface to the ESV says that it 'seeks to be transparent to the original text, letting the reader see as directly as possible the structure and meaning of the original', reminding us of Philo's claim of the Septuagint that 'our translators found the expressions exactly suitable to the things signified. And these were the only words possible, or at least the words most apt, to render the things signified with perfect clarity'. Interestingly, the ESV Preface explicitly links the desire to be transparent to the interest in word-for-word translation. The sentence immediately preceding the one just cited reads, 'The ESV is an "essentially literal" translation that seeks as far as possible to capture the precise wording of the original text . . . Its emphasis is on "word-for-word" correspondence.' For this apologist, then, transparency requires word-for-word correspondence. To see the spiritual content ('the message'), the windows need to be both clear and placed in exactly the right arrangement, corresponding to the arrangement of the windows in the 'housing' of the source text.

More prosaically, we might find ourselves speaking in terms of the imagery of commerce. As we saw in Chapter Two, this is a very common set of metaphors in Western discussion of translation: the message is a cargo, which must be transported/translated over a linguistic border. As every businessman knows, the packaging of a product is often just as important as the product itself, particularly where there are great distances to travel, or where the product is delicate; care should be taken that the packaging is appropriate to the product. This is, of course, how Jesus' parable of the wineskins (Luke 5.37-39) has often been interpreted: ignoring the enigmatic punch-line to the story has allowed many commentators to use it as a parable for 'the message and the medium'.

When Jerome speaks of sometimes making an exception, in scriptural translation, from his normal practice of translating 'sense for sense', he seems to have this sort of consideration in mind. He did not want to follow the word-for-word practice of Aquila, whereby readers would 'look at the surface instead of the real meat, and [be] put off by the unprepossessing clothing of its style rather than finding the beautiful body underneath', and yet he believed that in Scripture 'even the order of the words is of God's doing'. The inner conflict he experienced on this is symptomatic of an entire history of thinking about translation: the problem is that the underlying theory of meaning (and therefore also of translation) links signifiers to signified by apparently unbreakable chains: how important, then, are the words? Looked at one way, they are profoundly unimportant, yet looked at another way, the metaphysical link between a word and an idea may be strong enough to confound any attempt at freedom in translation.

Neither Jerome nor any other translator working with this model of meaning has ever resolved this problem, which remains as one of the puzzles with which theoreticians wrestle. It has produced a good deal of muddle and confusion in theorising about translation, but has not prevented its progress, perhaps because the muddle itself has allowed practitioners to develop a quite pragmatic and flexible literalism, which has proved serviceable over many centuries. The writers of the KJV preface were certainly conscious of the difficulty, and at the same time did not find themselves crippled by it. Nor, as we have seen, have been the many translators who have followed the holy marriage translation, who have juggled 'the spirit' and 'the letter' in a more or less principled fashion. To one particular group of literalists operating in this way, we will shortly turn. The greatest expression of neo-Platonic literalism in English, though, remains the Douai-Rheims Bible, particularly as revised by Bishop Challoner between 1749 and 1763. In it the ideal of using words as literal windows of crystalline clarity on the eternal verities within is beautifully realized.

Gametic literalism

As we have seen, there is a certain tendency within what we have labelled 'neo-Platonic literalism' to begin to reify the links between signifiers and signified, so that a word is thought of as 'meaning' some 'thing itself' (whether it be an 'idea' or an 'object' or however it is characterised), to which it is in some way linked. This in turn can lead to supposing that there can also be strong lines of 'equivalence' between two words in different languages which 'mean' the same 'thing':

All practising translators, as well as those who seriously reflect on the matter, know that the above diagram does not represent reality. It breeches at least three of the key insights which have allowed linguistics to make such strides in the century since Saussure.[1] First: words may be *used by* a language-user to refer to things (existent or non-existent) but they are not 'tied' to those things by invisible strings. Second: Within a language, it is the differences *between* words, which define how they may be used. Third: 'Each language has a distinctive way of segmenting experience by means of words',[2] so that they map reality differently: words cannot, then, be 'equivalent' to each other in any straightforward way. All this is known, and yet, as we saw in Chapter One, a thinker such as Grudem, when discussing biblical translation, proceeds as if it were not. The reason for this, as we saw there, is the overwhelming presence of the Holy Marriage translation of the Bible, which establishes a set of such 'equivalents' in the translator's mind – a series of correspondences which are so strong as to override any other consideration, so that one begins to think of the Greeks (for example) 'having a word for' the English 'heart'. From the pre-supposed equivalence between 'heart' and καρδία, an equivalence sanctified by the holy marriage KJV, it is even possible to project the existence of 'the idea' itself, so that the acid test for an innovative translation, for

---

1   Insights which can be attributed, respectively, to Frege (and Wittgenstein), to Saussure himself, and to Edward Sapir.
2   Nida and Taber, 1969, p.21.

Grudem, is the question: *'But is it the same idea?'*[1] It is from statements such as this that we might conclude that Grudem is a neo-Platonic literalist, who believes that words straightforwardly represent 'things' or 'ideas'. However, I believe this would be an unfair assessment – in fact, as we will shortly see, Grudem has other and better-founded motivations for his literalism, and his apparent endorsement of a long-defunct theory of meaning is only a side-effect of his commitment to what I propose to label Gametic literalism. That is, to a (conscious or unconscious) assumption that the KJV does represent a series of agreed 'correspondences' between source and translation texts, and establishes a set of tests which all subsequent translations must pass.

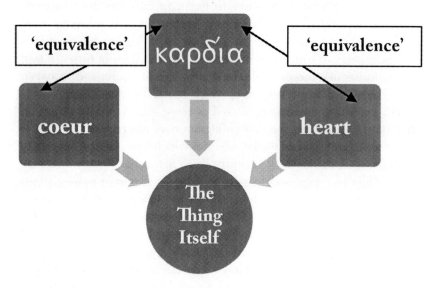

The fantasy of Gametic Literalism

Neo-Cabbalistic literalism

There is another kind of literalism whose motivation is rather different, and which can be shown to produce a different sort of 'word-for-word' correspondence. This is the strain identified by Seidman as distinctly Jewish, and as being characterised by a quite different set of metaphors:

> The rabbinic notion of translation can productively be read through the lens of circumcision, in the sense of a transcription that signals affiliation in which the body of language – the letter – is marked as Jewish. Translation, in this mode, must be

1   Grudem, 2005, p.32. Emphasis in original.

> understood in terms of the signifier rather than the signified, and
> thus as transformation rather than equivalence.[1]

The imagery here knows nothing of the neo-Platonic spirit which animates a text; rather, the corporeal reality of language is emphasised, and a text is seen not as kind of zombie which only spirit can bring to life, but rather as an entity already charged with significance. Words are like people: they are bodies. Just as Hebrew bodies are made according to the Lord's will but capable of 'improvement' by circumcision,[2] so also words may be circumcised or uncircumcised. Seidman illustrates this understanding of translation with the case of Aquila's new Greek version of the Hebrew scriptures, completed in accordance with the hermeneutic principles of Rabbi Akiva in the 2nd Century CE. Aquila produced what is usually described as a very literal ('almost unreadable')[3] Greek text, which aimed for complete word-for-word concordance with the Hebrew. In this conception of translation, words of the target language are captured and circumcised, so that translation is a type of conversion: just as Aquila himself was converted to Judaism and circumcised, so the Greek translation of the Hebrew scriptures which he produced was a kind of 'circumcised Greek'. Thus, whereas the patristic reception of Aquila's translation emphasised its 'slavish' concordance with the Hebrew, and bemoaned its scandalous mutilation of the beauties of the Greek language,[4] 'the rabbis . . . celebrate a Greek Bible that bears the distinctive stamp of its Hebraic allegiances, the methods of the rabbinic academy, the whiff of Semitic tents. Nor do they see this stamp as a mutilation: the Greek retains its grace, even in Semitic garb and under the Hebraic knife.'[5] It is seen as a fulfilment of Genesis 9.27, in which Japheth (standing for the Greeks) is prophesied as the bringer of the beauty of that culture into the tents of Shem.

As well as the corporeal nature of the guiding metaphor here, we may note the 'role reversal': whereas in the patristic tradition the target language is seen as the aggressor, and the spirit of the source document is the thing taken captive, in this rabbinic metaphor, it is the target language which is captured and altered by the altogether more powerful source language. This conception of translation, which is logically and historically associated with the rabbinic idea of Torah as something both

1 Seidman, 2006, p.86.
2 Genesis Rabbah 46.1, cited in Seidman, 2006, p.89.
3 Seidman, 2006, p.94.
4 Ibid.
5 Ibid.

concrete and breathed out by God, has a profound effect on what we believe to be *die Aufgabe des Übersetzers*, as Walter Benjamin put it.[1] The task of the translator is not to capture the spirit of the original, but to make whatever alterations to the target language are necessary, to absorb it into the source. This is key to Benjamin's conception of *die reine Sprache*, ('the pure language') which he sees as 'concentratedly concealed in translations'. Famously, Benjamin's ideal translation is an interlinear, in which there is word for word correspondence and which speaks in a new language formed from the encounter of source and target.

It is also possible to see this idea at work in the Buber-Rosenzweig translation of the Hebrew scriptures, to which we made reference in Chapter One. The authors' preferred term for it was a *Verdeutschung* of the scriptures, but they were happy to make whatever changes to German were required for it to be (in Seidman's terms) a circumcised language, fit to be accepted into the world of scripture. Gershom Scholem, in a speech addressed to Buber in 1961, expressed it thus:

> *There was a utopian element in your endeavour. For the language into which you translated was not that of everyday speech, nor that of German literature of the 1920s. You aimed at a German which, drawing sustenance from earlier tendencies, was present potentially in the language, and it was just this utopianism which made your translation so very exciting and stimulating . . .*[2]

Rosenzweig insisted on what he called *die Wörtlichkeit des Worts*, and the obligation which falls on a translator to preserve it:

> [I]f we believe that . . . any human utterance may conceal the possibility that one day, in his time or in my time, God's word may be revealed in it, then in that case the translator must, so far as his language permits, follow the peculiar turns of that potentially revelation-bearing utterance, whether by direct reconstruction or by implication.[3]

The problem for the translator is that it may be almost any of 'the peculiar turns' in the text which becomes, in God's good time, the means of revelation. Although Rosenzweig's remark applies to *any human utterance*, the problems are particularly acute in the case of scripture. If, with a certain rabbinic tradition, we regard *every feature* of the Torah as *significant* – every jot and tittle, down to the white spaces between words – then how can this be reflected in translation? 'The Law that God gave

1   *The Task of the Translator*, Benjamin, W, 1923, tr. Zohn, in Venuti, ed, 2000, p.15.
2   Scholem, 1971, cited in Rosenwald and Fox, 1994, liii.
3   Rosenzweig, 1925, tr. Rosenwald and Fox, 1994.

to Moses was written in black fire on white fire.'[1] In some traditions, the 'white fire' is God's own skin.[2] Not only does the Torah have seventy facets, each with an infinite number of reflections, but 'biblical language is motivated at all levels; as Word it is called on to found and speak the world . . . It is homologous with the real – a sort of vast ideogram.'[3]

Such a conception has, in the Western Christian tradition, commonly been characterised as the route to madness or despair, at least as regards the question of translatability. In a system which does not distinguish between the sign and signified, linguistics is impossible. Yet it does go to the heart of the problem we identified at the beginning of this chapter, which we introduced by means of the innocuous idea of Robbins' repetitive texture. Buber and Rosenzweig, in the course of their lifetimes, did come to an answer of sorts. Like Aquila, they did not attempt to address the 'literality of letters' in the source text, but concentrated on words, and particularly on roots. Their translation methodology involved establishing Leitwörter, 'leading words'. A Leitwort is 'simply a word or word-complex that the translator must translate consistently in all its reccurrences, i.e. must translate in such a way that wherever the Leitwort recurs in the original, its equivalent recurs in the translation.'[4] Thus, in their rendering of the account of the Tabernacle in Exodus (Namen), the Hebrew root dha ('ed) is a Leitwort, so that wherever it recurs, the German must use the same 'equivalent' root, which seems to be settled as gegen, conveying the idea of 'witness' or 'testimony'. Thus, Exodus 30.6 reads:

> *Gib sie vor den Verhang, der über dem Schrein der Ver**gegen**wärtigung ist, vor das Verdeck, das über der Ver**gegen**wärtigung ist, wo ich dir be**gegnen** werde.*
> (Put it in front of the curtain which is over the ark of recollection, in front of the cover which is over the recollection, where you and I will collect together).[5]

---

1   Tanhuma, Genesis 1. Also Rashi on Deuteronomy 33.2 and Yeroushalmi, Shekalim 6.1. Cited in Rojtman,1998, p.3.
2   Ibid, xi.
3   See Midrash Rabbah, Genesis 1.1., cited Ibid, p.9. 'Motivation'is a term used in linguistics when the sign is thought of as having a relationship other than an arbitrary one with the thing signified. Thus 'splash' is clearly phonologically motivated. The idea of 'motivation at all levels' is the guiding thought behind such extraordinary works as Jeff Benner's 2005 Ancient Hebrew Lexicon of the Bible, as well as modern rabbinic works such as Munk's 1983 The Wisdom in the Hebrew Alphabet.
4   Rosenwald and Fox, 1994, xxxix.
5   My translation. It is clear that English is here pushed further beyond its

Much of this seems to fall comfortably within the ambit of the distinctively 'Jewish' translation tradition which Seidman identifies. 'They knew that they were creating a translation that Hebraized the German language . . . '[1] However, there are also a number of question-marks, and the simple division of traditions into 'Christian' and 'Jewish' varieties is, in the end, untenable. To show this, we will make a brief excursus, examining the strand of Christian 'Jewish' translation.

Christian neo-Cabbalism?

There is a vigorous strand of 'Jewish' literalism within the Christian tradition: as we identified in Chapter One, protests against the 'holy marriage' translation are often expressed in terms of a word-for-word literalism, which seems more comfortably described within the 'Jewish' category than the 'Christian'. Cases in point are Robert Young's *Literal Translation of the Bible* (1862), Joseph Rotherham's *The Emphasised Bible* (1872 to 1902) and especially A E Knoch's *The Concordant Version of the Ancient Scriptures*, described by one reader as distinguished by its 'utter incomprehensibility',[2] but sitting comfortably within the tradition, exemplified by Aquila, of presenting the scriptures in a kind of circumcised English. Rotherham's version's circumcision is particularly evident, as a result of his invention of new sigla to show grammatical features of the souce text. The influence of this kind of literalism may also be detected in the ASB and the NASB, the latter describing itself as 'a word-for-word translation that is accurate and precise.'[3]

Perhaps the most extremely 'Jewish' Christian reading of the Bible

---

limits even than Buber and Rosenzweig push German. Interestingly, Everett Fox's The Five Books of Moses, which is an English version completed self-consciously along the same lines as Buber and Rosenzweig, cannot manage a Leitwort rendition of this verse, reading instead: 'And you are to put it in front of the curtain that is over the coffer of Testimony, in front of the purgation-cover that is over the Testimony, where I will appoint-meeting with you.'

1   Plaut, cited in Seidman, 2006, p.180.

2   Dewey, 2004, p.134.

3   There is, further, more than a whiff of it in some of the arguments of the 'essential literalists'. Thus Grudem entitles one of his pieces: Are only some words of scripture breathed out by God? (in Grudem etc, 2005, p.19.) Mixed with his other arguments, some of which as we saw above have a neo-Platonic basis, there is the idea that every word in the source must be represented by a word or words in the translation. Although all translators would agree with this in a sense, Grudem wants the connections to be tangible in a way which he does not define but perhaps could be expressed in terms of Seidman's 'circumcision'?

was that of John Hutchinson (1674 – 1737) and his followers, who read the consonantal script of the 'Old Testament' as a kind of Christian Kabala in which vocalisation opened up a vastly expanded horizon of possible interpretations. 'Such complicated word play was well within the infinite capabilities of the Almighty, and part of the multi-layered message of the Bible. The Old Testament became a sort of code-book containing all the secrets of the universe, which now became available to the creative Hebraist.'[1] As Katz reminds us, 'Many histories of the Bible tend to emphasise those thinkers in the past whose beliefs seem comfortably like our own, or may be seen as helping move us in that direction.'[2] In fact, in their time the Hutchinsonians (and the Swedenborgians after them), 'dominated whole areas of the English theological establishment.'[3] The Hutchinsonians did not express this hermeneutic in the form of translation activity; how could they? Full-blooded cabbalism represents a dead-end as far as translation goes, which might be one explanation for the movement's decline and ultimate demise, within a Christian tradition which (as we saw in Chapter One) tolerates difference but whose mainstream insists on the universality and translatability of scripture.

James Barr's machine gun

Much more long-lived was the 'biblical theology' movement, whose late flowering in the form of *TWNT* (and its English version *TDNT*) received such a thorough machine-gunning by Barr and his imitators in the 1960s.[4] The 'biblical theologians',[5] like Buber and Rosenzweig, emphasised focus on Hebrew (and Greek) roots, and attempted an hermeneutic based on reading theology from linguistic features of the source languages. In the course of his devastating critique, Barr invented two new fallacies which, I believe, although not directed at the practice of biblical translation, have had a significant effect upon it, as we have already seen in preceding chapters. The 'root fallacy' is directed at the belief that 'in Hebrew [or Greek] there is a "root meaning" which is effective throughout all the variations given to the root by affixes and formative elements, and that therefore the "root meaning" can confidently be taken to be part of the actual semantic value of any word or form which can be assigned to an

1   Katz, 2004, p.159.
2   Ibid.
3   Ibid, p.165.
4   Barr, 1961.
5   Barth, Kittel, and many others. The list of contributors to TWNT provides the fullest possible list.

identifiable root . . . "[1] Rather, Barr pointed out, the semantic value of a word can be determined only by looking at its use in context – synchronically rather than diachronically, and with reference to the understanding of actual language-users, rather than a reconstruction of its etymological past. Thus although in English the word 'holy' is from the same root as 'healthy', this does not entail that they mean the same thing.

Barr's second fallacy, 'illegitimate totality transfer' is defined as 'The error that arises, when the "meaning" of a word (understood as the total series of relations in which it is used in the literature) is read into a particular case as its sense and implication there.'[2] He uses a range of examples to show that, of course, a word cannot be understood as always conveying the totality of what we have reconstructed as its full semantic potential, and this applies particularly to common words such as λόγος – a full theology of history and the Word cannot be read from each instance of the word's use.

Barr did not have much to say about translation, restricting his remarks to affirmations of the translatability of scripture – a translatability which he saw as being undermined by the misty romanticism and lack of scientific rigour of the 'biblical theology' movement.[3] However, Barr has had a profound influence on English translation in a number of ways, as a natural bed-fellow for Nida's 'scientific' approach. His two 'fallacies', taken together, seem to imply that the translator is safe to ignore etymological roots, and that she or he should concentrate instead on use in context. This in turn is one of the main drivers in the abandonment of concordance and of the preservation of repetitive texture as a legitimate objective in translation. As we will see below, these implications do not at all follow from Barr's fallacies, but they have acquired such momentum that they are often 'taken as read' in the literature.[4] Some of the most

1   Barr, 1961, p.100.
2   Ibid, p.218.
3   See Barr, 1961, pp.264 – 265.
4   See for example Silva, 1994 (1983), pp.18-32. Silva religiously repeats Barr's case against 'the monstrous regiment of shoddy linguistics' (p18), and it informs the whole of his book, a work whose stated aim is 'the relatively modest goal of determining the most accurate English equivalents to biblical words.' (p31). Like Barr himself, Silva entertains the fantasy that there are such 'equivalents', and it is easy to see how this would affect an approach to translation. Although Silva does recognise cases where exploration of a root is relevant (for example where a word in use is transparent to its root – see p.48) in general his approach to semantics ignores the communicative clues which

harmful effects of Barr's arguments arise not from their conclusions (which are completely valid) but from the tone in which they are conducted, which represents an easy ridiculing of any kind of philological sensitivity to source texts. It is, of course, of no value to speculate as to how English biblical translation might have progressed, had there been no Barr (1961) and no Nida (1969). The Buber and Rosenzweig Bible, although largely completed before Rosenzweig's death in 1929, was for obvious and tragic reasons not finally printed and widely distributed until the 1960s, by which time its originally envisaged target audience had been murdered or dispersed. An English translation of Torah along their lines was not attempted until the 1970s.[1] By this time, the major English translation efforts of the 20th Century which we mentioned in Chapter One were well under way; they would not benefit from its example, but from the strictures of 'scientific linguistics' represented by Nida and Barr.

There is no doubt that Buber and Rosenzweig also fall foul of Barr's etymological fallacies. Consider, for example, Rosenzweig's assertion that 'the tetragrammaton was never a mere name, but always made its appearance with the full voltage of the theological charge with which it had been loaded at the Burning Bush.'[2] This might have served Barr well, as a textbook case of 'illegitimate totality transfer'. For the 'root fallacy', he might have chosen the whole discussion of the use of עֵד (' *ed*) in Exodus, which culminates in the statement 'I believe that we can trace beneath these two roots a single root in common, encompassing the whole semantic territory of being-made-present, remaining-present. (Thus 'edah . . . means by etymology "the generation of the people present at a given occasion."')[3]

Yet, it would be a mistake to conclude from this, that Buber and Rosenzweig's approach is fundamentally flawed. Although their discussions of particular cases make plentiful reference to

---

arise from repetitive texture. As an aside, it is worth noting, with Silva (p.19) the overwhelmingly positive reception of Barr's work – surprising, because he seemed to be attacking something mainstream. It is almost as if a classroom of naughty children is brought to order by a teacher who, having been called away for a moment, and returns to find chaos. The pupils return to their seats and are secretly relieved to be brought back in line. Perhaps there is always an element of guilty pleasure attached to the examination of roots, in the Christian tradition.

1   'The Five Books of Moses'. See bibliographic information under *Abbreviations*.
2   Rosenzweig, The Eternal, in Rosenwald, ed., 1994, p.111.
3   Buber, On Word Choice in Translating the Bible, in ibid, p.81.

etymological roots, and in language which frequently detonates the
land mines which Barr identified, to write them off would be to fail
to do justice to the *Leitwort* technique. *Leitwörter* are not in the
end motivated by fallacious assumptions about root meanings, but by
something else altogether. Thus, Buber, for example, talks again and
again about Leitwörter in terms of their use in the establishment of
verbal patterns in the text. Discussing the translation of the Hebrew
kippur, he says: 'It has been one of the strongest confirmations of our
method that we have been able to reproduce such verbal patterns
in both their breadth of manifestation and in their unity.'[1] He goes
on to distinguish between 'absolute word choice' and 'relative word
choice'. The latter is:

> aimed at preserving the biblically intended relation between two
> or more words related by their roots, or sometimes merely by their
> sounds . . . In the Bible, then, alliteration and assonance, and to a still
> greater degree repetitions of words, phrases and sentences cannot be
> understood in aesthetic terms alone; rather such patterns belong for the
> most part to the matter and character of the biblical message itself, and
> rendering them rightly is one of the central tasks of the translation.
> Extremely important connections are being made when we attempt
> within a passage – and sometimes within a larger portion, within a
> whole book, within a sequence of books – to reproduce a single Hebrew
> root with a single German one.[2]

It is the *patterns* of words or sounds, then, which are so important.
There is nothing in this argument which requires the fallacious
identification of a single universal meaning for a given root. Indeed,
Buber declares elsewhere that 'There is no "content" to be smelted
from the biblical ore. . . . '[3] Rather, what he and Rosenzweig are
interested in is the 'formal principle' of rhythm: 'By rhythm here we
understand . . . the auditory connection, manifested in significant order,
of a constant with a variable. The constant can be purely structural –
the recurrence of cadence, of tempo, of quantity. Or it can be phonetic –
the recurrence of sounds or sequences of sounds, of words or sequences
of words.'[4] What seems to be asserted here is that *rhythm*, which may
be established by verbal or phonetic repetition, is (in our terms) a
communicative clue. *Repetitive texture*, then, in Robbins' terminology,
represents a feature of texts which may be honoured in translation. In

---

1   Buber, 1930, in Rosenwald, ed. p.81.
2   Ibid.
3   Buber, 1926, in Rosenwald, ed. p.28
4   Ibid.

what follows, I hope to pick up this suggestion, and propose a fourth kind of literalism which does not fall foul of the perils represented in the other three: it depends neither on defunct epistemological assumptions nor on fallacious etymologising; and it does not consist of prostration before an authoritative 'holy marriage' translation. Rather, it simply takes seriously the communicative clues arising from verbal repetition, clues which may be used both to construct the relevant interpretation and to deconstruct it.

Deconstructive literalism

In the introduction to *The Control of Biblical Meaning: Canon as Semiotic Mechanism*,[1] George Aichele sets out his ground rules, amongst them this one: 'I choose the RSV translation because I regard it as a "literal" translation of the ancient manuscripts . . . Every translation betrays and transforms its source text, but a literal translation is more likely to record problems and defects that appear in the source text. Such problems and defects hinder the clear transmission of the canonical message, and thus they are of particular interest here.'[2] Aichele's text is a self-conscious attempt to deconstruct the idea of a Christian canon. In order to do this, he senses the need to access the *repetitive texture* of the original: how else can the text be turned against itself and opened up to the force of deconstruction?[3] Any kind of writing represents 'ideology at work', and this applies just as much to *re-writing* in the form of translation. As he is interested in the 'ancient manuscripts' themselves, he wants to find a form of translation which so far as possible 'reproduces the uncertainties of the source text's meaning, not the interpretations that would resolve them.'[4] In the course of the discussion, he correctly identifies the logocentric tendencies in Nida's 'dynamic equivalence' and refers to 'the general rejection of the theory of literal translation by Christian Bible translators'[5] as evidential of the desire to control the meaning of source texts to which the book's title alludes.

What Aichele has noticed is that if the interpreter wants to 'see' the source text, he or she would prefer not to have another interpreter

---

1   Aichele, 2001.
2   Ibid, p.3.
3   Much of the argument in the main body of the book relies on concordant translation of key words and word sequences. See for example 'The Humanoid', p.p151-172, in which 'the Son of Man' is the target.
4   Ibid, p.72.
5   Ibid, p.74. He acknowledges in a footnote that of course there are some 'fairly literal' Christian translations (such as the RSV).

standing in the way. The problem with a dynamic equivalence translation, then, is that it does not permit deconstruction of the source text. The translation represents an ideological undertaking which *itself* can be readily deconstructed, but does not provide access to the source. Aichele might perhaps have under-estimated the extent to which a 'literal' translation *also* represents a thoroughly ideological undertaking. As we saw earlier, the idea of a translation which is 'transparent' to the source text in this way is itself misconceived. However, what I would like to draw attention to here is the formal similarity between his argument and some of those of the proponents of 'essentially literal' biblical translation who, looking from an intellectual and ideological perspective radically different from Aichele's, have notice the same thing.

Thus, Ryken suggests that 'A good translation preserves the full exegetical or interpretive potential of the original biblical text. Conversely, a translation is inadequate to the extent to which it diminishes the interpretive potential of the original text.'[1] One of the ways this is achieved is by careful attendance to concordance: 'Literary texts tend to contain word patterns and image patterns . . .'[2] Ryken shows that it is important, for example, in translating Ruth, to translate the repetition of כָּנָף ('wings') in 2.12 and 3.9 concordantly: whereas Boaz' wish that Ruth be protected under the Lord's wings was merely conventional piety, her desire to be protected under Boaz' wings was an authentic challenge. Similarly, C. John Collins shows that if the eleven occurrences of μένω in John 15 are not translated concordantly, it means 'a failure to convey the intended meaning of the discourse. . . . We ought not hide verbal parallels from the reader when those verbal parallels have a bearing on the same topic.'[3]

Now, of course Ryken and Collins, whilst advocating concordant translation on the one hand, also desire, on the other hand, to maintain the control over meaning to which Aichele refers, by implicitly linking concordance to thematics. In other words, concordance is seen as desirable because it reinforces the theme ('the message', again) of the text, to which it is seen as a servant. They leave unexamined the question of what to do when the phenomenon of concordance might be turned *against* thematics, to undermine it – to deconstruct it. One man's exegesis is, however, another's deconstruction. A concordant translation of a text might serve equally to reveal Aichele's 'defects and problems' or Ryken's 'full exegetical potential' – to reinforce its 'intention', or to undermine it. I will argue that it does both.

1   Ryken, 2002, p.140.
2   Ibid, p.220.
3   C John Collins, in Ryken, 2002, p.311.

The perfect translation

I propose to deal with this under the above heading, in order to be clear that this is not to be achieved in this world. The perfect translation is the one whose relationship to a source text is such that it permits both the construction of the relevant interpretation of that text, and its deconstruction. It takes seriously both Ryken's advocacy of a translation which provides 'the full exegetical potential', and Aichele's of one which provides all the 'defects and problems' – requirements which, in the end, amount to the same thing. This translation is also the natural result of our conclusions about the nature of relevant communication in Chapter Two. We saw there that 'the relevant interpretation' of a text describes a curve, not a point. The 'relevant interpretation' turned out to be not a stable, single interpretation, but a series of possible interpretations corresponding to different levels of reader attention and forming a curve (see figure 6).

The perfect translation, then, is one which does not attempt to produce a target language text with 'a meaning', but one which produces a text with a range of possible interpretations, including those which cut against the grain of the text and therefore require a higher level of reader attention.

The perfect translation is one which has read the source text in the light of all the communicative clues it provides – both those identified by Gutt (and which form the subject matter of Chapters Three, Four and Five of the present work), and those outside the categories he establishes – especially the communicative clues from repetitive texture, which are so important in any reading beyond 'the plain sense'.

In order to attempt such translation practice (and, to repeat, no attempt to do so will finally succeed in this world), something like Buber and Rosenzweig's *Leitwörter* will be needed. The reason for this is that, as we have seen, complete concordance is impossible. Benjamin's ideal of the interlinear fails in the end because, although it permits *deconstruction*, it does not permit *construction* of the relevant interpretation. The perfect translation permits both, and to achieve this, decisions must be made. Buber and Rosenzweig were very selective about their Leitwörter, both in terms of *selection* and *application*. In selection, they chose Leitwort renderings where thereby 'a meaning of the text is opened up or clarified, or at any rate revealed more insistently.'[1] This most obviously occurs in supporting the theme of a text, although as Mara Benjamin points out, 'Sometimes the

1   Buber, 1927, in Rosenwald, ed. 1994, p.114.

correspondence between the root-word in question and the meaning of the story is indirect, even subversive or ironic.'[1] The authors are quite open in declaring that what they are interested in is the *Botschaft* (the message) of the Bible, and they select *Leitwörter* to serve this objective. We thus find them considering but ultimately dropping possible *Leitwörter* which do not meet this purpose (for example *rosh* and *Ba'al*).[2] Rosenzweig was happy to describe the choice of *Leitwörter* as an ideological decision, a decision more difficult for him than it had been for Luther. Whereas Luther had a clear theological lens through which he interpreted the text, the translator of modernity (and still more of post-modernity, we might add) has a much less clear frame of reference. The text might speak to him in ways unknown, and this makes the choice of *Leitwörter* more problematic.[3]

We also find Buber and Rosenzweig being selective in their *application* of a Leitwort, once chosen. Thus although 'ed is given thoroughgoing Leitwort treatment in that part of Exodus where the Lord gives the precise specifications for the Tent, this treatment is not applied consistently throughout the Pentateuch or even in Exodus itself. The reason is that it would be impossible to do so – 'ed' is an extremely common root, and 'The boundary of linguistic possibility is also and unconditionally to be maintained, regarding the injunction to translate a word "everywhere consistently in scripture".'[4] Elsewhere, Buber commented that 'with words given little or no mental emphasis, this principle may be eased or annulled. In every case we ask about what will produce the higher value for the intention of the rendering, and make our decision accordingly.'[5] It is this realism and sensitivity to the actual problems of translation which make Buber and Rosenzweig's insights serviceable even within the communicative tradition. Buber's comments can be easily expressed in terms of how a passage achieves Relevance – what he and Rosenzweig have done is to notice the critical role which repetitive texture plays in how a text achieves a relevance; they want to honour it in translation, whilst recognising that it would be a mistake to allow it to elbow all the other communicative clues off the stage. Theirs is a translation approach which is fully aware that translation is a hermeneutical procedure, but at the same time makes room for the mechanics of repetition.

The Perfect Translation will choose *Leitwörter* which both serve

1   Benjamin, M., 2009, p.148.
2   Rosenwald, 1994, xli.
3   Rosenzweig, in Rosenwald 1994, pp.58-59.
4   Ibid. p.68.
5   Buber, *On Translating the Praisings*, cited in Rosenwald, 1994, xxxix-xl.

the intended relevance and undermine it, just as an original text does. The application of Leitwort technique which I wish to specify for the Perfect Translation is slightly more circumscribed than Buber and Rosenzweig's in some respects, and somewhat wider in others. The extension I would like to make is to extend the principle to all texts, not just biblical ones. There seems no principled reason, if Buber and Rosenzweig's insight is valid, to limit it to a certain canon. They themselves were not much interested in translating extra-biblical texts.[1] It is true that the Hebrew Bible, with its paronomasia, alliteration, and other forms of word-play, may be particularly suitable for *Leitwort* treatment, in the sense that it may represent one of its favourite ways of achieving relevance, but the passages where Buber or Rosenzweig seem to suggest that this is a unique and occult quality of the Bible are amongst the least satisfactory. It is also in these passages that Mara Benjamin accuses them of sidestepping the important issue of how these *Leitwörter* are thought to have got there – are they the work of the authors, or editors or redactors? Are we intended to infer only an unseen divine hand?[2] Related to this point is the manner in which I propose to limit the application of the concept. It seems to me that the *Leitwort* technique has at least questionable application, outside the work of a given author. For example, whilst it is clear that John's gospel uses μένω as a *Leitwort*, and that its translation accordingly is a 'no-brainer' for our Perfect Translation, it is not thereby proved that it is also a *Leitwort* in Luke. The complications in this argument, of course, arise from intertextuality and from canon. If Luke and John share intertextuality, either directly or via a third (Mark, or the LXX?), then a *Leitwort* may make its way between them. This is a matter for empirical textual criticism.

On the question of canon, I would like to make a proposal, which will bring us back to the phenomenon of the 'holy marriage' translation, with which the present work began. It is a proposal which addresses the vexed question of how a canon can be defined at all.[3] I would like to suggest that a canon is created only by translation, and comes into existence to the extent that a translator (or community of translators) decides to perform the translation using the same *Leitwörter* across the range of the works in question. Thus 'the

1 Rosenzweig did do a little – see Grace after Meals; but this was an early encounter with the puzzles of translation, and before he and Buber had invented Leitwort technique.
2 Benjamin, M., 2009, p.147ff.
3 See Aichele, pp1-12.

Hebrew scriptures' becomes canon only at the point at which they are translated as a body into Greek, and only to the extent that this is done according to common *Leitwörter*; the 'Christian scriptures' only becomes canonical when the Greek sources are translated into Latin; Shakespeare only becomes a canon when Schlegel translates it into German, and so on.[1]

In support of this proposal, a few observations might be made. The first is that as a matter of history, this does seem to be what happens – the question of what is in the canon is usually resolved at around the same time as it is translated. This is natural because, of course, the translation cannot be commissioned and performed until the source text has been defined – and this forces a decision which perhaps had previously been left open. In this sense Jerome's work of defining canon and translating it may be seen as a unitary exercise.

The creation of a canon's fundamental driver, though, is what Aichele correctly identifies as the 'control of meaning', and translation is the principal way this is achieved: an authoritative translation sets up a range of 'authorised equivalents' – what we have called a 'holy marriage', which can be very successful in giving an apparently fixed, stable meaning to a group of disparate source texts. As we saw in Chapter One, it is in the nature of such translations to make subsequent and different translations impossible.

The canonical translation, conceived this way, is also an instance of the fourth, elusive stage of Steiner's 'hermeneutic motion' – that of compensation or restitution. The source text is 'raised' by translating it with canonical *Leitwörter*, placing it in a certain company rather than another. Thus, the decision to include John's Apocalypse in the New Testament is not defined by the decision to include it within the covers of a certain codex or book, not even by a decision to regard it as 'authoritative' (how can a work whose referential meaning is so radically uncertain be 'authoritative' anyway?). Rather, it is defined by the decision to translate it using *Leitwörter* from the other books of the canonical New Testament, and not *Leitwörter* from (for example) the Nag Hammadi collection of what used to be known as 'gnostic' texts, or some other group. In this way, translation creates canon.

The weakening of canon is also thereby a predictable consequence of any translation practice which does not use common *Leitwörter* throughout. Crossan's 'The Five Gospels', or the 'Good as New' translation, or 'The Restored New Testament', all of which take

---

1   Steiner, 1998 (1975), p.400.

a relaxed view of what is 'in' or 'out', are yet another unintended consequence of Nida's focus on idiomatic translation. Once the *Leitwörter* are lost, those thousands of threads which bind the canon together, giving it its own distinctive repetitive texture, break, and the canon seems no longer 'sacred'. If, for example, the canonical Christian scriptures (however they are precisely drawn) were translated with no *Leitwörter* at all, we would have no particular reason for identifying the Elohim of Genesis 1.1 with 'the Lord' at the end of Revelation, or any of the other designations of the divine in between – *a Relevant interpretation could not be constructed.*

Lest we move too quickly to form the conclusion that the loss of the concept of canon is not to be regretted, we should also remember that it is only the presence of *Leitwörter*, shared through the whole canon, which allow us *to deconstruct it.* The ties which bind are also the points of maximum weakness. If, for example, I wished to expose the inner contradictions in the Christian idea of a God who was present at creation and throughout history, but who we were still waiting for and asking to come, at the end of the final book of the Bible – I could only do so, with the benefit of *Leitwörter* holding them together.

As will probably be clear, my present work allows me to remain agnostic as to whether the Perfect Translation of 'the Bible' should use common *Leitwörter* or not. Answering this question would require much deeper consideration of the issues of canon than is possible here. In the meantime, it seems clear at least that if and so far as we consider 'Luke' and 'Acts' as the work of a single 'author', they should be translated accordingly. Only thereby do I stand a chance of performing a target text which permits the reader to form what I regard to be the Relevant interpretation of the text *and* to question and deconstruct that interpretation.

The Perfect Translation, then, will choose *Leitwörter* which will both serve the intended relevance and undermine it, just as any original text does.

Final remarks:

The experimental translation

The translation which follows, in the Appendix, is not (far from it!) the Perfect Translation, but an Experimental Translation, of the first two chapters of Luke's gospel, as it appears in the main text of Nestle-Aland 27th edition.

'Experimental' means just that – it is an experiment to see whether and to what extent a 'perfect' translation of any text is possible, if perfection is defined as above – as that which permits both construction of the relevant interpretation, and its deconstruction. In terms of the concepts used in Chapter Two, it aims above all to provide 'outstanding value' to the reader – that is, it should reward attentive reading richly, whatever the underlying motives for the attention. It aims to reward either a reverent or a suspicious reading. If it were 'perfect', it would of course also appropriately reward a casual reading – but this, I fear is the part of the relevance curve where it is least successful.

The approach used, then, is to pay very careful attention to each of the 'communicative clues' we have identified, in order to allow the reader to form (my, the translator's, conception of) the relevant interpretation of this text, as well as allowing him or her to see the contradictions and problems in that interpretation. The experimental nature of the project has encouraged me to err on the side of the latter – that is, to make every attempt to honour a clue in translation. This can be seen in, for example, my attempt to honour the prominence which attaches to the use of the perfect (and pluperfect) tense forms, by duplicating the English verb-form which translates it; the attempt to re-perform alliterative word play in various places (for example in Gabriel's greeting to Elisabeth); the semantic explication of some proper names; and many others – but above all, in accepting a high density of *Leitwörter*, which are translated concordantly (for example ἄγγελος, 'angel', and its cognates are always translated with some variation of 'story' and 'telling'; ἅγιος, 'holy', and its cognates are always 'scorching' and so on). The density of *Leitwörter*, and therefore the degree of verbal concordance with the source document is higher than any translation known to me – and this is the result of both very considerable effort, and of the fact that I have only had two chapters of Luke to juggle with.[1] Although the translation may be 'wrong', then – and it is clearly 'wrong' against any Gametic criteria – I do promise that it is motivated by the desire to achieve interpretive resemblance to the source text. Where it reads very idiomatically in English, this is not because it sounds good to me; and where it reads strangely, this is not because I am trying to be literal.

I have also erred wherever possible on the side of innovation, rather than compliance with the ἱερὸς γάμος, the Holy Marriage translation which has preoccupied us throughout this work and perhaps for the last four centuries. This is not because I regard innovation as better than compliance, but because when (for example) Simeon's words have been heard and translated in the same way for 400 years, it is time for him to be heard and translated differently – even if that means, in the ears of many, 'incorrectly'.

---

1   Although in doing so, I have had a mind for the rest of Luke and Acts. I have tried in the Experimental Translation to perform an interpretation compatible with the balance of the Lukan corpus, or at least not obviously at odds with it.

Appendix

Experimental Translation of Luke 1–2

1

That which happened, happened; there were those who learned at first hand.
Then, still more served the word, by passing it on.
Some set hands to order these reports, and
It seemed the honourable thing
To me, too,
Theophilus,
God's Excellent Friend,
That I should write for you: something clear,
Wherein you might recognise the foundations
Of all those words from the beginning, which echo around us.
Because from the very start I have followed it all, followed it very closely.

❧

Now in those days, when Herod was still 'King of the Jews', there was a certain Assessor, whose name was Zachary, of the Assessor Day Rota 'Abia'. He had a wife named Elisa, also of Aaron's family. And they tried to do right, both of them, in the eyes of God at least, going about things scrupulously in line with Ya's rules and regulations. But they had no children, because Elisa was barren, and by now both of them were well on in their days, well on.

Now then, according to the inherited customs of the Assessorship, the turn of his Day Rota came up, and then, by lot, his chance as Assessor to go into the Sanctuary to burn the incense. And as usual the tribe was outside, chanting the hour of the incense burn.

Then it was it appeared to him: Ya's Story Teller – standing there, standing to the right of the altar of incense! Seeing him like that, Zachary was troubled, and fear swept over him. But the Story Teller said to him:

> Do not be afraid, Zachary.
> How can I put this?
> Your complaint was heard:
> You will have a son.
> (Your wife Elisa will bear him.)
> So many will be delighted;
> It's the joy you have longed for,
> An adornment to your life.
> At his birth you will name him:
> Call him Johan, 'Ya's Joy'.
> And Ya's eyes will be on him,
> Because yes, he'll be great.
> No wine or saki, though:
> Right from the mother belly,
> A scorching breath will scour him.
> He'll drive before Ya,
> And Elijah, 'My-god-is-Ya!'
> Will powerfully breathe again,
> So that fathers' tough hearts
> Will be turned back into children's,
> Those who think they know best
> Will be brought into line
> And the tribe will be moulded,
> Moulded into a vessel
> Fit to receive Ya.

But Zachary said to the Story Teller:

> I don't know about this. I am an old man – and my wife is well on, well on in her days.

And the Story Teller, picking his words, said to him:

> I am Gabriel – 'God-Overwhelming;'
> I am he who withstands,
> Withstands before this God's eyes.
> I was sent to speak to you,
> To Tell what, after all,
> Is surely a welcome Story.

You don't trust my words?
Well look, in return
I will teach you the meaning of silence:
No power to speak
Until the days come
When 'then' becomes 'now'
And time delivers my Story.

And there was the crowd, expecting Zachary to come out, and wondering at how much time he was spending in the sanctuary. When he did come out finally, he couldn't speak to them – and they realized he had seen - he must have seen - a vision in the sanctuary. There he was, gesticulating at them but remaining dumb.

Now then, he finished the days of his service, and went back to his hometown. After these days were over, sure enough his wife Elisa conceived. But she hid herself for a whole five months, saying 'So many days of nothingness among men. Then, Ya looked in on me, and took it away – but what a way to do it, what a way to do it!'

In the sixth month, Gabriel the Story Teller was again sent from the presence of God, to a town in Galilee, called Nazareth, to a maiden who was betrothed, betrothed to a man of the house of David, whose name was Josep. And the name of this maiden was Mariam. So, he went in to her and said:

Girl, I give you greetings;
Ya greets you too,
And grants you a gift.

Now she was quite troubled by these words, and her mind disputed what this greeting seemed to mean. But the Story Teller said:

Mariam, do not be afraid.
Your gift is from God.
Look: your womb will conceive,
You'll give birth to a son.

Name him Xavier: 'Ya-Saves!'

Because he will be great,
Called a son of a high-up,
The throne of his father,

'Beloved' king David,
Will come to him now,
Given by the God Ya;
And he'll be King over Jacob's house,
For ages and ages,
No end to this Kingdom, once it has come.

But Mariam said to the Story Teller:

How can this possibly be? Not from any man *I* know.

And the Story Teller chose these words in reply:

A scorching breath of wind
Brings this to your door.
But the power of the high-up
Will shield you, protect you,
For the one to be born,
Is the scorched one,
The one called God's son.

Look at cousin Elisa –
She called 'barren' has conceived,
She's conceived in old age,
It's six months already.

When God expresses a view,
It's accomplished in fact.

So Mariam said:

Then let me be that expression: Look, Ya's girl submits.

And the Story Teller left her.

So, naturally, Mariam got up and in a very few days hurried straight to the hills, to a town in Judea, to Zachary's house, and, calling hello, she went in to Elisa. Now then, when Mariam's hello reached Elisa's ear, the infant in her belly gave her a good kick, and a scorching breath scoured through her, and raising her voice until she was shouting, she said:

Good words for you, girl!
Woman, good words!
And good words for your womb,
Good words for its fruit!

How did you get here?
Why come to me?
Goodness me, mother to Ya?
When you came in,
And your voice said hello,
As it came to my ear,
My own belly's baby
Gave me a good kick
(it must have been joy).
Be confident, girl:
As Ya has spoken, as he has spoken to you,
It will all end happily.

But Mariam said:

Is this then the shape my life is to take
To somehow enlarge this Ya?
The breath of a slave-girl to adorn
The plans of a saving God?

When he looks down on my damaged state,
He sees what he can do –
Through me, great things,
From a position of power –
And, then, they'll call me happy
For all generations to come.

His very name is a scorching fire;
And his kindness is quite something
For those who fear him
Down through the generations:

He grabbed with his arm,
He yanked rulers off thrones,
He scattered their thoughts,
However heart-felt or high,
He emptied the rich,
And fattened up beggars,
He sought out the damaged,

And put them in charge,
So: he took the boy in hand,
Israel, 'Struggles-with-God'.

Just his way of remembering:
The terms were discussed
With 'High-Father-of-Many,'
And Abraham & Sons
Have felt the force of this kindness
Down through the generations.
And will do forever.

Now Mariam stayed with her for the next three months, but then turned round and went home.

As for Elisabeth, her time of waiting for the child was filled up, and she gave birth to a son. When neighbours and relatives round about heard that Ya had dealt her such a great kindness, they shared her joy in the gift.

Now then, on the eighth day they went to circumcise the lad. They were calling him 'Zachary', after his father's name, but, choosing her words carefully, his mother said: 'No, on the contrary, he is to be called Johan'. But they said to her that there wasn't a single person in her family called by that name. So they were gesticulating at the father, to see what he wanted him called. And asking for a slate, he wrote these words: 'Johan is his name.' And everyone wondered about that!

At that moment, though, the tongue in his mouth was released, and suddenly he was speaking, giving good words to God. Now, then, it was fear that swept over those neighbours of theirs. Soon all this was spread through the whole district of Judea, and everyone who heard, whether they expressed it or held it in their heart, was saying 'What will this lad be? – for Ya's hand was in this'.

And the scorching breath swept through Zachary, the father, and his words of interpretation were:

Ya is the God of good words for Israel!
He saw the problem,
And fashioned a rescue for his tribe,
Like the horns of strong oxen,
He protectively circles;
The house of David, his son, is kept safe.
Just as he said he would,
Scorching the mouths of interpreters,
Down through the ages –

Safe from our enemies,
From all those who hate us;
Dealing kindly with our fathers,
Keeping in mind the terms
Of that scorching deal
Abraham got out of him:
The one he swore to,
To pull us out of enemy hands,
If only we would serve him,
In line with his rules and his rites,
And let his eyes smile on us
All of our days.
And you, little lad, will be called
The highest interpreter of all:
You will run ahead of Ya,
Clearing the roads for him,
Making it safe for his tribe,
Serving them notice
About letting sin go!
The lungs of our God
Exhale only kindness.
He will look in on us
Like a dawn from on high,
Lighting up those in darkness,
Those prostrate before death,
So our feet can take those first steps
On the good road to peace.

Now, the little lad grew up, and his breath grew strong. But he was kept out of the way until the days when he would be shown to Israel.

2

Now then, in those days Caesar Augustus issued a decree which the whole occupied world was to honour by being registered. (Now this one was the registration before that of Cyrene, when he was Hegemon of Syria.) So everyone went to register, each to his own town. Joseph also went up country from Galilee, from his town of Nazareth, to Judea, and because his forefather was David, he was of his house. So he went to the town of David, called Bethlehem, with Mariam, who was betrothed to him; betrothed to him but already pregnant.

Now then, while they were there, the day came for the child to be born. And she produced her child, a son: her firstborn. She wrapped him in swaddling clothes, but laid him down in a feeding trough, because circumstances were not welcoming for them in the roadside inn.

There were shepherds in that area, as there always are - the world being their backyard - watching the watches of night, and herding the herds of sheep. Suddenly, Ya's Story Teller stood over them. And the honour of Ya was apparent all around them, and they were fearfully afraid. But the Story Teller said to them:

> Do not be afraid,
> For look, I Tell a Story of welcome:
> Something great – a gift for all tribes.
> For you, this very day:
> Someone to make you safe:
> Ya the Anointed,
> Is born in David's town,
> And here's the sign:
> If you go there
> You will find a baby,
> Well wrapped,
> Wrapped in swaddling,
> But lying in a feeding trough.

Now then, from the sky beyond, quite unexpected, a vast army, praising God, saying:

> Whoever's honour's highest up, higher still is his;
> On the ground, God grant you peace;
> He seems to like folk here.

Then, now, they were gone! The Story Tellers went off to the sky beyond, leaving the shepherds speaking back and forth – 'Let's go!', 'We must to Bethlehem!', 'How was it expressed?', 'I must see!', 'What has come?' and 'Ya himself let us know'. So they went, all in a hurry, and found Mariam, with Joseph and sure enough, the baby, lying in a feeding trough.

So they saw. And they told what had been spoken and how it had been expressed to them, about this little lad. Of course, everyone who heard them wondered a bit, about what these shepherds told them. But Mariam herself kept trying to put together the different expressions they used, and the different strands entwined in her heart.

And the shepherds turned back, honouring and praising God about all that they had heard and seen, just as it had been told to them.

Eight days later they circumcised him, and they called his name Xavier, 'Ya makes us safe' – what he had been called by the Story Teller, even before he was conceived in the mother-belly. Now, Ya's Law is quite clearly written: it is written that, 'the infant male which first opens its mother's birth-canal is to be called a scorched one, set apart for Ya.' However, Ya's Law also says other things – says a sacrifice can serve instead – 'a pair of turtledoves or two young pigeons.' So, when their eight days of cleansing were over, according to the Law of Moses, they took him to Jerusalem to see how things stood with this.

And look, there was a man in Jerusalem, whose name was Simeon. This man was careful to keep right with others, but he was longingly waiting for all Israel to be called to account, and there was something of the scorching breath about him. This scorching breath had blown him something – blown the information that he would not be allowed to see death until he had first seen Ya's Anointed. And, this breath blew him to the Scorching Place just as the parents of the lad Jesus went in to do the customary legal stuff. And he took him gently in the crook of his arm, gave good words to God, and said:

> Master! At last I can go in peace –
> By the promise you expressed before,
> Because my eyes saw your planned salvation,
> In a shining face, for all the peoples,
> A light to reveal what's best and worst in all nations,
> And what honour there is in your own tribe, Israel.

His father – and his mother – were wondering about these things said about him. And Simeon reassured them with good words, but he said to Mariam, the mother:

> Look, this child lies,
> A contradictory sign,
> Revealing hearts' thoughts
> A blade cutting your life in pieces –
> Yes, you too, Mariam.
> He will pull down
> And raise up
> Many in Israel.

Also there was Anna the Interpreter. She came from good family – that of Phanuel, and the tribal-branch of Aser. She was well on in her days, well on: she had lived with her man for seven years after her maidenhood, but then was a widow until her eighty fourth year, and during that whole time, never left the Temple, night or day, but stayed there observing the fasts and making her complaint. Now, at that very hour, her trust returned! And so she was at last talking openly about it to God, and to everyone in Jerusalem longing for release.

※❀※

When all these things had been done in accordance with Ya's Law, they went back to Galilee, to their own town of Nazareth, where the young lad was to grow, to master himself, and to be filled with knowledge of life. So, the gift of God seemed present in him.

※❀※

Now his parents used to go to Jerusalem every year for the feast of the Paschal Lamb. And when he had grown to the twelfth year, they went up there accordingly. But this time, when the feast days were completed and they turned back home, the lad, Xavier, remained behind – but his parents didn't know. Having laid down the law with him to be in the road-caravan, they were on the road for a whole day, and kept looking out for him amongst relatives and those who knew him. But they didn't find him, and turned back to Jerusalem to look for him.

Now then, it took three days to find him! He was sitting in the Scorching Place in the midst of the Rabbis – listening to them and questioning them. And everyone listening to him was amazed how he put things together, and by his judgment. As soon as they saw him, they lashed out, and his mother said to him: 'Child, how could you do this to us? Look, your father and I were in agonies looking for you.'

And he said to them:

> Why were you looking for me like that? Did you not know, know that I would have to be amongst my father's friends?

But they didn't understand this expression he used, even though it was spoken for them.

So, they went down with him, back to Nazareth, and he submitted to their discipline. But his mother continued to turn over all these expressions in her heart. And Jesus struck forward in every way, growing in knowledge of life, in stature, and as God's gift among men.

※❀※

Bibliography

Biblical versions

Biblia Sacra Vulgata, 390-405? (5th ed, 2007)

Contemporary English Version, 2000 (1995), British and Foreign Bible Societies, UK

Complete Jewish Bible, 1998, Messianic Jewish Publishers, USA (David H. Stern)

Clarence Jordan's Cotton Patch Gospel, 1969, Smyth & Helwys, USA (Clarence Jordan)

Das Neue Testament, 1989, übersetzt von Fridolin Stier Kösel-Verlag, Patmos-Verlag, Germany (Fridolin Stier)

Die Bibel in gerechter Sprache Gütersloher Verlagshaus, 2006, Germany (Bail, *et al.*)

Die Bibel, Luther Übersetzung, 1984, Deutsche Bibelgesellschaft, Germany

Die Volxbibel 2.0, 2005, Volxbibel-Verlag, German (Martin Dreyer) Elberfelder, Die Bibel, Elberfelder Übersetzung, 2005 revidierte Fassung, Voltmedia

New Testament, 1768, London, UK (Edward Harwood)

Holy Bible, English Standard Version, 2001, Good News Publishers, USA

Good as New: A Radical Retelling of the Scriptures, 2004, English, Winchester UK and Washington USA (John Henson)

Good News for Modern Man: The New Testament in Today's English Version, 1966,1976,1992, American Bible Society, USA (Eugene Nida)

Holy Bible, New Living Translation, 1996, 2004, Tyndale House Publishers, Inc, USA

Holy Bible, New Revised Standard Version, 1989, Anglicized Version 1995, National Council of the Churches of Christ in the United States of America, publishers various

Holy Bible, Revised Standard Version, 1952, Publishers: various, UK

Holy Bible, Revised Version, 1901, Publishers: various, UK

La Sainte Bible, Nouvelle Version Segond Révisée, 1978, Société biblique française, France

La sainte Bible traduite en francais sous la direction de l'École biblique de Jérusalem, 1955, Publisher: various, Paris, France

Nestle-Aland Novum Testamentum Graece, 1993, 27th edition, 9th correction, 2006, Greek New Testament, Deutsche Bibelgeselschaft

New American Standard Bible, 1963, Lockman Foundation, USA (Revision of American Standard Version, 1901)

New Testament in Modern English, 1958, Harper Collins, UK (J.B Phillips)

The New Testament of Jesus Christ translated faithfully into English, 1582, English, Douai, The English Roman Catholic church, (Gregory Martin)

Restored New Testament: A New Translation with Commentary, Including the Gnostic Gospels, Thomas, Mary and Judas, 2009, W.W. Norton & Co, New York and London (Willis Barnstone)

Septuaginta Id est Vetus Testamentum graece iusta LXX, 260 BCE? interpretes ed. Alfred Rahlfs, Editio altera (2006) Greek (Ptolemy II Philadelphus)

Tha Halgan Godspel on Englisc, 990? (4th edition, 1907), George Putnam, New York, USA (ed. Benjamin Thorpe)

The Concordant Version of the Sacred Scriptures, 1930, Concordant Publishing Concern, Los Angeles, USA (A.E. Knoch)

The Five Gospels: What did Jesus Really Say? 1993, Polebridge Press, USA (Robert Funk/Roy Hoover, The Jesus Seminar)

The Gospels, 360? Joseph Bosworth (4th edition, 1907) Visigothic (Ulfilas?)

The Holy Bible, 1611, (New Cambridge Paragraph ed. 2005) 'The King James Version' or 'Authorised Version', rights vested in the Crown, UK

The Jerusalem Bible, 1966, Publisher: various, UK

The Later Version, 1388, (Cooper ed. 2002), The British Library

The Message: The Bible in Contemporary Language, Eugene H. Peterson, 1993, Nav Press, USA

The New English Bible, 1961, Oxford University Press, UK

New International Version, 1978, Zondervan, New York Bible Society International, USA

The New Testament, 1968, Collins, UK (William Barclay)

The New Testament: A new translation, James Moffatt, 1926, Hodder and Stoughton, UK

The New Testament, Freshly translated, 2004, Kevin Mayhew Ltd, UK (Nicholas King, SJ)

The New Testament, New King James Version, 1979, Thomas Nelson, USA (Arthur Farstad)

The newe Testament as it was written and caused to be written, by them which herde yt., 1526, William Tyndale, (Cooper ed. 2000) The British Library

The Revised English Bible (the New Testament), 1989, Oxford University Press, UK (revision of NEB)

The Street Bible, 2003, Zondervan, USA (Rob Lacey)

The Unvarnished New Testament, 1991, Phanes Press (Andy Gaus)

Traduction Œcuménique de la Bible, 1988, Société biblique francaise, France

Zürcher Bibel, 2007, Genossenschaft Verlag, Germany

Translation Studies

Baker, Mona, *In Other Words: A Coursebook on Translation*, ,Routledge, 1992

Barclay, William, *The New Testament*, 1968, Collins, UK

Benjamin, Walter, 'The task of the translator' in Arndt (ed.), tr. Zohn, *Illuminations: Essays and Reflections*, Schocken Press, New York, 1969

Brayford, Susan, *Translation*, in *Handbook of Postmodern Biblical Interpretation*, A.K.M Adam (ed.), Chalice Press, St. Louis MO, 2000, Derrida, Jacques, *Signature, Event, Context*, in *Limited Inc*, tr. Weber and Mehlman, Glyph, 1977

Derrida, Jacques, *Writing and Difference*, tr. Bass, Routledge, 1978

Derrida, Jacques, 'What is a Relevant Translation?', tr. Venuti, in *The Translation Studies Reader*, 2nd edn, Routledge, 2004

Die Bibel in gerechter Sprache Gütersloher Verlagshaus, 2006, Germany (Bail, Crüsemann, Domay, Ebach, Janssen, Köhler, Kuhlman, Leutzsch, Schottroff)

Die Bibel in gerechter Sprache Gütersloher Verlagshaus, 2006, Germany (Bail, Crüsemann, Domay, Ebach, Janssen, Köhler, Kuhlman, Leutzsch, Schottroff)

Dryden, John, *Preface to Ovid's Epistles*, J. Tonson, 1680

Eco, Umberto, *Experiences in Translation*, tr. Alistair McEwen, University of Toronto Press, Toronto, 2001

Eco, Umberto, *Mouse or Rat? Translation as negotiation*, Weidenfeld & Nicolson, 2003

Gadamer, Hans, *Truth and Method*, 2nd revised edn, tr. J. Weinsheimer and D.G.Marshall, Crossroad, New York, 1989

Genette, Gérard, *Palimpsests: Literature in the Second Degree*, tr. Newman and Doubinsky, University of Nebraska Press, Nebraska, 1997 (1982)

Gentzler, Edwin, *Contemporary Translation Theories*, Multilingual Matters, Bristol, 2001 (1993)

Goodwin, Phil, 'Ethical Problems in Translation: Why we might need Steiner after all', *The Translator*, (2010)

Halliday, M.A.K., *Language as Social Semiotic: The Social Interpretation of Language and Meaning*, Hodder, Newcastle-upon-Tyne, 1978

Heaney, Seamus, *Introduction to Beowulf*, Faber and Faber, UK, 1999

Hervey, S.M., Loughridge, I Higgins, *Thinking German Translation*, 2nd edn, Routledge, 2006

Johnson, Will, 'Making Sanskritic or Making Strange? How Should We Translate Classical Hindu Texts?' in Long (ed.), *Translation and Religion: Holy Untranslateable?*, *Multilingual Matters, Bristol*, 2005

Lecercle, Jean-Jacques, *The Violence of Language*, Routledge, 1990, Milgrom, Jacob, *Leviticus*, Doubleday, New York

More, Thomas, *Letters*, in *Complete Works*, Yale University Press, New Haven CT, 1991

Munday, Jeremy, *Introducing Translation Studies*, Routledge, Abingdon, 2001

Muschard, Jutta, 'Relevant Translations: History, Presentation, Criticism, Application', *European University Studies, Linguistics*, series XXI, vol. 163, (1996)

Neusner, Jacob, *Judaism and the Interpretation of Scripture*, Hendrickson, Peabody MA., 2004

Nord, Christiane, *Translating as a Purposeful Activity: Functionalist Approaches Explained*, St Jerome, Manchester, 1997

Palumbo, Giuseppe, *Key Terms in Translation Studies*, Continuum, 2009

Quine, Willard van Orman, *Word and Object*, MIT Press, Cambridge MA, 1960

Reiss, Katharina, *Translation criticism: the potentials and imitations (Categories and criteria for translation quality assessment)*, tr. Rhodes, St Jerome, Manchester, 2000

Ricoeur, Paul, *Sur la Traduction*, Bayard, Paris, 2004

Schleiermacher, F., tr. Lefevre, André, 'Translating Literature: The German Tradition from Luther to Rosenzweig', *Approaches to Translation Studies*, vol.4, p.74f

Seidman, Naomi, *Faithful Renderings: Jewish-Christian Difference and the Politics of Translation*, University of Chicago Press, Chicago IL, 2006

Shamma, Tarek, *Translation and the Manipulation of Difference: Arabic Literature in Nineteenth-Century England*, St Jerome,Manchester, 2009

Somers, Harold, 'Machine Translation' in Baker (ed.), *Routledge Encyclopedia of Translation Studies*, Routledge, 1998

Steiner, George, *Real Presences*, Faber and Faber, 1989

Steiner, George, *After Babel*, 3rd edn, OUP, Oxford, 1998

Toury, Gideon, *Descriptive Translation Studies and Beyond*, John Benjamins, Amsterdam, 1995

Venuti, Lawrence, *The Translator's Invisibility: A History of Translation*, Routledge, 1995

Venuti, Lawrence, *The Scandals of Translation: Towards an Ethic of Difference*, Routledge, 1998

Williams, Alan, *Rumi Spiritual Verses: The First Book of Masnavi-ye Ma'navi*, Penguin Classics, 2006

Biblical translation

Aichele, George, *The Control of Biblical Meaning: Canon as Semiotic Mechanism*, Trinity Press, Harrisburg PA, 2001

Barker, Kenneth (ed.), *The Making of a Contemporary Translation: New International Version*, Hodder & Stoughton, 1991

Barr, James, *The Semantics of Biblical Language*, Oxford University Press, Oxford, 1961

Barton, John, *The Nature of Biblical Criticism*, Westminster John Knox Press, Louisville KY, 2007

Beekman, J. and Callow, J *Translating the Word of God*, Zondervan, Grand Rapids MI, 1974

Benjamin, Mara H., *Rosenzweig's Bible: Reinventing Scripture for Jewish Modernity*, Cambridge University Press, New York, 2009

Berry, Lloyd, *Introduction to the Geneva Bible, 1560 Edition*, Hendrickson, Peabody MA, 2007

Bonnes Nouvelles Aujord'hui: Le Nouveau Testament traduit en Français courant d'après le texte Grec, First Edition, Editè les Sociètès Bibliques, Paris, United Bible Societies (1975)

Bosworth, J. *The Gothic and Anglo-Saxon Gospels*, John Russell Smith, 1865

Brawley, *Text to Text pours forth speech*, Indiana University Press, Bloomington IN,1996

Daniell, David, 'Translating the Bible' in S.E. Porter (ed.), *The Nature of Religious Language: A Colloquium*, Continuum, Sheffield, 1996

Daniell, David *The Bible in English*, Yale University Press, New Haven CT, 2003

Danker, Frederick in B. Taylor, J. Lee, R. Burton, and R. Whitaker (eds.), *Biblical Greek Language and Lexicography: Essays in Honor of Frederick W. Danker* , Eerdmans, Grand Rapids MI, 2004

Dalferth, Ingolf, and Jens Schröter (eds.), *Bibel in gerechter Sprache?: Kritik eines misslungenen Versuchs*, Mohr Siebeck, Tübingen, 2007

De Waard, Jan, and Nida, Eugene, *From on language to another: Functional equivalence in Bible translating*, Nelson, Nashville TN, 1986

Dewey, David, *A User's Guide to Bible Translations*, InterVarsity Press, Westmont IL, 2004

Fee, Gordon and Mark Strauss, *How to choose a Translation for all its worth*, Zondervan, Grand Rapids MI, 2007

Funk, Robert Walter, *Language, hermeneutic, and word of God: the problem of language in the New Testament and contemporary theology*, Harper & Row, New York, 1966

Gargano Innocenzo OSB, *Holy Reading: An introduction to Lectio Divina*, tr. Vitale, Canterbury Press, Norwich 2007

Gignac, Alain, 'A Translation that Induces a Reading Experience: Narrativity, Intratextuality, Rhetorical Performance, and Galatians 1-2' in Porter and Boda (eds.), *Translating the New Testament: Text, Translation, Theology*, Eerdmans, Grand Rapids MI, 2009

Gössman, E.E., Moltmann-Wendel, and H. Schüngel-Straumann (eds.), *Der Teufel blieb männlich: Kritische Diskussion zur Bibel in gerechter Sprache; Feministische, historische und systematische Beiträge*, Neukirchener Verlagsgesellschaft, Neukirchen-Vluyn, 2007

Grayston, K., 'Confessions of a Biblicall Translator', in *New Universities Quarterly*, vol. 33 (1979)

Grudem, W., in *Translating Truth: The Case for Essentially Literal Bible Translation*, C.J Collins, W Grudem, V.S. Poythress, et al., Crossway Books, Wheaton IL, 2005

De Hamel, Christopher, *The Book: A History of the Bible*, Phaidon Press, 2001

Hatina, Thomas R., 'The Perfect Tense-Form in Colossians: Verbal Aspect, Temporality and the Challenge of Translation' in R. S. Hess and S. E. Porter (ed.), *Translating the Bible*, Sheffield Academic Press, Sheffield, 1999

Hill, Harriet, *The Bible at Cultural Crossroads: From Translation to Communication*, St Jerome, Manchester, 2006

Katz, David S., *God's Last Words: Reading the English Bible from the Reformation to Fundamentalism*, Yale University Press, New Haven CT, 2004

Levinas, Emmanuel, 'Franz Rosenzweig: A Modern Jewish Thinker', in *Hors Sujet*, Fata Morgana, Saint-Clément, 1987

Levinas, Emmanuel, 'The Strings and the Wood: On the Jewish Reading of the Bible', in *Hors Sujet*, Fata Morgana, Saint-Clément, 1987

Lewis, C.S., *English Literature in the Sixteenth Century*, Clarendon Press, Oxford, 1954

Long, Lynne (ed.), *Translation and Religion: Holy Untranslatable?*, Multilingual Matters, Clevedon, 2005

Long, Lynne, *Translating the Bible from the 7ᵗʰ to the 17ᵗʰ Century*, Ashgate, Surrey, 2001

Metzger, B.M., *The Bible in Translation*, Grand Rapids MI, 2001

Newman, B.M., and E.A. Nida, *A Translator's Handbook on the Acts of the Apostles*, UBS, 1972

Nida, Eugene, *Toward a Science of Translating: With special reference to principles and procedures involved in Bible translating*, Brill, Leiden, 1964

Nida, Eugene, *Signs, Sense, and Translation*, Bible Society of South Africa, Capetown, 1984

Nida, Eugene and Charles Taber, *The Theory and Practice of Translation*, UBS, Leiden, 1969

Nida, Eugene, and Johannes Louw, *Lexical Semantics of the Greek New Testament*, Society of Biblical Literature, Atlanta GA, 1992

Pelican, Jaroslav, *Whose Bible is it?*, Penguin, 2005

Pearson, Brook, 'Remainderless Translations? Implications of the Tradition Concerning the Translation of the LXX for Modern Translational Theory' in Hess and Porter (eds.), *Translating the Bible*, Sheffield Academic Press, Sheffield, 1999

Porter, Stanley E., *Verbal Aspect in the Greek of the New Testament, with Reference to Tense and Mood*, Peter Lang, Bern, 1989

Porter, Stanley E., *Idioms of the Greek New Testament*, JSOT Press, Sheffield, 1992

Porter, Stanley E., 'The Contemporary English Version and the Ideology of Translation', in Hess and Porter (eds.), *Translating the Bible*, Sheffield Academic Press, Sheffield, 1999

Porter, Stanley E., 'Assessing Translation Theory: Beyond Literal and Dynamic Equivalence' in S.E. Porter and M.J. Boda (eds.), *Translating the New Testament*, Eerdmans, Grand Rapids MI, 2009

Prickett, Stephen, *Words and The Word: Language, poetics and biblical interpretation*, Cambridge University Press, Cambridge, 1986

Rajak, Tessa, *Translation and Survival: The Greek Bible of the Ancient Jewish Diaspora*, Oxford University Press, Oxford, 2009

Rosenwald, L., 'Introduction', in *Scripture and Translation*, M. Buber, E. Fox, L. Rosenwald, Indiana University Press, Bloomington IN, 1994

Rosenzweig, Franz, 'Scripture and Word: On the New Bible Translation', in *Die Schrift und ihre Verdeutschung*, 1926, tr. L. Rosenwald and E. Fox, Indiana University Press, Bloomington IN, 1994

Rosenzweig, Franz, 'Scripture and Luther', in *Die Schrift und ihre Verdeutschung*, 1926, tr. L. Rosenwald and E. Fox, Indiana University Press, Bloomington IN, 1994

Ryken, Leland, *The Word of God in English: Criteria for Excellence in Bible Translation*, Crossway Books, Wheaton IL, 2002

Silva, Moisés, *Biblical Words and their Meaning: An introduction to Lexical Semantics*, Zondervan, Grand Rapids MI, 1994 (1993)

Strauss, Mark, 'Form, function and the "literal meaning" fallacy in English

Bible translation', *Bible Translator,* vol. 56:3, (2005)

Thiselton, Anthony, *New Horizons in Hermeneutics: The theory and practice of transforming biblical reading,* Zondervan, Grand Rapids MI, 1992

Tuggy, David, 'The Literal-Idiomatic Bible Translation Debate from the Point of View of Cognitive Grammar' in K. Feyaerts (ed.), *The Bible through Metaphor and Translation: A Cognitive Semantic Perspective,* Peter Lang, Bern, 2003

Wasserstein, Abraham, and David Wasserstein, *The Legend of the Septuagint, from Classical Antiquity to Today,* Cambridge University Press, Cambridge, 2006

Pragmatics and Relevance Theory

Ariel, Mira, *Pragmatics and Grammar,* Cambridge University Press, Cambridge, 2008

Blakemore, Diane, *Semantic Constraints on Relevance,* Blackwell, Oxford, 1987

Blakemore, Diane, *Understanding Utterences: an introduction to pragmatics,* Blackwell, Oxford, 1992

Brown, Jeannine K., *Scripture as Communication,* Baker Academic, Grand Rapids MI, 2007

Goatly, A., *The language of metaphors,* Routledge, 1997

Green, K., 'Butterflies, wheels and the search for literary relevance', *Language and Literature,* 6 (1997), pp.133-8

Grice, H.P., 'Logic and Conversation' in P.Cole and J. L. Morgan (eds.), *Syntax and Semantics, Volume Three: Speech Acts,* Academic Press, Waltham MA, 1975Grice, H.P., *Studies in the Way of Words,* Harvard University Press, Cambridge MA, 1989

Gutt, Ernst-August, *Relevance Theory: A Guide to Successful Communication in Translation,* Summer Institute of Linguistics, Dallas TX, 1992

Gutt, Ernst-August, *Translation and Relevance: Cognition and Context,* 2nd edn, St. Jerome, Manchester, 2000

Hendel, R.S., 'Prophets, Priests and the Efficacy of Ritual' in D.P. Wright, D.N. Freedman and A. Hurvitz (eds.), *Pomegranates and Golden Bells: Studies in Biblical, Jewish, and Near Eastern*

Ritual, Law, and Literature in Honor of Jacob Milgrom, Eisenbrauns, Warsaw IN, 1995

Hill, Harriet, *The Bible at Cultural Crossroads: From Translation to Communication,* St. Jerome, Manchester, 2006

Leech, G., *Principles of Pragmatics,* Longman, Harlow, Essex, 1983

Levinson, S., 'Pragmatics and the grammar of anaphora', *Journal of Linguistics,* (1987) 23, 379ff

Pilkington, A., B. McMahon, and B. Clark, 'Looking for an argument: A response to Green', *Language and Literature,* vol. 6 (1997), pp.139-148

Recanati, F., 'On defining communicative intentions', *Mind and Language,* I (1986), pp.213-42

Searle, J., 'How performatives work', *Linguistics and Philosophy,* 12 (1989), pp.535-58

Sperber, Dan, and Deidre Wilson, *Relevance: Communication and Cognition*, 2nd edn, Blackwell, Oxford, 1995

Sperber, Dan and Wilson, Deirdre, 'Loose Talk', in *Proceedings of the Aristotelian Society*, vol. 86 (1985/86), pp.153-171

Toolan, M, 'International linguistics, relevance theory and stylistic explanation: A reply to MacMahon', in *Language and Literature*, vol. 8 (1999), pp.255-268

Wendland, Ernst, *Language, society, and Bible translation*, Bible Society of South Africa, Cape Town, 1985

Wendland, Ernst, *Contextual Frames of Reference in Translation: A Coursebook for Bible Translators and Teachers*, St Jerome, Manchester, 2008

Related Topics

Anderson, John M., *The Grammar of Names*, Oxford University Press, Oxford, 2007

Blackmore, Susan, *The Meme Machine*, Oxford University Press, Oxford, 1999

Boyer, Pascal, *Religion Explained*, Heinemann, 2001

Bök, Christian, *Enoia*, Coach House Books, Toronto ON, 2001

Chomsky, Noam, *Aspects of the Theory of Syntax*, MIT Press, Cambridge MA, 1965

Edwards, Mark W., *Sound, Sense and Rhythm: Listening to Greek and Latin Poetry*, Princeton University Press, Princeton NJ, 2002

Eysenck and Keane, *Cognitive Psychology: A Student's Handbook*, Psychology Press, Hove, 2005

Fish, Stanley, *Is there a text in this class?*, Harvard University Press, Cambridge MA, 1980

Fodor, J.A., *Modularity of Mind*, MIT Press, Cambridge MA, 1983

Fussell, Paul, *Poetic Meter and Poetic Form*, Random House, New York, 1979

Girard, *The Scapegoat*, tr. Freccero, Johns Hopkins University Press, Baltimore MD, 1986

Goatly, Andrew, *The Language of Metaphors*, Routledge, 1997

Goffman, Erving, *Interaction Ritual: Essays in Face to Face Behavior*, Transaction, Piscataway NJ, 1967

Haspelmath, Martin, *Understanding Morphology*, Hodder & Staughton, 2002

Hill, Leslie, *The Cambridge Introduction to Jacques Derrida*, Cambridge University Press, Cambridge, 2007

Lakoff, George, and Mark Johnson, *Metaphors We Live By*, University of Chicago Press, Chicago, 1980

Löbner, Sebastian, *Understanding Semantics*, Hodder & Staughton, 2002

Maher, John and Judy Groves,, *Introducing Chomsky*, Icon Books, 1996

Peterson, Eugene, *Eat This Book: A Conversation In The Art of Spiritual Reading*, Hodder & Stoughton, 2006

Pinker, Steven, *The Language Instinct* , Penguin, 1994

Radford Ruether, Rosemary, *Sexism and God-Talk*, SCM Press, Norwich, 1983

Robbins, Vernon K., *Exploring the Texture of Texts: A guide to socio-rhetorical interpretation*, Trinity Press, Manchester, 1996

Styles, Elizabeth A., *The Psychology of Attention*, Psychology Press, Hove, 2006

Ward, Graham, *The Postmodern God: Theological Reader*, Blackwell, Oxford, 1997

Lukan Studies

Alexander, Loveday, *The Preface to Luke's Gospel: Literary convention and social context in Luke 1.1-4 and Acts 1.1*, Cambridge University Press, Cambridge, 1993

Bailey, Ken, *Poet & Peasant and Through Peasant Eyes*, combined edition, Eerdmans, Grand Rapids MI, 1983

Barker, Margaret, *The Great High Priest: The Temple Roots of Christian Liturgy*, T & T Clark, 2003

Berger, Klaus *Formgeschichte des Neuen Testaments* , Quelle & Meyer, Heidelberg, 1984

Boismard, M.E., *L'evangile de l'enfance (Luc 1-2) selon le Proto-Luc*, Gabalda, Paris, 1997

Bracht Branham, R. and M. Goulet-Cazé (ed.s), *The Cynics: The Cynic Movement in Antiquity and its Legacy*, University of California Press, Berkeley CA, London, 1996

Brown, Raymond E., *The Birth of the Messiah: A Commentary on the Infancy Narratives in the Gospels of Matthew and Luke*, 2nd edn, Doubleday, New York, 1993

Bultmann, Rudolf, *Die Geschichte der synoptischen Tradition*, vol. 5, Vandenhoeck & Ruprecht, Gottingen, 1970

Cadbury, H.J., 'Commentary on the Preface of Luke' in F.J.F. Jackson and K. Lake (eds.), *The Beginnings of Christianity*, vol. II, MacMillan, 1922

Crossan, John Dominic, *Raid on the articulate : comic eschatology in Jesus and Borges*, Harper & Row, 1976

Culpepper, R. Alan, *The Gospel of Luke*, New Interpreters Bible, vol. IX, Abingdon, 1995

Esler, Philip Francis, *Community and Gospel in Luke-Acts: The Social and Political Motivations of Lukan Theology*, Cambridge University Press Cambridge, 1989

Evans, Craig A., *Luke, New International Bible Commentary*, Hendrickson, Peabody MA, 1995

Fitzmyer, Joseph A., *The Gospel according to Luke*, Doubleday, New York, 1970

Freed, Edwin D., *The Stories of Jesus' Birth*, T & T Clark, 2001

Green, Joel, *The Gospel of Luke, New International Commentary on the New Testament*, Eerdmans, Grand Rapids MI, 1997

Harnisch, Wolfgang, *Die Gleichniserzählungen Jesu*, 2001, Vandenhoeck & Ruprecht, Göttingen

Horsley, Richard, 'Hidden Transcripts and the Arts of Resistance: Applying the work of James C Scott to Jesus and Paul', *Semeia Studies*, vol. 48 (2004)

Jeremias, Joachim, *Die Gleichnisse Jesu*, 11th edn., Vandenhoeck & Ruprecht, Göttingen, 1996

Jones, Geraint Vaughan, *The Art and Truth of the Parables: A Study in their Literary Form and Modern Interpretation* SPCK, 1964

Jülicher, Adolf, 'Die Gleichnisreden Jesu (Zwei Teile in Einem Band)', DJG (1910)

Jung, Chang-Wook, *The Original Language of the Lukan Infancy Narrative*, Continuum, 2004

Klutz, T., *The Exorcism Stories in Luke-Acts*, Cambridge University Press, Cambridge, 2004

Klutz, T., *The Eighth Book of Moses: A New Translation with Introduction and Notes*, (provisional title) in R. Balcombe and J. Davilla *(eds.)*, *More Old Testament Pseudepigrapha*, 2011 (forthcoming)

Lagrange, M.J., 'Le Sens de Luc 1.1. d'apres les papyrus', *Bulletin d'ancienne litterature et d'archeologie chretiennes*, vol. 2 (1912)

Linnemann, Eta, tr. J. Sturdy, *Parables of Jesus: Introduction and Exposition*, SPCK, 1966

Malina, Bruce J, *The New Testament World: Insights from Cultural Anthropology*, Westminster John Knox Press, Louisville KY, 2001

Malina, Bruce J. and Rohrbaugh, Richard L., *Social Science Commentary on the Synoptic Gospels*, Fortress, Minneapolis MN, 2003

Marshall, H., *The Gospel of Luke*, The Paternoster Press, , 1978

Nolland, J., *Luke, Word Biblical Commentary*, Thomas Nelson, Nashville TN, 1989

Park, Hyung Dae, *Finding Herem? A Study of Luke-Acts in the Light of Herem*, T & T Clark, 2007

Parsons, M.C., *Body and Character in Luke and Acts*, Baker Academic, Grand Rapids MI, 2006

Parsons, M.C., *Luke: Storyteller, Interpreter, Evangelist*, Hendricks, Peabody MA, 2007

Pilch, J., Sickness and Healing in Luke-Acts, in Neyrey (ed.) *The Social World of Luke-Acts: Models for Interpretation*, Hendrickson, Peabody MA, 1991

Radl, Walter, *Das Evangelium nach Lukas, Kommentar, Erster Teil: 1,1 – 9,50*, Herder, Freiburg, 2003

Robinson, J.M, P. Hoffmann, and J.S. Kloppenborg (eds.), *The Sayings Gospel Q in Greek and English, with Parallels from the Gospels of Mark and Thomas*, Fortress Press, Leuven, 2002

Schaberg, Jane, *The illegitimacy of Jesus: A feminist theological interpretation of the Infancy Narratives*, Sheffield Phoenix Press, Sheffield, 1990

Schottroff, Luise, *The Parables of Jesus*, tr. Linda Maloney, Augsburg Fortress, Minneapolis MN, 2006

Sellin, Gerhard, 'Allegorie und Gleichnis: Zu Formenlehre der synoptischen Gleichnisse', *ZTK*, vol. 75 (1978)

Strobel, A., *Untersuchung zum eschatologischen Verzogerungsproblem*, Leiden, 1961

Theissen, Gerd, *The New Testament*, tr. J. Bowden, T& T Clark, 2002

Tucker, Jeffrey T., *Example Stories: Perspectives on Four Parables in the Gospel of Luke*, Sheffield Academic Press, Sheffield, 1998

Via, Dan Otto Jr., 'Parable and Example Story: A Literary-Structuralist Approach', *Semeia Studies*, vol. 1 (1974)

Wailes, S.L., *Medieval Allegories of Jesus' Parables,* Berkeley, University of California Press, Berkeley CA, 1987

Wright N.T., *The New Testament and the People of God*, SPCK, 1992

Wright N.T., *Jesus and the Victory of God*, SPCK, 1996

Wright N.T., *The Resurrection of the Son of God*, Fortress Press, Minneapolis MN, 2003

Wright, Tom, *Luke for Everyone*, SPCK, 2001

Young, Brad H. *The Parables: Jewish Tradition and Christian Interpretation*, Hendrickson, Peabody MA, 1998

Zaidman, B. and Pantel, .P.S., *Religion in the Ancient Greek City*, Cambridge University Press, Cambridge, 1992

Index

Lightning Source UK Ltd.
Milton Keynes UK
UKOW030003280213

206919UK00002B/78/P